MEDITATIONS
ON THE SIGNS
OF THE
ZODIAC

MEDITATIONS
ON THE SIGNS
OF THE
ZODIAC

by

John Jocelyn

Illustrated by Elmo Barnay

HARPER & ROW, PUBLISHERS
SAN FRANCISCO

Cambridge
Hagerstown
Philadelphia
New York

London
Mexico City
São Paulo
Sydney

1817

Library of Congress Cataloging in Publication Data

Jocelyn, John, 1890-1964.
    Meditations on the signs of the zodiac.

    1. Zodiac   I. Title
BF1726.J62   1980   133.5'2   79-3594
ISBN 0-06-066092-9

84   10   9   8   7   6   5   4   3

FOREWORD

THESE MEDITATIONS on the signs of the Zodiac have been written under the Aquarian impulse as a direct and distinct service to all who seek to cooperate with their Angel, the higher self, within them. They will prove of value to all who seek to know themselves as soul and spirit as well as body. They have been written in the hope that studying and meditating upon them will induce people to live a life that will be generative of those soul forces essential to the weaving of the "wedding garment," the robe which the Son of Man provides.

Aquarius is the sign of the Son of Man, which is the soul of man refined and purified in virtue of work done through many lives in all the twelve signs of the Zodiac. As man cleanses his astral body and generates soul essences through action in Christ-altruism and truth, the Son of Man is created and calls down and connects with the Son of God, "the Lord from Heaven."

Mankind is now being awakened to the truth of Spirit and the wisdom of love, and growing numbers will concern themselves with their "Father's business," which is not to get more personal power for themselves, but to grow in *soul*. This spiritual science of the stars is then the *true* psychology, science of the soul, for it educes the soul of man to give birth to the Christ within, as man raises and refines himself through the spiritual life of the Christ everywhere extant and accessible to man as he wills to live the true, the beautiful, and the good.

CONTENTS

YOU ARE MORE THAN YOUR SUN SIGN

IN this newly edited second edition, prominence needs to be given to what appeared in the first edition as a footnote at the end of the first chapter. It was in fine print and was overlooked by many readers, some of whom suggested that at the beginning of every chapter there should have been stated the period of the year when the Sun is in the sign. The omission, however, was intentional, for the author wanted the reader to free himself from the popular misconception that the influence of the Zodiac is concerned solely or primarily with the sign in which the Sun is found at birth.

Although it is important to know "in" which sign you were born, that is, the position of your Sun, you are, indeed, much more than your Sun sign. You are a *unique* individual and cannot be categorized, along with all humanity, in one of twelve types. In order to gain a comprehensive knowledge of yourself or of others, it is necessary to know also the sign-placement of the Moon and all the planets, as well as the hour of the day. The exact minute of birth determines the Ascendant (the rising sign "under" which one is born), the Mid-heaven, and the directions from which all the zodiacal and planetary influences come and imprint themselves on the infant at the moment it takes its first breath. On the average, a new degree rises every four minutes, thus even twins are not exactly alike.

Every individual is born when the unique and complex composite of all the various stellar influences best conforms to his destiny and need as a reincarnating Ego, which for its perfecting requires experience in all the signs in the course of its successive incarnations. Even in any single earthly life the individual character and destiny cannot be encompassed by a single sign. In fact, every person is to some degree related at birth and throughout life to all the signs. Therefore, irrespective of the signs dominant in one's nativity, it is essential that one be interested in all twelve signs of the Zodiac and strive to manifest the highest in all of them.

The date of the Sun's entry into the successive signs varies somewhat from year to year. The approximate dates are: Aries, March 21; Taurus, April 20; Gemini, May 20; Cancer, June 21; Leo, July 22; Virgo, August 23; Libra, September 23; Scorpio, October 23; Sagittarius, November 22; Capricorn, December 21; Aquarius, January 20; and Pisces, February 19.

While the Sun is passing through one sign in the course of a month, the rapidly moving Moon moves through all twelve signs. Thus every month the Moon is in each sign for about 2½ days. The planets move at varying speeds, and in the course of their journeyings we receive their influences mingled with those of the different signs of the Zodiac. For their exact positions, consult the ephemeris for any given date. Only when the place and precise moment of birth are known, can the ascending degree and the complete unique stellar picture be determined accurately.

Although generalizations may sometimes prove helpful, it is only this complete picture that can give you accurate self-knowledge, an understanding of which may enable you to meet your destiny more consciously, courageously, and even gratefully. It may also help you to measure up to your highest potential and, in freedom, be a more creative and responsible microcosm, cooperating with the ever-creating macrocosm.

November 1969   Beredene Jocelyn

10

THE DIVINITY OF THE ZODIAC
AND THE MAGNITUDE OF MAN

In an age when humanity has become conscious of cosmic space, the traditional and conventional religious views are inadequate to fit the changed conception of our universe. As larger clothes are needed for the growing child when it has outgrown its old ones, so enlarged spiritual concepts are needed for evolving humanity. This principle was recognized by Christ Jesus when he said, "I have yet many things to say unto you, but ye cannot bear them now" (St. John 16:12).

Vanguard individuals and increasingly larger numbers of persons are now mature for a cosmic view of man himself. Man is striving to know more about the physical structure of the universe, and is being lured to journey into cosmic space. Marvelous have been the beginning achievements. However, if they are pursued along the same lines, with reference only to the material nature of the universe, no more can be learned about the cosmos than can be learned about a human being by examining a corpse. What can thus be known about the man's life processes, his animation, his willed action, feeling, and thinking, and his Ego-nature?

The physical body soon disintegrates after the soul and spirit have departed from it. Why do not the solar system and starry worlds fall apart? Many people consider the cosmos a machine, but even a machine cannot operate endlessly without some direction by a thought-endowed being. According to Einstein,[1] "The scientist's religious feelings take the form of a rapturous amazement at the harmony of natural law which reveals an intelligence of such superiority that compared with it, all the systematic thinking of human minds is seen as an utterly insignificant reflection." Man's directing Ego is single and undivided, whereas the world of stars is sustained by a great multiplicity of spiritual beings, the Divine Creative Hierarchies. These supersensible beings are invisible to physical sight, yet a part of their creative activity is revealed to sense perception in the grouping of the stars, in the orderly motion of the planets, and in the light streaming from the heavens. If you move your arm, or walk into another room, purpose underlies the movement. Should not the movements of the planets be as purposefully directed and meaningful?

Although the physical earthly forces of nature provide man with food for the body, his soul and spirit are maintained by their relation to all the plurality of spirituality living in the stars. To physical sense perception, man appears to be enclosed within the boundary of his skin. In reality, he is, in his entirety, a being of body, soul, and spirit, born out of the cosmos and sustained by the cosmos as well as by the substances of the earth. He is not, as some say, just a grain of sand on a cosmic beach, the Earth. He is himself a cosmic being. He is a little world, a microcosm, inseparably related to the great world, the macrocosm, the vast realm of Spirit, including the majestic Zodiac, the Great Cosmic Man.

Why is the average person unaware of this? A comparison may make the answer clearer. A TV set is constantly surrounded by what is being broadcast from many stations,

---

[1] Albert Einstein, *The World as I See It* (London: John Land the Bodley Head, 1939), p. 28.

some even thousands of miles away, yet it is without pictures and sound until it is attuned to one of the broadcasts. It is a matter of attunement. In the case of the human being, it is a matter of consciousness. Cosmic conquest does not require a journey into space; it involves a heightened, intensified, and expanded consciousness. Highly evolved Egos can be conscious of the spiritual forces and beings of Venus, for example, or of the Sun, or Saturn. These influences are not localized to the shining stars we see in the sky. They fill the entire spheres bounded by the orbital paths of the respective planets. We are perpetually immersed in them and also in all that streams to us from the Zodiac, which is as a womb in which our entire solar system is evolving. We are inseparably united with them all—each individual in a unique way—in our waking consciousness and in sleep, throughout all our earth-life, and also during the "sphere-life" between death and a new birth. Everyone is at least vaguely aware that, without any visible external reason, the mood of one day differs from that of another, one hour from another, and often even one minute from another, but few can, in full Ego-consciousness, know of the influences broadcast from the cosmos.

In ancient times the consciousness of all mankind was oriented to the spiritual world and its beings, far more than to the physical world. In order to become conscious of himself as an independent Ego or "I," and to become a free being, inwardly free to make his own decisions and use his own creative powers, it was necessary that gradually, throughout ages of time, he awaken fully to the physical world and be asleep and oblivious to spiritual reality.

Not all humanity, but most of Western mankind, do regard themselves as independent Egos, and they have developed the intellect in working creatively with the physical resources of the earth. Thereby material progress has been

13

promoted, but we have been blinded to the Spirit and led to believe that we are one-earth-life beings. Having become free in the sphere of the Ego, there is great danger that we be enslaved to material existence and remain in spiritual night. It is the time now, in our century, to awaken to a clear consciousness of our own soul and spirit nature, and to the spirituality of the cosmos, while still retaining our complete Ego-consciousness and control, and without withdrawing from practical earthly life. If humanity is to progress, acquaintance with the spiritual side of existence is imperative.

The viewpoint of the author of this book is: "Ever do we disclose larger vistas of truth as we reach higher levels in spirals of ascent. Our attitudes are determined by the altitude we have attained. Without elevation, no view is whole; and without an approach to a cosmic view, we must perforce live —grope rather—in illusion and error." We must find a conscious connection with the spiritual cosmos. Every phase of human existence can be enriched and enlivened by such a cosmic, spiritual impulse, for example, education, psychology, astronomy, art, healing, and religion. It will dispel fear and insecurity in our personal life and enable us to face our destiny with equanimity.

To promote inner peace and world understanding, we need to know how man is placed in the whole universal order. A clue as to how to begin is found in the injunction that was given to the pupils in the Mysteries: "If you want to understand the center, investigate the circumference, for it contains the key." To know man, we must turn to the circumference, the Zodiac. Here we enter upon holy ground and must approach this domain of infinitely sublime spiritual beings with humility and reverence.

In order to comprehend to some degree our relation to these exceedingly lofty beings, let us first direct our gaze downward to the kingdoms below us. Through the fact that

14

we bear mineral substances within our physical body, we have something in common with the mineral kingdom. The plant, too, contains mineral elements, but it has something more, namely, life and the power of inner growth. Its physical body is interpenetrated by a body of life forces, termed the etheric body. The animal shares both the physical body and the etheric body with the plant and has, in addition, the capacity for sensation and movement from within its own being. This is because the animal has a third member, known as the astral body, desire body, or soul body. Man is not the highest animal as many people think. Man has a fourth principle which the animal lacks. It is the Ego, which enables him to say, "I am," "I think," "I speak." There are three latent higher members which will be referred to later.

Think of the vast difference between man and mineral! Yet man is only three stages above the mineral. Try to conceive of the sublimity of beings who are nine, eight, or even seven stages above man. These supersensible beings, the highest of the Spiritual Hierarchies, are called the Seraphim, Cherubim, and Thrones—the First Hierarchy. It is they who comprise the twelve differentiated groupings which we call the Zodiac, which, remember, forms as it were, the womb of our solar system. As a teacher was once a student and as a mother was once a child, so these exalted divine beings came from an earlier solar system in which they passed through their lower stages, until they were so advanced that their solar system could be transformed into our Zodiac and they could rise to mighty, creative, cosmic deeds and make the great sacrifice which gave birth to our solar system.

Beyond them is the Divine Trinity, the Threefold Unity, the godhead, who gave the ideas and aims for the new solar system to the Seraphim. The Seraphim inspired the Cherubim to apply their highest wisdom in making the plans workable, so that the Thrones, in turn, could transform the plans

15

into active reality by pouring out their own being. This substance of the Thrones was the primeval fire, a dark warmth. It was worked on from within by the less evolved, yet exalted beings of the Second Hierarchy—the Spirits of Wisdom, the Spirits of Motion, and the Spirits of Form, also called Dominions, Mights, and Powers (Elohim). From without there streamed in the influence of the First Hierarchy—the Seraphim, Cherubim, and Thrones. From the twelve directions of space, they organized the warmth and laid the foundation for the twelvefold differentiated warmth we bear in our twelve-membered physical body today, from Aries-head to Pisces-feet. (Only the briefest hints are given here. For details, see Rudolf Steiner's *Occult Science—An Outline; Spiritual Hierarchies; Universe, Earth and Man;* and numerous other books.)

This initial warmth stage of our solar system is called the Saturn Period. It was followed by a night interval, after which the warmth, on the one hand, densified to air or gas, and on the other, it rarefied to light. To man-in-the-making was added the etheric body, the life body of formative forces, raising this evolving being to a plant-like status. The First Hierarchy continued to be active during this Sun Period, from the periphery, the Zodiac. Further densification in the succeeding Moon Period produced the fluid element, and the commensurate rarefication, sound; and man acquired the astral body, through the sacrifice of beings of the Second Hierarchy. Man-to-be then had sensation and was in an animal-like stage.

It was not until our present Earth Period that very gradually our solar system differentiated into the planets as we know them and densification brought the solid state of the Earth. The Ego is the new member that man has acquired. It is this that makes him human and through which, from his own free will, he will develop from selfish egotism, to love, which, like the Sun, rays forth to all, for Man is becoming

16

the Fourth Hierarchy, named the Spirits of Freedom and Love. At the end of the Earth Period, love should be a part of everything, as wisdom is now.

It has been a slow process to member the Ego into evolving man. In earlier ages of the Earth-evolution, human beings were still guided by a group-ego and felt a part of a tribe, or family. The individualization took place gradually, until at the time of the Christ Event, man matured to independent Ego-consciousness and is now himself a responsible creator. The Ego or "I" is not physically visible, yet it is cognizable. It was bestowed by the Spirits of Form, or Elohim, as similarly, the astral body had previously been a sacrificial gift from the Spirits of Motion; and the etheric body, from the Spirits of Wisdom; and the warmth for the physical body from the Thrones, who, with the Cherubim and Seraphim, from the circle of the Zodiac, gave the initial twelvefold organization to that warmth.

To this day, we owe our physical body only partially to heredity; the form we owe to the sublime beings of the Zodiac: the head to Aries; the throat and larynx to Taurus; the symmetry, lungs, shoulders, arms, and hands to Gemini; the rib cage, breasts, and stomach to Cancer; the heart to Leo; the lower metabolic organs, solar plexus, and spleen to Virgo; the kidneys and loins to Libra; the organs of reproduction to Scorpio; the hips and thighs to Sagittarius; the knees to Capricorn; the calves and ankles to Aquarius; and the feet to Pisces. The seven inner movements within this twelvefoldness have their source in the planetary system, from Saturn to Moon. It is the work of the Ego, in this marvelous "temple of God," to transform the soul forces— thinking, feeling, and willing—from life to life in different environments and heredity and with experiences in purely soul and spiritual environments between incarnations in the earth-school.

All the beings of the Spiritual Hierarchies of the Zodiac

17

and of the planetary spheres—the many mansions of our Father's house—are active in man's entire life between birth and death, and also in each journey through the cosmos from death to a new birth. When the soul and spirit are released from the physical body, the beings nearest to man —the Third Hierarchy: Angels, Archangels, and Archai, connected with the Moon, Mercury, and Venus spheres—evaluate the earthly life and begin to arrange the needful destiny for the next incarnation, for we do reap what we sow. They prepare the Ego to free itself from its backward gaze, so that with the help of the Second Hierarchy, it may experience cosmic activities in the Sun, Mars, Jupiter, and Saturn spheres, before passing to the realm of the Zodiac. There the cosmic germ for the next physical body receives impulses from Aries to Pisces, head to feet, preparatory for the descent through the planetary spheres, where a gradual diminution of consciousness brings the Ego finally through the Moon sphere to a new birth on Earth for more schooling and further evolution.

If life is eternal, it must include existence before birth as well as after death. For individuals with heightened consciousness, reincarnation is a cognizable fact. For others it is the only reasonable explanation of the tremendous differences in human beings and their varied destinies, not only among people on separate continents but also within the same family.

Any pride in present achievement gives way to humility when we realize that in our Earth Period we are only at the midway station. We have yet to evolve the three spirit principles: the spirit-self, life-spirit, and spirit-man. Very few vanguards have developed them to an appreciable degree. All mankind will evolve them somewhat in the course of their future incarnations, and fully in the future planetary existences, called the Jupiter, Venus, and Vulcan Periods, through

18

which the Earth will pass in the future, before the beings of our solar system reach the stage of creativity when they can participate in the birth of a new Zodiac and solar system.

What has been described in barest outline is seen in detail by the highly trained spiritual scientist, who has developed the supersensible faculties slumbering in every human being, and whose findings can be comprehended by any unprejudiced thinker. Natural scientists have to change their theories from time to time. Interestingly, while this article is being written, the morning newspaper has on its front page, "Famed Astronomer Hoyle Thinks He May Have Been All Wrong," for twenty years, about the nature of the universe. The spiritual scientist does not theorize. He presents what his heightened consciousness is able to verify at firsthand from the Memory of Nature, guarded by the Saturn Beings. This Akashic Chronicle, as it is also called, is the cosmic memory in which is recorded everything that has occurred since the inception of our solar system.

Spiritual cosmology traces the source of all that arises and passes away within our ever changing, finite, planetary configurations, to the infinitely sublime divine spiritual beings of the Zodiac, sometimes referred to as "the twelve points of permanence." These points of permanence beyond time are also beyond good and evil, although the effects of their influence, as it passes into time in the planetary spheres, work out on our Earth as the opposition between good and evil.

It may seem strange that this divine twelvefold permanence should be called the Zodiac, meaning "circle of animals." It is not so strange when one knows that during the Ancient Sun Period, it gave rise to the earliest beginnings of the animal kingdom. Moreover, any unprejudiced observer of human nature notes in man resemblances to the animal representations, when rightly understood, and one still finds

19

traces of animal traits. These are effects working in time in lower spheres. Nevertheless, the symbols for the twelve signs of the Zodiac represent, in their pure essence, the oldest, most advanced, and sublime beings who gaze continuously upon the godhead, the Divine Trinity. Of them it can truly be said, "As it was in the beginning, is now, and ever shall be, world without end."

There is no chance or accidental coincidence in the recurrent reflection of the heavenly pattern in earthly life. We find it in the twelve sons of Jacob, the twelve tribes of Israel, the twelve disciples of Christ Jesus, and the twelve Knights of the Round Table. They are ordered by the twelve facets of the one zodiacal diamond. Spiritual realities have their image in earthly events and in human life, but man has largely lost his perception of these things. This disconnection in consciousness, this spiritual darkness, had to occur for man to become a free being. A compensation for this darkening was provided by the cosmos through the Christ Event, the significance of which we as yet only very, very dimly surmise. Christ brought to the Earth the forces which enable us gradually to attain a consciousness of the spirituality of the world of the stars and livingly to realize our connection with the all-embracing and eternal spiritual life of the great universe.

For an approach to this consciousness, we need an enlarged—a cosmic—concept of the Christ, the sublime Sun-Spirit who incarnated in Jesus of Nazareth from the Baptism till the Mystery of Golgotha, when he became the Spirit of the Earth and "the Lord of all the heavenly forces upon Earth." Christ is the being who in the Sun Period selflessly gave himself up in utmost devotion to the Twelve Voices of the Word of Worlds. He united in himself, in their fulness, the all-embracing secrets of the divinely creative Twelve Voices, which kindled in him such *Light* that he can say, "I am the light of the world." He belongs to our cosmos as a whole and spreads life throughout all our universe. For those who direct their thought to him during waking life, he becomes their guide through the cosmos—their Spiritual Sun —during sleep and between death and rebirth.

When there dawns on us the nature of the sacrifice and ceaseless activity of a multiplicity of spiritual beings throughout long, long periods of time, our hearts are filled to overflowing with reverence and gratitude and humility. We no longer take pride in thinking that we are the highest creation. Gratefully we acknowledge the resplendent gifts given to us by the divine beings who made us in their image, and we recognize that image in our fellowmen. We recognize, also, our responsibility in the process of world-becoming, our responsibility for every thought, feeling, and action, knowing that nothing happens in our innermost being without consequences that extend to the Zodiac.

It is hoped that this book will contribute to self-knowledge, which is at the same time world-knowledge. The original *Meditations on the Signs of the Zodiac* were written more than twenty-five years ago. I have added relevant material written by the author since that time and have also made revisions in keeping with his style and his own later development. The book goes forth as a bearer of glad tidings of the magnitude of man that arouses no egotism; rather does it inspire humility and reverence in contemplation of the divinity of the Zodiac.

October 1965   Beredene Jocelyn

MEDITATIONS

ON THE SIGNS
OF THE

ZODIAC

Aries - The Ram

THE EXUBERANCE of spring is characteristic of the vernal sign, Aries. As nature produces myriads of forms, so the mind of Aries is fertile with ideas, but the forces of other signs are needed to bring them to realization. As the first sign of the Zodiac, it is pioneering, progressive, ambitious, and desirous of leadership. In this sign we find the beginning of things, be they personal, local, national, international, or cosmic. As the first of the fire signs, and the one ruled by Mars, it is enthusiastic, energetic, self-confident, independent, frank, impulsive, militant, and either rash or courageous. This fiery force can ruin or it can retrieve the soul for the Spirit, depending on whether or not the lower Ego is cognizant of the higher self. As the first of the cardinal signs, Aries is extremely active and grows restless under restraint.

Aries rules the head and is symbolized by the *ram.* The "sheep," in chapter ten of St. John's Gospel, are not to be thought of as representative of dumb creatures that instinctively follow the herd. The reference is really to masculine sheep, to rams—Aries, the head-forces and the Ego-impulse—that is, to human beings in whom the Ego is active. The *idea of self,* of human individuality, is strong in Aries. Here is found the archetype of the Ego, the "I AM," the I-dentity or Ego-hood of man; here is the *will-to-be-man*ifest. Aries imparts initiative to the individual and gives the power to pioneer. The Ram is a leader, not a follower.

Among the most distinguishing characteristics of this sign of primal power and mental head-force are activity and ambition—the desire to be at the head of things. Incessant changeful action is its forte or its folly. When there is essentially manifest a consciousness not yet coordinated by the higher self, the native lacks the balance and harmony which wholeness gives. Then the exuberance of projected energy may produce a riot of rapidity resulting in the will to override and to rule. Too often, and to their hurt, Aries individuals are exponents of speed acting in space, forgetful of the forces of physical form and the limitations of their earthly bodies; then, like a boomerang, there returns to them the fruit of their own ill-conceived, fitful, forceful, outrushing, tempestuous folly.

So overwhelming is the force of this sign that it causes chaos and disorder, unless there is true light and a ballasted purpose. Too often, Aries is vapid and colorless, devoid of direction and accomplishment. One might truly say that the only definite purpose of Aries souls who are not properly balanced is the power of expansive, explosive, disruptive impulsiveness; for the Aries force forever flies off a center to the periphery and beyond, in abandoned centrifugal energy, at last to become scattered in space in mere diffusion. This frequently produces negation and barrenness in the native who is unaware of himself as a being of soul and spirit and who is not cognizant of the purpose of life on Earth. As a result of uncontrolled primal power not focused on a definite purpose, Aries may readily fly off the handle as it were, or shoot like sparks off an emery wheel.

Aries souls often suffer much because of this overload of out-rushing energy, unless fixed signs bring ballast and stability, and common signs bring thought-power and spiritual light, and unless Libra, the Scales, the complementary sign of Aries, brings the needed balance, equilibrium, and poise.

It is also because of this excess of uncontrolled force that ideals remain mere ideals, instead of being made the reality that they should become, as actual living things, creative and operative, instant with real power. Overestimation, leading to promise without performance, proves often the bane of individuals born in or under Aries, because intense idealism and vision are carried almost wholly as head or mental force with insufficient will and feeling to turn the vision into a concrete accomplishment. Yet, as the Aries individual rectifies his life by controlling his exuberant force and transmuting his rash impulsiveness, the correction brings into his life the needed balance and reliability that make him a valuable worker in any pioneering venture.

If one would understand Aries, one should be keenly aware of its incessant incitement to impulsiveness and to disruptive excess and extravagance where energy is concerned. When there is a lack of matured consciousness, and when the feeling forces are devoid of purpose and firmness,

as a result of one's failure in past lives and the current one
to devote oneself to deep meditation, the Aries person moves
through life unaware of the guiding principle and wise direc-
tion of the Christ; at least the earthly Ego does not obey the
guidance of the higher, spiritual being, the Angel, or the
"Lord from heaven." Were the Aries individual aware of
this influence and were he obedient to it, he would not have
to learn the hard and painful lessons that come in the mar-
riage relation, where difficulty arises because he himself, or
his partner, fails to measure up to the ideal expected.

The Christ, speaking of the man who has become spiritual-
ly intelligent, says, "Henceforth I call you not servants
[earthly Egos blind to truth because of their unlighted
brain]; for the servant [lower Ego] knoweth not what his
lord [Christ-Angel Being] doeth; but I have called you
friends" (St. John 15:15). The time is now here when ad-
vanced and evolved souls commune consciously with and
act on the guidance of the Christ-Angel, for the servant may
now advance to being admitted into the light of "the Lord
from heaven." All Aries souls will make definite progress and
be accomplishers if they heed these words and unite the
lower Ego with the higher Christ-being. Not until such union
occurs will the full lesson of Aries be learned and wild im-
pulses and erratic action be ended. So long, however, as the
"servant," the lower Ego, remains willful and uncooperative,
it can not carry out the requests of the Lord from heaven,
the Angel-being who knows the truth.

In the Gospel of St. John, the Christ repeatedly speaks
of the "I AM," as in the statements: "I AM the light of the
world," "I AM the door," and "I AM the way, the truth, and
the life." All these sayings show the depth and the force of
Aries as indicating the "I AM" presence, and it would be
well for all souls, not only for those born in or under Aries,
to think about it long and often if they would become alive
to and be guided by the higher being of the solar Christ-man

within. For egotism and the darkness will only be exchanged for the light of the world and for Christ-altruism as man attains a conscious knowledge of this higher Ego.

"In the beginning was the Word." Man, made in the image of divine beings, is revealed in the speech or word of Aries, ruled by Mars. In the ancient Mysteries, it was disclosed that in virtue of the fact that certain Moon-beings were able to gaze on Mars, the capacity for speech was organized into man's etheric body. The twelve macrocosmic signs of the Zodiac correspond to the twelve senses of man. Aries is correlated with the *sense of speech*. The inner dynamics of the organs of speech reside in Aries. Man's capacity to regain and to use the "Lost Word" is contingent upon his becoming holy. When this time comes, he will become god-like and speak life into being, but not before. As we meditate upon this vernal sign, Aries, we realize how essential it is for man to refine himself in his soul, so that, raising his quality to higher octaves of spiritual power, he can release in his speech Christ-constructive building forces. Today, speech is prosaic, if not profane, yet language is derived from spiritual sources and should be used as an instrument and power of the wisdom of love and the spirit of truth. Man needs to regain awareness of the sacredness of speech.

Man, in his full significance and dignity as man, is bound up with speech. To those who know, the human voice tells all, for it is indicative of the whole character of the individual. It is the soul that expresses itself in sound, and one who is alive to it, realizes its strength or weakness, its temperament and talent, in fact, the whole coloration of the soul. The character of a people, likewise, is contained in, and can be known by, the configuration of its special speech or language.

The majority attach to a word some common mental image or degenerated concept, which has displaced the original, true concept derived from spiritual sources, and souls imperfectly developed or unbalanced mistake very easily what the word images for them for the actual idea. This is the reason why so many are lacking in the ability to build up a conceptual world of their own that could raise them to a higher level than that imparted by the common currency of words of the time. Most people today are slaves of the common quality of the spoken language; they fall prey to the vernacular of the day, and become the victims of the tyranny of community power and dupes not only of slogans, advertising, and authorities, but dupes also of demagogues and dictators, rather than being exponents of the upbuilding, illuminating spirit of truth. The destiny and genius of Aries is *truth*, and the truly balanced Aries soul is content with truth only.

Ill-direction in thought and action, error, a flair for the false and sometimes for the fatuous become the lot and lesson of Aries persons whose nativities show unbalanced factors or inharmonious aspects; yet even these can make the intense idealism of this sign into a growing reality, provided they have the will to search for truth in spite of all obstacles, so that their idealism ceases to be intangible, for Aries is the sign of truth as well as of speech, and without truth no true speech can be formed, for human speech is a mystery of God. While touching on speech, it might be mentioned that a well-aspected Mercury in Aries often makes linguists, for Aries has a flair for language.

In Aries is the element of the primal, undifferentiated consciousness. Out of this virgin element so chaotic, man must derive organization and balanced activity. At first, this outrushing force flings the man about severely through the intensity of desire, which burns in him and sometimes consumes him in that fire. Unique in this sign is the intense instinct factor, a quality more akin to the animal than to man becoming Christ-conscious. It is through this avenue of instinct that Aries expresses itself in abandoned disorder; in outrushing rashness, ram-headed impulsiveness, changeful activity, and digression; in a riot of rude strength and extreme self-will; in excess and extravagance; in explosiveness, combat, and courage; and even in foolhardy militancy and madness. Willful and headstrong when young, many Aries persons fail to achieve the necessary caution and control even in their mature years and they continue to go to extremes. Self-restraint, calmness, poise, and consideration for the feelings of others are not the virtues of Aries souls, unless they have worked upon themselves for the sake of the soul and spirit. The vigorous riot of life-activity, taking its rise in Aries, can never be adequately or properly utilized until a means of true self-control and self-direction is acquired through the harmony of balance and the ballast derived from the fixed signs conjoined with the mental-spiritual comprehensiveness conferred by the common or mutable signs.

Aries is a sign of male power, and it pushes one forward into positions of power through the pioneering of new fields and purposes; here do we find the quality of initiative. No success will be assured, however, in new ventures unless one has gained definition and direction, for this sign lacks the power of coherence. Equilibrium is the essential element that the person must perforce seek if he would evolve effectively. The forces of Aries are fiery and fast, but unless they are balanced by the influences of other signs, they are devoid of coherence and lacking in definite plan and purpose, thus leading the negative souls in this sign into a high degree of error, inaccuracy, or gross exaggeration. The most evident trait of Aries is intense activity, fired by ambitious, projective energy which must take command and be at the head, for Aries cannot follow, it can only lead.

The fiery, forceful character of this sign may be seen in the vulcanian genius of the dynamic conductor, Arturo Toscanini, whose Sun, Mercury, Neptune, and Part of Fortune were in Aries. The combination of the Sun in Aries, the Moon

in Sagittarius, and the Ascendant in Leo—all fire signs—
contributed to his intense brilliancy as well as to the power-
ful dramatic force that he expressed in music.

The influence of instinct, so marked in Aries, is at the root
of the disruptive, impulsive explosiveness in its natives when-
ever there is lacking a proper sense of direction because the
spiritual self-consciousness is not yet awakened. It is in this
sign that self-consciousness must come to expression, as must
a growing power of self-controlled destiny. Aries draws out
the awareness of self and shows the sower of the seed who
is founding the personality and shaping its particular destiny.
In Aries, the animal nature must become tamed and con-
trolled, so that the Christ may take up residence in the soul,
for this is the sign of the Sacrificial Ram and of the Lamb of
God slain for the redemption of the world, making possible
the eventual reunion of the Earth with the Sun.

It is significant in this respect that the Incarnation of the
Christ in Jesus of Nazareth, giving a new direction to the
entire evolution of the Earth, occurred when the Sun, by
precession of the equinox, was in Aries, marking the *turning
point of time*, from B.C. to A.D. An early symbol of the
Christ, arising out of cosmic wisdom, pictures a lamb or ram
with its head turned backward, as though looking into it-
self, indicative of the birth of the Ego-consciousness. Sur-
rounding the head is the Sun-Aureole, with its four directions
of space, linking the Christ-Sun-Being with the Creative
Powers of the Zodiac.

Today we need to realize that knowledge becomes a posi-
tive power only when it is made so by the light of the wisdom
of love and truth. This realization comes to active expression
in an individual only as he makes an increasingly conscious
contact with his own inner Christ-Spirit. Many imagine they
are in contact with this higher self when it is only some
earthbound, deceiving astral human soul, or their own Luci-
feric Angel. The voice of the Christ is the word of truth.

Today, most people on our planet cannot take the Christ-truth, nor do they seek it. Hence no peace can obtain in the world, for this peace must first be made manifest and realized in individual men and women as a leaven, to leaven the lump.

The leaders of men have too often followed animalistic instincts rather than human principles, and have failed to pioneer new paths of truth. Progress toward understanding and peace—the peace that Christ "gives," but "not as the world gives"—can only be achieved as man ceases to live by "bread alone, but by every word that proceeds out of the mouth of God." Man must be moved out of the darkness and aroused out of his apathy if our civilization is not to perish. When men spurn the spirit of truth, they deny the Christ of the cosmos and the beings of the Spiritual Hierarchies who made man in their image. Aries forces, either in a nativity or operative by transit or progression, should remind us to open our souls to the Christ-truth and to pioneer work in its behalf with fiery ardor.

Mars is the counterfeit of the Spirit when personal desires are served. The Mars cycle that began in 1909 and ended in 1944 produced two world catastrophies—World War I and, twenty-one years later, the global war. Contrasts can be resolved only by the formation of a new mind in mankind, the mind of Christ, whereby the intellect, the unlighted brain in man, will receive solar illumination. The new order of life will no longer sanction the exploitation of the weak by the strong nor the submergence of the individual in the state.

There are various levels of meaning in each sign of the Zodiac. A brute nature is one of the lower expressions of Aries; it is evident when one is of the opinion that might is right. The great wars should have revealed man to himself and made him manifest his manhood; his Ego should have become openly revealed in these ordeals. He should see himself as an Ego and decide on which side he will stand—

whether on the side of the rulers of darkness, symbolized by the butting ram, the ignorant personality, the lower nature blinded by matter, on or the side of human self-consciousness, the illuminated intellect, which is Christ-conscious and dedicated to truth.

The perversion of the virtues of Aries has led mankind into a world of lies and lust. The evil of error produces illusions and a distorted perspective, a view that is out of focus and untrue in the light of the Christ. Through this distortion men have become indifferent to truth, and in World War I the majority were not only confused in their minds as to the actual purpose of the war, but they were also left completely ignorant as to the causes that had led to it. In the second conflict the purpose was more evident, but the awful ignorance as to the nature of man remains, for man does not consciously recognize himself as a being of soul and spirit. The counterfeit of the Spirit, Mars, has led and bled mankind through these two world cataclysms, and only the true spirit of Christ with "healing in his wings" can bring real peace.

Overloaded with exuberant life-force, the Aries individuals are so overwhelmed by ambitious activity and animation that it becomes imperative for them to realize the "one thing needful" in their lives, which is to work to gain a fully controlled direction of their fine, rich forces through a knowledge of life and true awareness of themselves as beings of soul and spirit, temporarily animating a body. Life on earth is a continuing process of unfolding consciousness. Human beings started out in a state undifferentiated in God. Gradually they become Ego- or "I"-conscious; many are still in the process of growing out of their mere racial or national consciousness. The next stage for each individual is to become Christ-conscious and to grow into a consciousness embracing the world and the cosmos.

Aries individuals evolve best if they wisely coordinate their thoughts and actions through intensively profound and willed thinking. They can give a new direction to their lives if they have a right attitude toward life and gain a true knowledge of themselves, recognizing the real nature of Aries as fiery. As Scorpio purifies the desires through regeneration, which brings rebirth, Aries purifies thinking and raises thought power, compelling correction and advancing toward truth. Until truth is manifest as a living fact in life, Aries individuals cannot become the real pioneers they could be, for it cannot be stressed too often that Aries has for its inner, esoteric essence the educative action of *truth* through the power of the living Word or *Logos*. The road of approach to the spirit of truth is rocky and steep, hence a strong will is required if one would be a pilgrim on this Path. Only after one has received the pentecostal baptism of the Holy Spirit will he have a love for truth and work for the truth in love. Only as one serves this fine purpose can one bring to expression the pioneer spirit inherent in Aries, as it was expressed and manifested by the Aries-Sun man, Thomas Jefferson.

The intense idealism animating Aries makes its natives promise far more than they can perform, and they overload themselves with projects beyond their strength. Because of this unfortunate trait, they unintentionally often make themselves appear untruthful. Their excessive good intentions engender the reverse of veracity; and they may enlarge on circumstances to such an extent as to appear to be deliberately lying.

In the sequence of disciples in his Last Supper, Leonardo da Vinci assigned Peter to Sagittarius; however, this does not preclude the possibility of Peter manifesting traits of Aries, for every nativity comprises various zodiacal influences besides the Sun sign. Peter is an excellent example of promise outweighing performance—the result of the sheer riot of overwhelming mental force springing out of intense idealism, along with rash impulsiveness and the will to be a leader and never a laggard. "Peter said unto him, Although all shall be offended, yet will not I. And Jesus saith unto him, Verily I say unto thee, That this day, even in this night, before the cock crow twice, thou shalt deny me thrice. But he spake the more vehemently, If I should die with thee, I will not deny thee in any wise" (St. Mark 14: 29-31).

In Peter's denial of Christ we see the weakness that is too often manifest in Aries, for the spirit is willing but the flesh is weak. Even though the physical courage may be there, the intellectual strength great, and the spiritual impulse present, the spiritual stamina may not be sufficient; and, without this inner spiritual strength, there is a state of unbalance; no proper link exists between the lower earthly Ego, the "servant," and his Lord. As a result, where true courage should have been present—the courage that comes of the Christ—there was satanic fear, and Peter denied all knowledge of the One who alone could have furnished the strength, the spiritual light to stand with God against all the world without fear. We see this tendency today in a fear-ridden world, where people fear the death of the body but not that of the soul; many do not even believe in the soul. Peter's hasty drawing of his sword and cutting off the servant's ear in the hour of betrayal is yet another example of his Aries rashness and of his failure to trust the Spirit for protection.

We see the same Aries impulsiveness and rash independence in Peter's refusal to have his feet washed by the Christ. But when the Lord told Peter that he could not be his disciple unless he agreed to having his feet washed, Peter avidly asked that the Lord wash his hands and head as well; he wanted to be every whit clean, clean all over.

Persons with Aries dominant have fine intellectual strength; the will-to-be-manifest is very intense because of the idea of self, and this gives them the great power to pioneer and to lead. Yet this leadership and pioneering invariably fall short of perfection, sometimes because the spiritual *will* is so much less developed in the individual, and because there is no coordination between the spiritual man, the Lord from heaven, and the earthly personality, the servant. And where there is no conscious link between the lower earthly man and the higher spiritual being, there is no proper power to pioneer, to lead a movement, to spread a teaching, or to become the spokesman for masses of humanity.

Once a bridge has been built between the lower and the higher man, once the baptism of the Holy Spirit has filled one with life, the Christ guiding and strengthening the soul, then truly has that man become a "new creature." This "new creature" is evident in Peter in the first half of the Acts of the Apostles, following the pentecostal baptism with spiritual fire. Peter, the pioneer for Christ, was the main spokesman on the day of Pentecost and on numerous other occasions, and he was repeatedly arrested, imprisoned, and enjoined to silence by the rulers, but no earthly power could stay him or frighten him, for as he said, "We must obey God rather than men" (Acts 5:29). The multitudes, as well as the magistrates, marveled at his boldness: "Now when they beheld the boldness of Peter and John, and had perceived that they were unlearned and ignorant men, they marveled; and they took knowledge of them, that they had been with Jesus" (Acts 4:13).

It is the purpose of life and the need of all men to become Christ-conscious, which means that a bridge must be built from the lower, earthly brain-bound man to his higher being, the heavenly man. In proportion to one's power to correlate with and do the bidding of the Christ within, are love and wisdom operative and our knowledge of truth enhanced. No college or school, only the lighted human Ego in the Earth-school, can give the tuition that gains the only degrees honored by the one great schoolmaster, the Father in heaven.

Aries gives a strong sense of personality and selfhood. In it is the deeply buried seed of the original, archetypal essence, the living core of the Ego, which has to blossom and bear fruit for the Christ. But, when the personality, which after all is only a part and not the whole, projects itself, a balance is required. A foil must be found to set against Aries as a complementing force, and this will be found in its complementary, opposite sign, Libra, the sign of supra-personality, which contains the whole and its parts.

If Aries evokes the idealism of truth, that truth becomes consummate in a love of justice, which is the justice of love engendered in the light of Libra, the right hand of Aries' left hand. Until one balances Aries through Libra, he will say with Pontius Pilate, "What is truth?" but will not stay, nor work, for an answer. For only as the physical, earthly personality becomes moulded consciously by the supra-personal, spiritual, heavenly man, will Christ-consciousness come to birth.

Aries comes forth from the plane of intellect and rules through egotism, until the complementary sign, Libra, impels one to make a choice, for it is Libra that must choose the way, the road of return to God by way of the spiritualized intellect. In Aries, the intellect must become lighted by the Spirit if separation and darkness are to be overcome and if union and illumination are to occur. This is the marriage of the Lamb, for which Aries people must work. It means the end of egotism and the beginning of an active altruism. Unless the Spirit is awakened, Aries people are active only in their own interests.

The martial energy of Aries fires its natives with so intense a cerebral activity, setting up so much diffusion, as to make proper thinking well-nigh impossible; as a result, they are unable to marshal ideas with sufficient definition and clarity to create harmony and balance. The living fire of rash moods often produces most peculiar prejudices, so that the first impressions of the Aries souls are not always true; on second thought, their views are often altered. Second thoughts, deeply meditative, are essential for Aries. In fact, their best road to balance is by way of second thoughts wisely applied. Yet Aries souls turn time and again to people, places, or things that had proved detrimental or disappointing.

The evolved Aries individual is fertile with constructive ideas and is prompt to act. He will fight for the rights of man, and sometimes the Ram, or the Lamb, will sacrifice itself and take pride in such martyrdom. Most Aries souls make their lives a school of very hard experience, for they are the souls that back up and leave, instantly taking offence at measures or laws they consider odious or unfair.

Aries is the sign of a *new cycle* and of the *pioneer*. It marks the vernal equinox and the new life of spring. In the spring season, we see in the physical world the newness of life, and it rejoices our hearts. But we should be reminded at the same time of that other, higher newness of life, which St. Paul had in mind when he said "old things are passed away." Any period when Aries forces prevail is propitious for pioneering some new purpose and for propagating a spiritual activity which, with consistent practice, will bring the eventual triumph over death, for Aries is the sign of resurrection and the Resurrection.

The essence of Aries is the urge that impels persons to new ideas, plans, thoughts, or proposals. New schemes throng their brains in quick succession, and they are ever embarking upon new enterprises, large or small, commensurate with the consciousness of the Ego. Once they see the aim or end of a plan and their will is aroused, they are rarely swerved from their purpose to bring it to accomplishment, being ever spurred on by the mental picture of the plan which they envision. But patience is scarcely a virtue of the Ram, and the impetuous approach of the Aries natives, ramming ahead and forcefully pushing their way forward, brings them too often to grief or undoing. Unless the nativity indicates an aptitude in dealing with detail, they are better fitted to lead, organize, and create, rather than personally to carry out their plans in practice.

The aim of Aries is *action*, but action must have wise

direction and must be governed by forces founded on truth. This is the sign whose ideal and destiny is the spirit of truth, and Aries souls must make themselves ready to receive and to realize the truth. This can only be done by consistently working to approach the truth, which is the *Great Work*. As much as we have taken into ourselves of the Christ-truth, so shall we be free from bondage to the lower earthly Ego.

Fine spiritual qualities inhere in Aries, for there is an excellent sense of righteousness with the courage and enthusiasm to work and serve to make righteousness prevail on earth. Today there is a desire, an urge, to dissolve the deceptive, backward systems everywhere, as the kingdom of man fails and is bound to fail without the light of the kingdom of God. Once the Aries individual gains stability, he gains definition, and with definition he finds his direction and the power to move forward, making fine progress and going fast and far. When he reaches devotion, he may rise to the power of sacrifice.

THE DAWN

Would he who made all worlds and man
Omit to give the good his plan?
Does order rule our lives or hate?
Will love abide and compensate?
Could all this loathsomeness remain
With Christ arrived to make man sane?
Here in this day disintegrates
The leprous sin of ancient hates;
The foulness of a day now done
Doth bring the *dawn* and *love* begun.
The *pioneer* doth pave the way
For love to come and have full sway.
The spirit speech make man so clean
And search his soul so much to glean
That grain of magic potency
Which brings to man Christ-majesty!

Taurus - The Bull

TAURUS, the Bull, the only earth sign that is also a fixed sign, tells of the energies of the earth and man's use of, and often bondage to, earthly things and forces. A fruitful energy, which may express itself for good or ill, manifests in this second sign of the Zodiac. Its vice is inertia—peace at any price. Its virtue is a successful, practical achievement bringing concrete results. The Taurean feels much at home on the earth. The evolved Taurean inwardly realizes that as the earth fructifies seeds and brings plants to maturity, so the earthly body must become enclothed by the higher, spiritual, heavenly man. He realizes that the earthly body has office and existence as a temple of God.

The Bull is indicative not only of great strength, but also of extraordinary digestive powers. Metabolism is the mode of Taurus. A marvelous expression of metabolism is found in the bovine species which chews the cud, digesting, redigesting, assimilating, and transmuting food into other forces. Similarly, must facts, ideas, and experiences long be chewed upon, as cud, by Taurean souls, before they are assimilated and resolved into new truth.

Taurus-represents the primordial desire-force that must be transformed into the priceless possession of the perfected man doing the will of the Father. In Taurus, man's desires must be transmuted into spiritualized *will*. The physical must be used as the vehicle in refining and raising the soul's quality. Indicating this verity, there is, in addition to the symbol of the Bull, the picture of a coiled serpent. Its folded coils reveal the latent, concentrated energy and stored-up occult powers, held in silent, ready reserve, as in a granary of peculiar power, gained in the harvests of many earthly lives. The source of these powers is the soul, and their force of manifestation is contingent upon love and purity.

Taurus is seen then as a soul-source of power. Here is a magazine of mighty moods, a reservoir as it were, of concealed, confined, emotional force held in the bond of one great, intense feeling, which is often released in that peculiar occult quality of prayer and praise, which is true song. This sign rules the vocal cords and gives expression to the voice, for the life of the larynx manifests in Taurus, as well as the power of productive, physical labor, the means of making money and gaining by means of material concerns and the products of the earth.

Occult forces are held here in storage, kept latent against

the time, or the life, when they will be needed and become active for other earthly expressions of the Christed Ego. Just as the constellation of Taurus is the greatest in the Zodiac, so too is the sign the mighty reservoir for all of the faculties man has gained throughout his various lives on earth. In this sign is the secret source of storage. But, only those moving on the higher level of Christ-life can tap this vast storehouse of occult supply. The service of this intense sign is to sound out the senses and to build higher octaves of soul quality. With deliberation Taurus takes hold of the physical forces in man and, through earthly work, concretely manifests and creates in such wise as to generate, from the Spirit within, a heightened power of soul as a distillate.

Here, in this sign of latent power, we see and understand the great strength inherent in the British people, the forces of the British Empire. For, even though Aries rules England, Taurus rules the British Isles, and we see John Bull as a typical Taurean. Such Taurean Bull-spirit power came to expression in Queen Victoria. This tiny woman, with the cusp of Taurus-Gemini rising, carried and symbolized the strength that was Great Britain, standing in the vanguard of civilization and committed to the ideal of spiritual freedom. In the strength of Taurus, the mighty sign holding the Pleiades, Queen Victoria possessed the forces to bond and build the vast congeries of nations as far-flung as the British Empire, a Commonwealth of free nations, foreshadowing a new age of friendship of all nations and peoples. Such was the focal point, the mighty well-spring of archetypal spiritual power inherent in this little, but colossal woman.

Insofar as physical forces are concerned, no sign exhibits greater stolidity and solidity than Taurus. It rules finances and foundations handling funds, and it gives the ability to earn and to disburse money. More than any other sign, Taurus not only gives a forte, but also much finesse in the transaction of financial affairs and their management. Highly evolved Taureans, in their largess, may be called doers of the bountiful. The practical power to earn money and to energize activity through money and the concerns of physical property is part of the expression and experience of Taurus. Its natives invariably encounter intensely significant happenings connected with money and property, which arrest attention and provide spiritual lessons on the earth and after death.

The purpose of planetary life and of repeated births of both man and planet is to incorporate in man-in-the-making a new member, the *Ego,* for which it was necessary to make the involutionary descent into earthly density; now, there follows the evolutionary ascent into spiritual realms, by way of the wisdom of love, both man and planet being raised to the magnitude of the Sun-power itself. In this process of densification, purification, and sublimation, perhaps the most telling test and turning point occurs in the first earthy sign, Taurus, which is also the first fixed sign of the Zodiac. For, true to the ancient symbol of the coiled serpent, there lie concealed in Taurus the profound depths of desire, which must be transmuted into spiritualized will. Although the mood of matter becomes the manifest mode of Taurus, these intensely physical experiences are being proffered to the soul solely to lead the man to mastery, never to master the man or to subvert that in him which is spiritual. The desires and rude strength, secretly concentrated in the Taurean, must be touched by the magic of transmutation through the indwelling Christ-Spirit, and the thinking must be lighted by Spirit-truth. Otherwise, the principle of *will* will be at war with the desires of these Taurean souls, and it will often run amuck in the world, until such time as fleshly desires are transformed through true vision and purity. The keynote and destiny of Taurus centers in the *obedience* of the lower man to the higher, spiritual self, the "Lord from heaven."

The sum and substance of Taurus is not only the solid and

the stolid, and the power of patient persistence working into a soul-spiritual distillate or essence—this alchemy it does work—but also the secret of sound and the utterance of speech; for Taurus manifests the power to vocalize and to form and pronounce the word. True song sounds forth from Taurus and often it gives the genius to set down the harmonies of heaven, as we see in Beethoven, with the middle of Taurus rising, and Uranus therein, making his power still more dynamic, forceful, and spiritually charged with the compassionate warmth of Christ-love. By studying a picture of Ludwig van Beethoven and listening to his music, one comes to understand far more deeply the mighty purpose and power in this sign of the Bull than by reading the most skilled description of it. The powerful composer of heavenly harmonies, song, and symphonies, Johannes Brahms, had his Sun in Taurus. In Franz Schubert, we also see Taurean power on the Ascendant, although the forces are toned down and rendered angelic by his Moon joined to Jupiter in Pisces, and his Sun in Aquarius.

To those who can see and know, Richard Wagner appears in a Taurean garment inwardly and outwardly, although the Eagle sign, Scorpio, may be evident, because of his Uranus in Scorpio opposing the Taurus-Gemini Ascendant. He had Venus and Mercury in Taurus; and his Sun as well as his Ascendant shared the cusp of this sign of song. Taurean traits appeared throughout his life. It may seem irrelevant, but it is still of psychological interest to show the close, though often subconscious, relationship and kinship of souls woven by the soul-spiritual forces of the signs of the Zodiac, as people meet and move in their earthly life. There is a fine example in Richard Wagner, who served the London Philharmonic Orchestra for six painful months. The bright spot of his life there was his summons to the royal box, where Queen Victoria highly praised his marvelous music. Queen Victoria's Ascendant, Sun, and Moon were in the early degrees of Gemini on Wagner's Ascendant and Sun. Both shared the Taurus-Gemini cusp and were attuned to each other in their physical-soul-spiritual forces.

In the galaxy of opera stars and singers, we find a large number of Taureans, for Taurus is the sign of song and sound. We may say again that true song is real prayer and praise to God, just as is the song of the birds. And, as the song of the birds open the buds on the trees, so does the peculiar soul-spiritual energy in and behind vocalized sound, when true, build the forces for the Spirit and open the soul to the love of wisdom and truth, which is God. Sound, then, as a source of soul forces, manifests in the sign Taurus as it becomes audible in earthly, human tones. The quality and power of human speech, as a creative, healing power, is perceived by the seer as arising in the forces of fixed signs, but especially in this sign of song and voice, Taurus, that brings it to a focus, as it were, and gives it direction, its quality being sensed, if not heard, by the timbre of the tone.

The voice expresses the soul through sound, in audible speech and tone. In the voice can be heard, and felt, and known the mind and the emotion of the individual, as well as the quality of his soul. The speech uttered by the human voice tells the spiritual knower the whole truth about the man. Although there is a measure of truth in Tallyrand's statement that "Speech was given us to conceal thoughts," and it is quite apropos as regards diplomatic relations among nations, the dramatist and poet Ben Jonson spoke the truth when he said, "Language [voice] most shows a man: Speak, that I may *see* thee! It springs out of the retired and inmost parts of us, and is the Image of the parent of it, the mind. No glass renders a man's form and likeness so true as his speech." He who hears the harmonies of heaven or senses the sound of the zodiacal tones has come into union with God, with the voice of God, and with his vision. Through in-tense meditation upon the Zodiac and spiritual study of the stellar script, one is raised from the dead. One rises out of the corpse of present-day convention, brain-bound abstraction, and the lack of love to which they lead, as well as the degenerating love of ease and self-indulgence that are the bane of Taurus.

Since Taurus manifests the physical forces of song and sound, the throat becomes either the strength or the weakness of those souls born in or under this sign, in accord with the quality of the Ego and the destiny-debt due for liquidation. But, on the whole, Taureans suffer more from an oversupply of strength than from its paucity. They often give way to fear, and then laziness and self-indulgence often beset them, which may lead to stagnation because of their selfish love of ease. Such a regimen all too soon breaks down the stamina of the body for lack of a natural, healthy, physical activity and the absence of a mental-spiritual life. We see now all over the world the spreading of this kind of disease as man refuses to exert himself in the sense of spiritual life.

As Aries flies outward from a center, in irradiating, flinging forces, in purely centrifugal fashion wild with waste, so Taurus behaves in exactly the opposite manner. It throws its forces into a center in centripetal action. Aries is exhibitive and expressive; Taurus, inhibitive and compressive. So persistent are the moods of emotion, so compressed the feelings, that Taureans are faced with a collision of their thought and their feelings. Thus, contradictory states are the result, which often make the Taurean impossible to deal with. The emotional forces become so conflicting and entangled with the thought that the moods declare themselves in a sullen silence which is more eloquent than speech. Undeveloped Taureans are to themselves and often to others quite impossible, because of their torrential, destructively dangerous emotion. Of the twelve senses, Taureans need to develop the *sense of thinking*. This sense of thinking, when rightly developed, can save them from their damaging emotional forces.

Materialistic thinking, the mere intellect, tends to dominate the Taureans, however, and they want nothing that cannot be set into earthly concepts. The heaven of the Taureans would have to be a glorified physical existence. To attain to Ego-consciousness and freedom, it was temporarily necessary for man to have his sight limited to the earth and to earthly conditions. Now the time has come when the human being must discover that he has within himself the whole cosmos. The power of the cosmos, the Christ, is condensed into a central focus in the man. This spiritual power must become usable and released in the earthly man, if he is to be raised to a divine status. To do this safely, one must become wise with love and add to his intellect the light of Spirit-truth, which is the voice of the archetypal Christ-Ego within. It is the voice that transcends the vocalization of sound in speech, the Taurean instrument, which the intellectual person in this fixed earthy sign must learn to listen to and hear well if he would find the Christ in himself, as well as the cosmic Christ in the Earth, for to hear the Spirit sounding in one's self is to hear the greater voice and see the higher, vividly vital vision of the Lord of the Sun. Veritably the voice and vision act as the word and the wand to wield the world and all humanity into a single unit of divine power made of God's substance, the light.

No soul becomes articulate or animated with Christ-life until the merely intellectual thinking of Taurus is transcended. A large part of humanity today, but especially the earth-minded Taureans, arrested by the boundary and bondage of the brain, believe the pinnacle of man is reached in the mind, that the brain is the end and essence of man. But, there is much more to man than the corpse-like thoughts he carries, the thoughts that have built this exterior physical fabric of civilization and that are now the cause of degeneration, hatred, and misunderstanding. The unevolved Taurean would be content to live on bread alone and not on every word that proceeds out of the mouth of God. There is far more to man than the earthbound thought power. In man there is that which transcends the physical, for beyond the body there is the soul, fed by the light of the Spirit. Yet the Taurean often sets limits to himself where light is concerned, by making his life a continuous residence in the earthly brain-bound concepts of the intellect unlighted by the Christ-truth light. It is as though one were to look at a picture not with the object of contemplating the essential idea which it expresses, but merely of examining and determining the various component colors of the paint—the physical substance of the paint employed, rather than the spiritual idea as it was conceived and expressed.

I knew one such Taurean who recoiled from the spiritual with real dread, because this idea left him bereft of his body and brain, his earthly physical garment. He felt that the idea of Spirit denied and deprived him of his sense of egohood; he was afraid he would lose his identity and be utterly swallowed up in the solar system, for he had no center of Christ-force to call his own. In such intellectual thought, we often find the Taureans to be the most naïve, if not naked, in the sense of soul and Spirit. This is the mode of science, however, a mode of thought without any sense for spiritual reality, which sees only the bare exterior part and never the spiritual whole. Only those who sense and see the whole can ever properly know the part, the physical body of man and of the Earth; the rest ruminate or merely speculate where they do not deliberately fabricate. In any event, the element of error gets in its deadly work, as witness the world today. It is the test of Taurus not only to become accurate in thinking, but also to become *obedient* to the higher nature.

The lessons of the Taurean souls get them invariably involved in very intensive experiences in connection with physical things, property, and money. They are usually adept at earning money and providing finance and income for others, for they usually have to furnish funds for others as a part of their destiny-duty; it is in the scheme of their life's lessons. Acquisitiveness seems to be the mainspring and goal of their activities; they give their time and energy to gaining physical rewards, and through this they learn very important lessons, sometimes through misdirecting accumulated funds. But, even here, the seeming evil works for eventual good as the personality is stripped of the hindering, spiritually blinding brain and body. I remember the case of one who learned and then lifted her life into the light, after death, when she saw in true perspective the results of her maladministration of the estate left behind.

Taurus souls seldom touch the Spirit and realize the *real* except as they pass through a period of extreme materialistic thought activity, and it is their intensely earthly, earthy endeavor that leads ultimately to a regenerated life, even after death. At last the soul then obeys the Spirit, and the fruit of the earthly experience, in the spiritual worlds after death, reverses the view, to permit the soul right vision. If the lessons have been learned, the next life may be one become Christ-solarized.

No sign more than this one, which inhibits and compresses the feelings, more often explodes at last in ruinous desires. In no other domain of the Zodiac is the element of misjudgment more evident, be it in thought, feeling, or desire, for the contradictory moods tend to make the man unreasonable. In this connection, I remember a man I used to look at with my soul before saying "Good morning" to him, for had I not done so, many a morning I would have received scowls, silence, or worse, in response, depending on the amount of alcohol he still carried. And it must be observed that the sensual appetites are large in Taurus. They are avid for food and have a tremendous capacity for it; it seems almost they have, like the bull, many stomachs.

The forces of will and of desires are held in latent potency in Taurus, and they lie concealed and coiled within the soul, suppressed and dammed back until some incident or provocation touches off the fuse, firing the pent-up power with the force of an explosion. It takes much to goad a Taurean into excited action, but once the boiling point is reached, he becomes furious and is actually beside himself with rage, like a mad bull, usually to the great surprise of the attacker.

If a Taurean can disengage himself from his fixity and phlegm—and this may occur when he receives the inner light—and if other things are equal in his nativity, his interest is aroused, giving him an ambition as great for the Spirit of truth and for "preaching the gospel and healing the sick," as that which earlier he had entertained toward his selfish, mercenary, and materialistic activities. Yet, for the most part, there persists in the Taureans a delaying if not a damaging materialism, an intellectualism that delights in a life conceived too wholly, if not solely, in the physical. Too often, their worship of the Golden Calf casts them far from the feet of the Master, the Christ. They remain old-fashioned and very conservative; they take themselves often for the cosmos itself, rather than for a part of it. To be of true service to the cosmos, one needs a baptism of divine love in pentecostal downpouring, thus to become lighted cosmically. When that occurs, man knows himself to be an instrument of the gods, serving the heavenly Hierarchies with a definite and well-ordered purpose.

In the youthful years, before his astral body is fully born at puberty, the Taurean shows a beautiful meditative, contemplative mood of calm and quiet kindness; but, with the astral body matured and the blind brain merged with the desires, the Bull's fixed forces are so aroused as to cast the maturing youth into a state of defiance that is likely to remain implacable. At this age, the force of opposing emotional moods becomes evident and often devitalizing. The placidity changes into passion, manifesting in stubborn recalcitrancy that renders reasoning or argument impossible. Intrinsically, the character of Taurus is genuinely honest, but there is often a lack of accuracy and sometimes an element of self-deception, which makes Taureans live in delusion. In fact, they will feed on fallacies and harm their true progress. In this connection, it is well to note that no correction or help will induce Taureans to rectify or transmute their faults or give up their fallacies, except when they yield to the advice of someone they love or greatly admire. Their errors in thought or in action can only be pointed out to them by those they esteem; but, once they realize they are at fault, they will remove the blemish, provided their will is ripe enough to do so.

As man emancipates himself from his spiritual ignorance, children will be reared and taught not only as though they were mere bodies of flesh or beings endowed solely with a brain; rather, their education will address itself also to the soul and spirit indwelling in the child. The nature of man in his true sevenfold content will be known and honored, and childhood will no longer be violated, as it is today, when the child is taught to read and write before the change of teeth at about the seventh year of life. The defiant and sensual character, however, the stubborn moods and emotions, the contradictory and often torrential elements in Taurus, can be redirected and transmuted before they develop, provided the start is made in infancy and the child is rightly reared through stellar insight and spiritual wisdom. I have known mothers who were at their wits' end over their Taurean children. Yet, it is true that this explosive force of the Bull spirit can be transmuted properly into the secret Serpent Spirit Fire if the proper means are used from the beginning, for this is the sign of the coiled serpent as well as that of the heavy-necked Bull.

Taureans must transform their egocentric attitude if they

are to move ahead in a positive way; otherwise, they remain obstinate and immovably stubborn because of their self-will, and such rigid resistance allows no proper expression. The best thing a Taurean can learn in life is that it is to his greatest advantage to recognize his phlegm and fixity. Let him face his large quota of prejudices and hates, and overcome his strong inner reserve and diffidence. His tempo is quite unhurried; so slow, in fact, that the destiny forces unfold belatedly, with all the phlegm that goes with this sign, the effects of his self-delusion being carried on and on, frequently to dog him after death. Early environment and parental influence are very critical factors in the case of Taureans. Their destiny will be largely determined by the type of parents the self-created destiny will allow the Ego to take. It should be realized by these souls that chastity is an important secret of their success, and that the conservation of their life forces and a life led in positive constructive Christ manner lead to illumination, whereas the waste of such forces results in a depletion or destruction of the soul.

The paradox of passion and peace finds its expression in Taurus, for with the quality of obedience and a nature that is trustful, conservative, gentle, and kindhearted, there is combined at the same time the fury of a vicious self-will, a stubborn recalcitrant spirit, whose force invariably matches the power of the opponent. But the best avenue for Taureans is to find a release in song, music, and art; and in this Venus sign, this forte is usually present. It is true enough that most people have to learn that there is no goal but God, but Taureans especially have to realize this fact on earth, rather than in the realm of the dead, for far more can be done, and faster progress be made, if this truth is recognized while the Ego retains tenure of its physical body.

A delightful sense of humor is of great help and happiness to Taureans. One is carried more buoyantly through life with such a quality of soul, for it enables one to maintain courage, and it helps others to keep poised in trying days, when darkness and difficulties loom ahead. The ability to see and to enjoy the comical side of a situation is British, despite the American notion that the British lack humor. Taurus rules the British Isles as a whole, and John Bull portrays exactly this second sign of the Zodiac, the Bull sign, whose force ever outmatches the power of his opponent. There is no sense of the comical that compares with this happy possession of the British, and when peril of war oppresses, it seems to reach its highest expression. Such a sense of humor may be traced in its psychic connection to optimism, which subconsciously discerns an unseen higher light.

Things not fully understood by a Taurean are sometimes simply ignored or even detested; and, if such ideas or proposals are pressed upon him, his fury is likely to be aroused in opposition, in virtue of the stubborn, unreasoning fixed-sign force. However, once get him to see and comprehend the idea or plan, he will be as steadfast in its persistent promulgation as previously he was opposed to it, whether for lack of interest or ignorance. Will power and persistence are present in Taurus, but they do not manifest until either ambition or interest are aroused, even though these incentives usually act with slowness, because of the fixed force of this most unhurried sign. But once an idea is grasped, or some task recognized as necessary, and a definite plan is reached, no pains, nor time or energy will be spared to gain the goal.

Taurus is actually the very "soil" of the soul. It is a soil that is rough, raw, and often rude, and it must be redeemed. This regeneration invariably takes place through physical forces inherent in earthly wealth, money, property, and all things included in the economic life. Especially, the way the metabolism of the body operates, creating a state of well-being as a result of the food taken in, contributing to health and generating the forces required to resist disease, is Taurean in its nature. Of all the fixed signs, Taurus is the most retentive, the life-force being held by matter more securely here than in other signs.

Just as the archetypal idea for the human Ego, the Christ-individual, is contained in the primal pioneering sign of male force, Aries, so the substance for the manifestation of man derives from the fixed earthly female sign, Taurus. In Aries is shaped the unique personal destiny, the principle that founds the earthly form, self-aware of its Egohood in its will-to-be-*man*ifest. Aries is the "sower" of the intellectual Gemini "seed" in the earthy substance of Taurus, the "soil" that in a literal sense also provides the elements needed for the growth of the higher kingdoms: plants, animals, and man.

Whereas Aries stands for the primal archetypal pattern of man, Taurus signifies the primordial substance of the manifested self, which was spoken into being "in the beginning" by the Word. Taurus holds the synthesis of past lives as psychic inheritance and basic possession. Here we see the strong conserving and retaining force, which can either retard or bring true ballast to the man as he evolves in will, in thought, and in feeling; for, Taurus is the most retentive of the twelve signs, and this power, the most concentrated, may be wisely used or wildly misused. In no other sign of the Zodiac are the life forces more suppressed or the impulses more inhibited than in this sign of the "soil," save in one respect, that of the voice and speech.

In Taurus, the energies of the earth become either a boon or a bondage, depending on whether the soil of the soul is redeemed or not, for in this sign is the reservoir of forces, the storehouse of past harvests, held as concentrated power; the quality of compression and conservation is held over from past lives, to be retained inherently. The truth about reincarnation—repeated lives on Earth—becomes evident by observing men and women in their humanity, but it is especially evident in Taureans who are able to release matured forces long held in storage from the past. In Taurus, the forces of past lives are either manifested on a higher octave of power, or the Taurean is submerged by his own sense of suppression. In this respect, we may point again to the ancient symbol of Taurus, the coiled serpent, realizing that in Taurus lie concealed abysmal depths of often searing but ever searching desire that ultimately must be transmuted into will. It is the concealed quality, which we would emphasize as the cause of conservation and concentration in this sign.

What the world calls "practicality" is often said to be the trait peculiar to Taureans, for they are usually people with a capacity to collect the coin of the realm. It is their forte to deal with the physical and financial, to make money, with some success, for their lesson in evolution binds them to the energies of the earth. The truly practical, however, is at the same time the spiritual. Today, humanity suffers and civilization breaks down wherever this true, spiritually real practicality is disregarded. The evolutionary task of the Taureans is to acquire this power of the truly practical. They are the souls that need to be "born again," theirs is the great work to raise themselves to far higher octaves of consciousness, to be regenerated and re-educated. And, according to their power of *will*, their vision will vitalize their activities, refine their souls, and elevate their minds, while their consciousness will be heightened and vastly expanded. In Taurus one discovers in the end that the only worthwhile possession is spiritual self-possession.

It must be kept in mind that Taurus is a sign of great reserve and retention, deep-rooted in the past. Taureans are fixed in purpose and plodding, possessing for the most part more endurance and a stronger body than individuals in other signs of the Zodiac. Being practical, and embodying the drive of silent *determination* and great perserverance, Taureans make concrete the energies of the earth. Their forte is endurance; their vice is obstinacy. As a certain amount of

salt is good, but too much ruins the food, so the commend-
able Taurean quality of determination, carried to excess,
easily turns into stubbornness. Great reservoirs of energy can
be tapped on need, and then the strength, and often the
obstinacy of the Bull, become apparent. Extremely strong-
willed, they can be led by persuasion, but never driven.
These are the men who mould and make things; manu-
facturers and builders. Although it is in the province of the
Aries souls to create the abstract idea, which they pioneer
and promote in their idealism and inspiration, it remains for
the Taureans actually to translate the idea into reality by
moulding and giving shape to matter. Thus, Aries idealizes
while Taurus realizes. Aries is the architect, but Taurus the
builder.

Through the forces of conservation and compression in this
fixed, earthy sign, Taureans are non-adaptable and averse to
change or innovations. Whatever knowledge and skill they
have, they bought at the price of experience, for their fixed
mental attitude binds them to the effete and outmoded, fol-
lowing tradition rather than truth. Taureans, like Pisceans,
love peace at any price, yet once aroused, they take on the
force and fury of the bull and run amuck, losing control of
themselves.

Taurus is ruled by Venus, and so this sign is often a furnace
of affection, with strong healing forces, which make Taureans
good masseurs, doctors, nurses, etc. However, if we keep in
mind the negative Venusian quality of this sign, we may
gain some insight into what makes these natives sensuous if
not sensual, given to worldly pleasures and to venting their
animal desires, very fond of food, and usually inordinate
meat eaters, somewhat slovenly in dress and appearance. Of
course, these habits obtain only in those living principally
in their desires, which then have full and sweeping rule over
the true man, the higher self. When, on the other hand, these

souls turn to the Spirit and walk on the way of *will*, they show vast powers of concentration and a matchless perseverance.

There is no sign that may compare with Taurus for the storage of life forces; thus, its vitality is great. This over-supply of life can be an asset or an evil, depending on the mode of life, whether it is lived in the spiritual will or in the fleshly desires. No one can move farther ahead on the path of return to God than a highly developed Taurean using his will, and none can be flung down farther than a Taurean serving his fleshly lusts in an abandoned manner. In any event, this negative Venus sign, more than all others, gives to its natives intensely pronounced experiences; happenings that tend to turn and attune the Ego to far higher octaves of true living and thinking, in the future.

If one studies Taurus, its place in the nativity, and the planets it holds, and its ruler Venus, one sees behind the scenes of one's own life its stored-up forces and qualities; these are the abilities, faculties, and powers held in abeyance and not active in this life, at least not in the larger part of it, but sometimes expressed at the end of life, as in the case of Swedenborg, whose Moon and Uranus were conjunct in Taurus in his fourth house, indicating the latter part of life.

In a world-historical sense, Taurus tells of the past when the Bull was properly worshipped, when the Sun, by precession of the equinox, stood in Taurus during the Egyptian civilization. In this symbol of strength, man increasingly sought to master the outer, material world and his own inner world of animal instincts. Its forces have worked on and moulded the material, so that its potent occult content will now be used to raise the man to spiritual height and power, to lead man to his true strength by way of the spiritualized will, working to sublimate the flesh, through a proper transmutation, in virtue of the interior alchemy of the Christ in man and in the planet.

When we think of Taurus, we think of the tremendous, and we realize that this mighty constellation is the largest in the Zodiac, and at the end of it are the Pleiades, a group of stars said to lead to bad sight or blindness, intense ambition, and often violent death. Yet, whoever has Taurus dominant and has the will to become wise, can generate the "oil" to light the lamp of his soul, enabling him to *see*, for in this sign of latent occult power lie concentrated the forces that bring illumination. It is a question, however, of the spiritual will getting the mastery over the animal desires, for if Taurus lives in its lower phase, it gives expression to the lust of life, fondness for ease and luxury, as well as a tendency to spend itself in drinking and feasting. Taureans stagnate and may tend to die while living because of their stubbornness in avoiding true thinking. They are often so lazy as to have no desire for concentrating their thoughts. Their cynicism too often shows an utter disregard for the eternal verities, the reality of the truth of the Spirit.

Taureans are often impervious to true religion or to spiritual science, yet even though they shy away from esoteric teaching, they are usually fatalists, their professed indifference or scepticism to truth being comfortably set aside in this thought, because of their psychic or inner feeling. If at all religious, they incline to ceremony and ritual, the Venus influence moving them with music and song.

Taurean feelings being very intense, a terrific concentration of fixed force, these souls are either one's faithful friends, kind and affable, or relentless enemies and unappeasable foes, unless one can appeal to their feelings. They must be most choice and careful in selecting a marriage partner, for in this negative Venus sign there is a likelihood of mistakes, and the more so if the marriage is contracted in younger years. Very pronounced, soul-shaking, and mind-arresting experiences are likely to occur in Taurus and in a second house configuration—experiences that work actively to turn and transform the man by their magnitude, experiences that jolt him out of his contented gravitation toward the purely earthly.

One can learn much about Taurus if one understands the animal representative of this sign, the cow, a ruminant that is primarily digestion and that eats daily about one-eighth of its weight. It seems weighed down by the gravity of the earth. This is especially evident if one observes a herd of contented cows, lying in the pasture, slowly chewing the cud, reluctant to raise their heavy heads. How different they are from a flock of birds flying through their rightful element, the air, and how remarkable the agility with which the birds move their heads!

Our wonderful scientific civilization is the result of our working with the earthly, with the things that can be numbered, measured, and weighed; but this lifeless technology will become a deadly thing with an evil effect, unless man discovers the spiritual forces of nature that lie hidden within the physical substance itself, for that truly is real which is spiritual, and this is the light that shines in the darkness. An idea of the deeply intense materialism of our age may be gathered from the answer given to the question, "What is real?" by a celebrated physicist, who said, "That is real which can be measured; that is not real which cannot be measured." This is the danger today, the danger of the darkness of the brain, which takes the Taurean number, measure, and weight as the only reality, with no allowance for the spiritual imponderables.

Man remains in bondage to his body and brain, a slave to the energies of the earth, unable to transcend the merely intellectual, thinking in terms of the sense-perceptible only, and looking to nothing more than a physical heredity, until the Spirit illumines the darkness. Not till then does man become a true builder in and with the fixed forces of this earth sign. This power of Taurus becomes fertile and fruitful in the measure in which the Man, Aquarius, is able to synthesize this sign with the two other fixed signs, Leo and Scorpio, the Lion and the Eagle. Here is the mystery of the Sphinx declared and the true measure and power of the balanced or synthesized man brought to realization.

We can learn from Taurus the tremendous role which conservation plays in our evolution as Egos, for the power to preserve the forces of the past lies concealed in the secret reservoir sign once depicted in ancient zodiacal symbology as a coiled serpent. Secrets of the soul in this sign are portrayed to those who can read the stellar script; and to note the facts and forces in one's nativity is to see what actual Christ-gold account we have in the spiritual bank, and how best to put our talents to use, whether we hide them or put them out to increase and higher use. For Taurus demands that we make the earthly forces amenable for the spiritual, and that we use all things of the earth for the sake of the Spirit and be obedient to the higher man. This balance of the earthly and spiritual insures progress.

Meditation on the Bull calls forth the picture of the Mithras Bull, which was sacrificed so that the rider's development might be furthered. As such, the Bull has become the token of complete surrender and the zodiacal symbol for the Gospel of St. Luke, the Gospel that, more than the others, speaks of love and compassion—the love that makes the supreme sacrifice. St. Luke presents Christ as a being who embodies self-giving love, who conveys to the Earth the warmth of love that streams through the universe from the exceedingly exalted beings, the Seraphim. It is in St. Luke's Gospel 23: 34, 46, that we find the words from the cross revealing the greatest depth of compassion and love, "Father, forgive them, for they know not what they do," and "Father, into thy hands I commend my Spirit," expressing humility, devotion, and utmost surrender.

LOVE'S LYRE

O common sense of Christ so rare,
O heaven's love on earth so fair,
Assign our souls that we may love
With all thy art as thou art *love*!
Employ us with thy works so well
That men shall rise from out of hell
Into thy heaven by new truth told,
Then shall their souls at last unfold;
Then shall thy seed take root and rise,
Sprouting its stem up toward the skies,
Shoot forth its leaves of joyous hope
Till Christ declare its blossomed scope.
Thy bud doth burgeon, then, the Rose,
That one sweet love all heaven knows.
O take we the time to till on earth
That soil, our souls, to bring thy birth,
To give ourselves to man entire
So we at last become love's lyre.

Gemini - The Twins

GEMINI, the third sign of the Zodiac, denotes the Twins, indicating the dualism inherent in this changeful sign of alternation. It is pictured also by two upright columns, one black, showing its exoteric expression, the acquisition of earthly knowledge by way of the intellect; and the other, a white column, portraying the esoteric expression, which leads to the Spirit and to the perception of truth by way of sense-free, pure thinking and the superconscious Christ-mind.

In Gemini arises man's sense of his *Ego*, which I-denti-fies his unique *seed* that is his to sow (Aries) in the soil (Taurus). It is through the "I"-factor and thinking, ruled by Gemini, that man is raised above the animal. In this mutable air sign, consciousness is at work in its objective and subjective expressions, reasoning on the myriad sense perceptions streaming from the outer world and on all the feelings and emotional experiences of the soul, seeking to bring all this to a harmonious synthesis. This mutability gives rise to incessant restlessness and constant changefulness; hence, the dualism and the contradictory elements in Ge-mini. It is, however, because of this dualism that there comes effective advancement, and students of the stellar script will, therefore, not stress or dwell so much upon the outer, double-mindedness of Gemini natives, but will seek esoteric meaning and spiritual purpose behind the striking alterna-tion and the extreme polarity inherent in this airy common sign.

The quality of the imitative and the forces of genius are both resident in Gemini and are expressed by Gemini souls in accord with their soul-age in evolution. In this respect, we are reminded of the parrot whose forte is to mimic easily and to chatter much. The close observer of zodiacal character-istics will even see a facial resemblance to the parrot in cer-tain Gemini individuals, as he will find a likeness to the monkey in others. An ancient esoteric symbol of this sign shows two apes, the first, a witless chattering animal, apishly imitative; the second, an ape who has become a transcen-dental man and, thus, divine. In short, in this sign engender-ing Ego-consciousness, man ranges in quality and degree from the earthly, egotistical man to the spiritually-born Christed Ego, with a sublimated soul expressing its latent genius as a transcendental being. We may point in passing to examples such as Plato, the divine initiate, and in more recent times to Richard Wagner and to Alfred, Lord Tennyson, all of them evolved Egos, strong in or under the influence of Gemini in this sublime sense of the transcendental —earthly men expressing their godlike genius. Such men of Gemini genius never "picked the brains of others" to secure their immortal gems, as some superficial critics would have it, but ever dressed anew with fresh views and new vigor the old ideas or ancient myths, which they raised to new light and quality to suit the new day and time.

Man makes his way to the brain-free power of the Spirit in virtue of the earthly intellect, enlightened and illuminated by the light of love and truth in Gemini and in the other air signs. The air signs are mental and spiritual in their development and manifestation, and Gemini connects the lower man of flesh to his higher mental faculties, until the earthly experiences at last call down true illumination through Spirit-light. Under or in this sign we may see souls that range from the most scatter-minded and superficial, mere dabblers in everything, to the most profound men of genius, wisdom-filled like those just mentioned. The quality and the power depend upon the stage reached in evolution. Much depends on the sharp focus, single-mindedness, and direction of the thinking.

Gemini is receptive to all ideas, for this is the force of the formative intellect, which gathers all sense-impressions and integrates ideas. Souls in this sign are ever seeking knowledge and information, even from their earliest years, and their parents and teachers are apt to be driven into a corner by their incessant questions on a vast variety of subjects. There is a great love for books and reading; hence, self-education continues throughout life. Gemini creates mental awareness. All things are tested by the intellect and the reasoning faculty.

Although Gemini is a positive mutable mental sign, its vice is diffusion. In its outgoing receptivity to all ideas, it lacks the capacity for concentrated mental application to one idea.

This makes for great versatility and volatility, as well as for the frequent vice of excessive volubility and loquacity, resulting in an enormous waste of speech forces. However, success is assured those who master their contrasting moods and conquer the restless mobility of this dualistic sign, for it is true that the Gemini individual often wishes to be in two places at the same time, and this dualism, the basic element of the Twins, forever portrays itself throughout life; two things of a kind are always occurring.

Concentrated thinking and intense feelings are lacking and need to be cultivated by most Gemini persons whose Sun, Moon, Ascendant, or planets are in this mental sign. Changeability can be a clog to their progress. Yet they are eloquent, sensitive, affable, democratic, genial, and humane, even when lacking in deep sympathy or true affection. They are remarkably dexterous and deft with their hands and in their thinking, and are expressive in their gestures, speech, and language. Their hands are usually in motion when they talk. At repartee, they are quick and witty. Although they are not domestic, they make the best servants because of their versatility, adaptability, and dexterity.

Gemini rules the brain and nervous system, as well as the twinned lungs, hands, arms, and shoulders, expressive of the symmetry of the human form. This duality affects the nervous system, through Mercury, and often we find Gemini souls riding the highest heaven one moment, and in the next they are flung down into the depths of dark despair, rapidly alternating from the grave to the gay, and from gladness to gloom. At one moment charming, childlike, brilliant, and joyous, they can revert to pessimism and cynicism as quickly as the ethers change.

Generally speaking, the Gemini Ego has a nature that is adaptable and expansive, the soul is impressionable and intelligent, comprehensive, and comprehending. They are the zodiacal souls who seek an all-round development through

seeing and knowing, their successes depending on their pow-
er of intense attention and on their ability to make their
thinking one-pointed by focusing it at will in concentrated
attention, and by achieving the ability to maintain continuity.

Gemini, the first mutable sign, Mercury-ruled, is as volatile
as the air it represents and as quick and mobile as quicksilver,
the Mercury metal. It is a sign of volatility with a rhythm
of such alternating polarity, from positive to negative states
of consciousness, that instability often appears in the char-
acter, as well as a thought-life that is superficial. From this
sign comes the dilettante, who manifests a surface-skimming
interest in ideas, things, people, arts, and whatever else. At
the same time, no sign gives a greater desire than Gemini
for an all-round excellence of expression in the sphere of
thought and still gives such deftness in the use of the hands
and fingers. Thus we see in this sign the duality of head
and hands, thought and action, as a composite power com-
bining physical activities with the faculty of thinking. Gemini
Egos will actually embrace and employ ideas and motives
that are deliberately opposite, contradictory in type and
tenor. The duality is such that it affects thought, so that
those who are evolved can seize upon ideas in their polarity,
bringing them to a synthesis or an over-all, whole view. Dif-
ficulties arise in the less evolved through superficial, inade-
quate thought power. When the negative aspects of Gemini
—superficiality, instability, and flightiness—are transmuted
through perseverance and endurance, then reliability and
loyalty are assured.

As the other Mercury-ruled sign, Virgo, is contractive, re-
served, and analytical, Gemini is expansive, outgoing, and
synthetical in its adaptive nature. Gemini is the sign of ego-
ity, and so the Ego must test itself by and through its environ-
ment; and according to the clarity of consciousness will
growth be made. Thinking and feeling interact here; the
individual reasons upon his sensations, for this sign is a link-

ing force that unites and shows relationships, the relation between rhythm and form, between self and substance, and between the self and its neighbors and relatives. There is usually destiny experience with brothers and sisters, and also with soul-kindred as well as with blood-brethren. Gemini rules, too, the outer means of establishing relationships by means of letters, writing, books, and speech; also the postmen who deliver the letters, as well as agents, messengers, middlemen, and intermediaries in general. It gives a passion for locomotion, a fondness for moving about, for walking and for travel, and its natives learn much from travel.

Thought moves with such intense speed in these people and along such varied lines that doubt forever arises and makes for indecision. Always at least two ways open up and make choice difficult, for the advantages of both ways are carefully examined and often leave one wavering, "sitting on the fence." Nervous restlessness, irritability, and worry must first be resolved before the Gemini natives become truly fruitful, proficient, and capable of clear judgment and right decision. Once Gemini Egos are able to synchronize their breathing system, that is, their lungs, with the brain and the nervous system, and then to integrate these rhythms with the cosmic rhythms, restlessness will be arrested, worry eradicated, harmony realized, and comprehensive understanding attained.

The Gemini individual invariably gives the impression of being well-informed in virtue of the susceptibility of his mind and his ability to adopt and adapt many ideas, together with his adroit faculty for imitation and his facile flair for imagery. But things, ideas, people, and whatever else that formerly attracted him may be dropped or discarded when something else suddenly arouses his interest. Although there is a certain superficial quality in a Gemini survey and study which fails to grasp the inner meaning or significance, yet the outer facts and peculiarities are quickly seen with keen observation.

The idea of the Gemini individual is to make many connections, and his desire is to expand his circle and to be abreast of everything. A sense for time and a wise use of it become a necessity, for there is never enough time for all his interests. The vice of this sign is its lack of intensity in thinking, which leads to surface-skimming of ideas, devoid of the power of possession and identification, that is, of making one's self one with the thought or idea. Only in virtue of such identification with the ideas can there be any real knowledge.

In Gemini man becomes a knower and gains knowledge through thinking. Yet the mode of Gemini is first to feel the experience, then to think upon the feeling-episode and to analyze the feelings by means of reasoning; then the more highly evolved Egos sublimate the experience in virtue of the soul's higher light, the touch with truth and with the teacher found in Gemini's complementary sign, Sagittarius. In short, thought must become informed by feeling and vice versa; also, the inner reasons must be found for action, hence the importance of motive. By reasoning on the service of suffering in love in all its various phases, from the lowest animal-man to the highest divine, angelic being—the gamut of the forces of feeling, ranging from elemental grossness to the highest, most exquisite etheric refinement—by experiencing this diapason of the soul's development in the physical body and through the force of feeling, the Gemini reasoner derives increased ability to think. The one sign above all others where man uses thinking as a touch faculty, as it were, is this sign Gemini, which rules the *sense of the Ego*.

Once we come to understand the foregoing, we shall know why Gemini people always reason upon their sensations and upon their feeling-experiences. By bringing much thought to

bear upon their feelings, and by bringing will into their think-
ing, the intellect at last can become lighted by intuitive,
brain-free cognition. Men and women make headway in evo-
lution as they become truly discerning of their own soul
and spirit, and of the Spirit of the Earth. To know the Zodiac
in its esoteric truth is to learn to know oneself as a Christed
soul. Such self-knowledge enables one to know all other
human selves—their woe and weal—bringing unity and
wholeness into life, and the will to be friendly and coopera-
tive, and thus to be an individual of creative good will.

The element of duality is of paramount significance to all
human souls, but especially so to Gemini people, for our
Earth is a planet of duality. It manifests pairs of opposites:
winter and summer, day and night, man and woman; and
God himself declares the phases of Father and Mother, a
Divine Duality, as well as a Holy Trinity. In Gemini is inher-
ent the dualism of the brain-free and the brain-bound, the
negative and the positive, the objective and subjective, the
exoteric and esoteric, the form and the life, the black and
the white, male and female.

Implicit in this symbol of divine wisdom is the perfect
purpose of divine love. Love and wisdom are a twain that
cannot be separated, and it is in this polarity that there
manifests the archetypal light of the Christ. Thus, in evolved
beings who have learned the lessons of the forces of the Zo-
diac, there is evident an ethereal loveliness expressive of the
divine and the heavenly; the Angel in them connects with
the lower earthly man of intellect. This means that work has
been well done through many lives on Earth and that the
lessons have been learned. Such souls have saved their lives
by losing their lower selfishness and by transmuting what
was evil in them. These souls no longer live for themselves,
but for the welfare of the whole world.

The esoteric element in Gemini is excellently expressed in

that part of the most highly occult prayer known, the Lord's Prayer, which says, "Thy will be done on earth as it is in heaven," for earthly man in his physical body endowed with a brain must evolve to the point where his personality becomes conscious of the Christ-Spirit. We human Egos must bring down into the forces of earthly form, the body and the Earth, those life kernels or archetypal forces that are the keynotes of the Spirit. These archetypal ideas are the *real* forces of all that is on Earth, every last manifestation of life on the Earth. These earthly forces and forms must become spiritualized, "born again," born of the Spirit. The archetypal heavenly region is the source, the ultimate cause of all things. The archetypal kernels originating there become clothed in physical form as a result of the arresting power of the Moon.

Out of the spiritual world there descends the divine directing idea. The spiritual archetype flows downward into and through the soul world—the astral sphere—and the etheric realm, down into earthly matter, where the form takes shape, and life comes to manifestation in the world of matter. It is this matter of the Earth that man must transmute and, in this metamorphosis, man must be "born again" through the Christ Etheric Essence, the creature at last becoming a creator. Thus the spirit leaves its lofty home to manifest in the earthly body, which is to be spiritualized. In this mystical marvel of metamorphosis made possible by the Christ, we may trace the building of the body, which then appears to be what it was called by the ancients, "the temple of God," and we may trace as well the creation of the Earth itself, which bears man in its evolution. We may discern in this dual sign, Gemini, the evidence of this divine-earthly duality. It is in the light of this wisdom-filled teaching that we may approach and comprehend the stellar script, for it is actually the thought and the wisdom of the Spiritual Hierarchies. Thus, he who would comprehend this thought must lose his profanity and in an oblation of loving reverence, must seek to perfect himself.

The Earth is already "born again," because the Christ has come and has entered the planet through the Man Jesus and the Mystery of Golgotha. The Christ, the ruler of the Sun, is the indwelling Lord of the Earth, and he re-connects now the Earth with its parent body, the Sun. Man likewise takes on now the Christ-consciousness and, together with the Earth, he becomes solarized or Christ-born. Thus the prayer, "Thy will be done on earth as it is in heaven," becomes for every one of us an invocation for the metamorphosis of man. But the soul become Christ-aware will move forward faster in its evolution through conscious creative spiritual activity. The thought faculty of Gemini, in sense-free, pure thinking, produces a power of thought that lifts man to the level of that light that is divine—the transcendental atmosphere of the wisdom of love and truth. In this manner the wisdom-filled genius works in men as mystical as Richard Wagner and Alfred, Lord Tennyson, for in highly evolved beings, Gemini is the sign of the sage.

Gemini, being the positive sign of Mercury, the messenger of the gods, creates an interest in all messages from all the worlds and all the gods. These are important to the Gemini soul for, having the desire to study and to acquire knowledge, it ever continues to learn from its total environment. Often one may meet with a Gemini individual whose education has been slight and elementary, yet who may give the impression of being well-informed and able to express his ideas eloquently. Even though his information may be scanty and his thought superficial, there is still evident in him that thought activity that leads to the forming of a comprehensive image, and this is the faculty of synthesis, which is the very reverse of the negative, feminine Mercury-sign, Virgo, for Virgo is analytical and sectional in its image-forming power. This is a very important difference worthy of exact examination and knowledge to the true student of the soul of man.

It is essential to gain *whole*, integrated views and ideas, full and complete in all respects, of things and of men, of worlds and of life, for they lead to truth and to divine wisdom, a wisdom that connotes wholeness as a matter of course. Self-interest or egotism is fostered by the intellect. Before man became intellectualized, he saw and heard and knew the spiritual worlds and beings. The descent, away from the Spirit and down into the physical and earthly personality, has mobilized egotism. The essence to be extracted from Gemini is *synthesis*. When man reaches this power of synthesis, he is reaching out to and recognizing the wisdom of love, the power that unites male and female as well as the divine and the earthly elements in the sign of the Twins.

The worst fault of the Gemini people who are not yet balanced in the sign is that of mental scattering; they are diffuse and disjointed in their thought life. Their interest reaches out to all points of the compass as though irradiating the full circle. They fly from a center to every circumferential fact and idea to gain a synthesis. This trait gives often to Gemini natives a fine and finished versatility; they fit in and fill every emergency. One would find many of our radio announcers and speakers with Gemini prominent in their nativities, for these men must be very deft and clever with their thoughts and speech.

The vice of many Gemini natives is lack of concentration. They are mentally dispersive, which makes them all too often scatter-minded. The genius of Gemini cannot come to flower unless the individual disciplines himself, to make his thinking *one-pointed*, functioning in sharp, forceful focus on any one thing or idea at will. Gemini souls must learn to select thoughts and ideas *at will*, making such ideas and thoughts their very own by acquiring a growing stability in their thinking. No true power is theirs until the superficial and surface-skimming quality of thinking is done away with, the desire to dabble being replaced by an intense power of concentration which makes the mind mighty.

Gemini people must learn to detach themselves from the vice of the shallow and the superficial, arising from their taste for an all-round development rather than for depth. It is their essential need to know the value of depth as well as of breadth, if they would not forever remain dabblers. They must learn searchingly to scrutinize ideas, teachings, statements, knowledge, things, people, and whatever else they meet in life, for unless they make a deep, scrutinizing survey, they either accept ideas without thinking, or they "pass by without seeing" the core of truth and thus they deceive themselves. They tend to seek the surface facts rather than the central core from which the circumference takes its rise, and because of such lack of focused or concentrated thinking, they miss the truth. Out of this lack of depth and profundity in thinking there arises the shallowness and the element of deceit and duplicity evident in those natives that are not yet balanced or matured, for where one skims all facts and ideas lightly, no depth can be found; the centering force is absent and so is the solidity of thinking and the proper use of will.

Gemini is a mental-feeling mill, where the soul is sheared and shredded, as it were, until the turmoil of testing at last tears off the blinders and enables the man to use the eyes of the soul to see the light and walk in it. All the deceit and dualism, the two-faced conditions one may so much deplore in Gemini people, are after all only experiences being churned by the soul in the mill of earthly life, to draw out eventually the light of wisdom. We cannot criticize or condemn these souls but must be ourselves about our "Father's business," transmuting our own blemishes of character and learning the lessons of life while we have the time, for the work must be done down here in the earth-school of physical form, and we find our earthly hours all too few, once we have a spiritual awakening. It is not only unwise, but dangerous, to study the stellar science unless we are ready to use it in improving our own natures and in helping others through our growing self-knowledge which is at the same time consciousness of our connection with the whole cosmos.

There are not just twelve zodiacal types. Each sign has its positive and negative aspects, making twenty-four characteristic expressions of sign influences. Freedom implies the power of choice, and choice involves good and evil. Every Ego is free to choose the positive or the negative, the good or the ill. The initiate Job states (2:10) in no minced language the truth that good and evil are opposite poles of One Reality, "What? shall we receive good at the hand of God, and shall we not receive evil?" Out of our fleshly weakness comes the strength of God, and there is no other road to perfection. There are certain movements today that blind themselves to the principle of evil, but it is by contending with evil that we develop greater good. The great Christ-exponent, St. Paul, speaking out of his gamut of sufferings, says, "And lest I should be exalted above measure through the abundance of the revelations, there was given to me a thorn in the flesh, the messenger of Satan to buffet me. For this thing I besought the Lord thrice, that it might depart from me. And he said unto me: My grace is sufficient for thee, for my strength is made perfect in weakness. Most gladly therefore will I glory in my infirmities, that the power of Christ may rest upon me" (II Corinthians 12: 7-9).

In this connection, we must stress something that is too often overlooked now, that is, that perfection comes through the power of polarization manifesting in all worlds, in men, and in spiritual beings. The Duality as well as the Trinity of God manifests in what is still a Unity. It was in the Ancient Persian Civilization, when the precession of the equinox had brought the Gemini Age, that man was most aware of this duality. He looked upon the world as being made up of two kingdoms—Light and Darkness. The Kingdom of Light was ruled by the good god Ahura Mazdao, or Ormuzd; the dark, material earth realm, by Ahriman.

In Gemini the soul is torn into two parts, the lower and the higher self; the factor of the twain is always at work in the sign of the Twins, and it is in the resolution of this duality of powers, one of earth and the other of heaven, that divine wisdom and love come to be born and become operative in man. In Shakespeare's play, *Romeo and Juliet*, we see the rival houses eventually reconciled through the love of Romeo and Juliet.

Many men of true genius, highly original and creative in arts, letters, poetry, and music, may be found in this sign Gemini. In its highest expression, it moves one beyond its ruler Mercury, to Mercury's higher octave, Neptune, the planet of creative musical and artistic power. In Gemini, experiences, energized by thinking, must be worked over and be lifted and lighted by the superconscious Christ-mind. This Christ-mind is supersensible and synthesizing, imparting ideas and images that are whole; not the disjointed sectional bits offered by the brain. As God is the whole, so must man, made in God's image, come to express this unity of the whole, which may be heard to be singing in the realm of archetypes.

So intense is the mental activity of Gemini that the mental moods change rapidly and tend to vanish into so much air. There is an incessant desire for new impressions and feelings, which the Gemini Ego seeks as grist for its mill. But so long as the Gemini native refuses to concentrate his mind and make it one-pointed, he lacks what he should win, for often in his far-reaching survey and compass he fails to master the single points of thought, to bring them into sharp relief and thus into full comprehension. But in the evolved soul, there is a power to hold integrated views and to manifest ideas that are rounded and whole, showing an exquisite nicety and balance in letters, art, or music.

The fixed signs bring stability and concentration to thinking, so as to focus the idea sharply and bring the mental activity to white heat, as it were. Only in this incandesence of thinking can there come about that integration of ideation so essential to the expression of genius. We see the effect of this fixed sign force in Richard Wagner, for he had the first degree of Gemini rising, with the Sun therein, also in the first degree, which means that he shared half of the forces of the preceding sign, Taurus, the sign that held his mental Mercury and his musical Venus. Thus the volatile thinking of Gemini was arrested and held in the fixed sign power of Taurus, and his Moon and Part of Fortune were in the fixed-air sign Aquarius.

Gemini functions well when combined with the angelic man of Aquarius, as it does when joined with the justice and judgment of the balanced soul in Libra. Then the Gemini soul has reached maturity. Such a soul was Plato. What a versatile genius! According to a probable nativity of Plato set up by Firmicus, he had Aquarius rising, with Venus, Mars, and Mercury therein, while the ruler, Saturn, was exalted in the Venus-sign Libra; the Moon was in Gemini, while the Neptune-sign, Pisces, held the Sun.

The genius of Gemini is likewise revealed in the nativity of Tennyson, for he had the Moon and Venus, the poetical, imaginative planets, rising in Gemini. He drew his inspiration down from heaven, in what he called his "waking trances." His poems are charged with the idea of man being still "in the making," moving "Forward, till you see the highest human nature is divine," and "Love will conquer at the last." In his works are many references to the dual aspects inherent in man, the male-female elements that complement each other, "The two-cell'd heart beating, with one full stroke, life." The blending of the two forces in man he declares in "The Princess": [1]

Not like to like, but like in difference,
Yet in the long years liker must they grow;
The man be more of woman, she of man;
He gain in sweetness and in moral height,
Nor lose the wrestling thews that throw the world;
She mental breadth, nor fail in childward care,
Nor lose the childlike in the larger mind;
Till at the last she set herself to man,
Like perfect music unto noble words;
And so these twain, upon the skirts of Time,
Sit side by side, full-summ'd in all their powers,
Dispensing harvest, sowing the To-be,
Self-reverent each and reverencing each,
Distinct in individualities,
But like each other ev'n as those who love,
Then comes the statelier Eden back to men:
Then reign the world's great bridals, chaste and calm:
Then springs the crowning race of human-kind.
May these things be!

As we study Gemini, we may find confirmed the truth that the progressive evolution of man and planet demands a development through differentiation, and the dualism we see at work in Gemini souls has a purpose as definite as it is divine. Through willed thinking, man sublimates the intellect to sense-free cognition. As thought becomes lighted with the Spirit, man can become active with a positive, powerful earthly and cosmic purpose. The human Ego residing in its

---

[1] Courtesy of Macmillan and Co., Ltd., London.

earthly members finds the higher Ego. The Man finds the Woman, and the Woman finds the Man.

The Biblical symbol for Gemini is "Solomon's Porch." As a porch serves as a protecting covered entrance to a building, linking the outer with the inner, creating a mediative or connective place, thus the human Ego connects the higher, divine triad of spirit in man with his three lower earthly members, which form the temple. But Gemini does not become *Solomon's* porch until the higher, spiritual triad informs, and interacts with, the lower members by way of the Ego's pure thinking, for Solomon is synonymous with wisdom.

This wisdom is the solar element, the wisdom of love, and we know that God gave Solomon "a wise and understanding heart," because Solomon sought this living wisdom above all things, the wisdom that showed the real motive and truth in and behind all things. The fullness of the solar spiritual truth is revealed in Christ Jesus—the Sun-god become Man, a divine-human Ego—the pattern of what man must become. In St. John 10:23, it is stated, "And Jesus walked in the temple in Solomon's porch." This shows the Man who has become fully integrated in all his forces, a Son of God, through a solar amalgamation of the potencies of the Zodiac, in that union which the air signs produce to unite the earthly, intellectual man with the Kingdom of Heaven and the Etheric Christ. According to Acts 5:12, the apostles acquired this solar Christ-power, "And by the hands of the apostles were many signs and wonders wrought among the people; and they were all with one accord in Solomon's porch."

In Gemini we see the Ego connecting the lower, earthly, brain-bound personality with the higher self. The life-urge is to link the intellect with the mind of Christ. By this means, one may achieve a synthesis which is the integration of ideation, finding and expressing the whole and not a part; and this means that the man of physical form relates himself to

and expresses the Solar Man, the genius of God within. It is
the chief function of Gemini Egos to comprehend this and
to make it a reality; hence, their versatility, the manifesta-
tion of many-sidedness and, in the highly evolved, that gen-
ius that shows the man has made contact with and has
recognized his higher Christ-self.

'Tis matter's mode, the intellect,
The earthly brain doth thought infect;
And now the mind must lighted be,
The Christing truth shall make man free.

The empty husk of earthy mind,
Man's darkened intellect, is blind
To Spirit's store of joyous youth;
The mind unlighted tramples truth.

What price to pay for intellect,
To set aside, no more detect
The Life of Spirit everywhere,
This mood of man so starved and bare.

The lighted Teachers of mankind,
With Christ, give sight to those now blind,
Reverse the rhythm from left to right,
From darkness to His Marv'lous *Light*.

Cancer - The Crab

CANCER is symbolized by the crab, an amphibious crusta-cean, which lives equally well on land or in water, and which early in its existence passes through stages of meta-morphosis. In this mysterious midnight sign inheres the mighty power of mutation, the impulse to jump, or leap over, to a new stage in evolution—that progressive growth which carries all life forward to new levels, be it in plant, animal, or man, or even the Earth itself in its various transitional "leaps" to new levels. The Earth has progressed through the Saturn, Sun, and Moon Periods, to this present mid-Earth Period, and it will evolve to the future Jupiter, Venus, and Vulcan Periods. To understand man and life, one needs to realize this marvelous mode of metamorphosis, which is the carrying-forward force of Cancer, for this is its secret.

No physical scientist can ever truly understand what carries evolution forward, until he knows the forces of this fourth sign of the Zodiac, Cancer. The jump forward and leap to a new level, which takes place between an ancestor and its descendant, no matter what the realm of life, from plants to planets—all that is carried forward of the spiritual, which alone endures—is brought about by the Spirit functioning through the powers inherent in Cancer. Even the symbol of Cancer, in both its modern and ancient form, shows plainly the gap, the leap, or jump-over from one spiral of life to another, indicating the very impulse of evolution served by this most mobile, fecundating sign.

Leap or gap

The mystery of metamorphosis in evolution inherent in the sign Cancer was brought out by Christ Jesus when he used a different symbology, that of the ass and her colt, the ancestor and descendant (Matthew 21). This was explained by Rudolf Steiner in his lectures on *The Gospel of St. Matthew*,[1] picturing the foregoing ancient symbol. The disciples

---

[1] Rudolf Steiner, *The Gospel of St. Matthew* (The Rudolf Steiner Publishing Co., London, and Anthroposophic Press, New York), Lecture XI.

had reached an important transition from one condition of consciousness to another. Christ Jesus had induced in them spiritual vision, enabling them to perceive in imaginative pictures the mighty events in the macrocosm. On rising into the spiritual worlds and learning of the forces there, a leap occurred in their development, and this was reflected in the physical world in the symbol of the ass and her colt. In this physical fact he showed the spiritual impulse of the sign Cancer.

This sign must be viewed as the motive power in inducing and bringing forth new life, the life of change, leaping forward and onward to higher spirals. To souls that observe truly and think deeply, this spiralling evolutionary force becomes apparent in the buds of early spring, for the buds have even the shape of a curl that unfolds as a spiralling form-force. Ordinary men, too, feel the beauty and the bounty of each springtide, and this new spiralling evolutionary life process makes the soul buoyant and joyous. The growth in God, which is evolution at work and operative in all things—plants, animals, men, and planets—corresponds to the sign Cancer, the midnight lunar sign, which parts one day from the next—figuratively, the ancestor from the descendant.

As man thus profoundly grasps the meaning of the signs of the Zodiac, he becomes aware of the language of life existent in the stars, for in the stars dwell divine spiritual beings. The stars are the letters and the language of the heavenly writing, and he who would read, write, and speak in that high tongue must know the truth of their love and wisdom. Man's consciousness expands as he reaches farther out into the cosmos and realizes the Spirit beyond the external form. That which separates from the old and leads to the new is the impulse that leads man forward, and this spiralling journey leads through repeated earthly lives, carried forward by the fecundating force inherent in this lunar feminine psychic power, Cancer. He who learns the language of the stars in this wise and lives the life, prepares himself for initiation, for the Zodiac is the signature of God.

As the Sun reaches its highest point on the ecliptic in Cancer, so the earthly life of Christ Jesus reached the climax of its power when he was able to lead his disciples to the attainment of spiritual vision, indicative of the change that eventually would take place through the Christ in the evolution of consciousness of all humanity. This is revealed in the cry, "Hosanna in the highest!"

The seasonal festival little known in our time is the summer festival on June 24th, when the Sun bears the same relation to Cancer as it does at Christmastime to Capricorn. This midsummer festival is called St. John's Day, after John the Baptist, the significant figure who announced the coming of the Christ and was the first to welcome him when he united with Jesus of Nazareth at the Baptism in the Jordan. In anticipation of this Coming, which marked the turning point of time, John the Baptist called on those who came to him to change their thinking and to make the leap toward a new understanding.

The greatest leap in all Earth-evolution occurred through the Christ. There was a leap-over from the Old Dispensation of Jehovah and the Moon to the New Dispensation of the Christ and the Sun. Jehovah then relinquished right and rule as the Plenipotentiary of the Moon in the education of humanity, to the Christ from the Sun, who came not to destroy the law but to fulfill it with his grace and truth.

Cancer, pictured as the ass and her colt, indicates the meeting and parting of forces and spheres, the old reaching out to the new, and the fructification that occurs as a result of the alchemy of both forces as the old condition is left for the new spiral in evolution. Only those who meditate upon Cancer in the light of this verity will know the import of this agent of evolution on the earthly plane of form and will be able to fathom the paradoxes of this sign where two contrasting forces meet—the negative lunar and the positive solar, accomplishing the leap-over from B.C. to A.D., the transition from Jehovah to Christ, from separativeness and tribal consciousness to the universal solar Christ-consciousness. This is the sign and the force in evolution in which the native is changing his old life for a new rhythm, and even if this newness of life may not transpire in this present incarnation, it will do so in the next earthly life, for the spiritual effects are retained and carried forward.

Metamorphosis in Cancer persons occurs mainly through feeling. The consciousness of Cancer is fed by feeling and emotion; all sensational life is active here and is instantly registered, from the coarsest physical feeling to the most exquisite, delicately nuanced spiritual touch, according to the purity and quality of the individual. Just as a lake reflects the immediate view above and about it, much as a mirror, so the sign Cancer reflects in the soul of its native the consciousness of feelings and forces from the environment and people. If the Cancer soul is pure and placid, there will be reflected the truth in people and places in which he or she moves; but if the soul is impure and perturbed, living in the senses rather than in the spirit, the morbid, lying, erroneous darkness will be registered in the aura and thus badly mislead and often wound the soul.

Cancer is so receptive to feelings and impressions from its surroundings that its natives do well to become wise to the Spirit and to purify the soul. This is vitally important if they would not respond to mere astrality or lunar lust, for this is easy for them to do, and so they attune and listen to, or become victims of, earthbound discarnate human beings, so-called spirit controls and "guides," either consciously or unconsciously. This path, if followed, leads to ruin. When man learns that he lives in close proximity with the so-called "dead," even though he cannot see them with his physical

sight, and that many people dying today die selfish or ig-
norant, or both, not having lived in the light while on earth,
then one can see that Cancer individuals would be wise if
they exacted from themselves a far higher degree of purity
as well as a more discerning, deeper thought power that
would call out spiritual truth, for this is how they would be-
come protected against that cesspool of the dead, the lower
astral world, to which masses of mankind gravitate after
death. These dead are very active in using and victimizing
the ignorant people on earth who live wholly in their feel-
ings and sensations. It would be a service royal to all souls
astrally aware, especially Cancer natives, if this comprehen-
sion could make them alive to the truth about the worlds in
which we live and about man as a being of soul and spirit.

Cancer is related to the Moon's sphere, and the Moon
rules the desire or astral world, the region of the soul's de-
sires. The astral world is exceedingly mobile, of terrific speed
and enormously rapid transformation. It is so formative and
plastic that it is easy to see why one is restless and change-
able when under the influence of the Moon and Cancer.
The physical counterpart of the lunar sphere is the sea,
and all water comes under the rule of Cancer, the first of
the three water signs.

The craving of the Cancer soul is for feeling; it thirsts to
live in an emotional ocean of sensation, touching everything
and everyone through the astral senses of the soul, for Cancer
rules the *sense of touch*. Thus Cancer natives ever project
that feeler-force, much like antennae that touch and take
in the message from the people and places about them.
One need not meditate long to see in their case how quin-
tessential is the quality of their purity and motive, for this
will qualify the type of their reception and the nature of
their impressions. The most sordid drunkards and mediums
may be found here as well as the most virtuous practical
mystics, like Cecil Rhodes, who formed and founded the

Union of South Africa, where many homeless people found a home, Cancer being the sign ruling the home.

The Moon's sign, Cancer, is the specializing agent for the soul's quality, coloring the particular earthly personality. It is Cancer which isolates the human Ego within the multitudinous mass of mankind and individualizes its unique color, through the force and firmament of its peculiar life of feelings and emotions. Cancer is concerned with the entire field of astral sensing. It is the head of the psychic trinity, comprising Cancer, Scorpio, and Pisces, and its life expression seeks outlet in its love for sensation, fame, and power. Its outstanding characteristic and insistent note is its love for insistence; hence the great tenacity of this sign, the quality of attachment which retains its hold long after all others would let go—like that of the crab, which holds on even if it loses its limb in doing so.

As Cancer rules the sense of touch, it is easy to see how the psychic feelings of the soul arise here, and why Cancer natives are so acutely impressionable and imaginative. Cancer serves the whole range of experiences in feelings and emotions; it is a psychic sign, hypersensitive and yet very selective. Readily does suggestion play upon the aeolian harp of the Cancer soul, and what sounds forth is by no means always harmonious. However, as the reception of the Cancer soul becomes more Christ-responsive, then, but not until then, does discriminative feeling become wisely selective and the personality truly positive.

Two traits then are outstanding in Cancer; the first is the quality of *touch* or *receptivity*, and the other is *selectivity*. The Cancer individual is a storehouse of moods, a sea of sensations and emotions and, according to his sympathies, antipathies, and apathies, his insight is sound or confused. The Cancer person uses feeling when he is thinking, much as a crustacean uses its feelers or antennae to make its way through the water, with the difference that the Cancer soul uses psychic-etheric feelers that extend into the astral sea of feelings, the world of desire. It judges everything in terms of emotions and feelings, sensation being its measuring rod. It is in virtue of these two traits that Cancer people are found to be fickle and changeable, the next field ever looking greener and the new friend more interesting. These are the souls that live and thrive on new impressions.

Cancer feels the need to *feel*, for the essence of this sign is emotion. If this oversupply of emotional life finds outlet only within its own limited "shell," it gives far too great a love for one's own family or children. Even if the feeling widens to include the community, nation, and race, it can be a deterrent to progress and be detrimental. There is far too deep a respect for tradition, heirlooms, old customs, and the like. When negative, Cancer souls talk about bygone days and still live in them, and this prevents proper progress. The mood of the miser inheres in this lunar sign when ill aspected, for this is a saving sign, one wherein household goods are hoarded and never used, except on high days and holidays.

Nourishing love is the special quality of the Cancer individual, for innate in him is the urge and desire to feed and tend others. If Cancer souls cannot tend their own children, they will take others' children or, failing this, animals. They must seek to nurture others in some way, for this is the nutritive sign that rules the breasts or mammae that nourish the child, and it also rules the rib cage which, like the shell of the crab, serves as a protection. In this midnight sign there is the mood of the maternal. Here, too, is the domain of the home and of family forces; most Cancer souls have a life-lesson experience with the home, the mother, children, family affairs, and property. They are affected most by family and domestic concerns, their faulty adjustment of feeling often proving a drag and detriment to their own individual development, and their smothering-mothering tendencies banefully influencing those around them.

Cancer is the great mother sign. It gives the desire to take care of whatever is in need of nurture; its inner urge is maternal, in men as well as in women. It is unusual, however, to find a mother free of selfish egotism, and thus Cancer mothers often injure their children's development by their wrongful indulgence and by shielding them too long from contacts with the outer world. Although sacrifices are often made by Cancer natives, yet consciously or unconsciously they expect affection and gratitude in return, and often they are much disappointed. As the true teacher knows that to be a successful educator he must eventually eliminate himself, so the true mother realizes she must in time step into the background and allow the child to be independent while she herself continues to love with no thought of return, that is, to love as do the Angels, without ceasing.

The hypersensitive nature of Cancer must not be regarded as a weakness, but treated with full understanding of its psychic quality, for only if one is a true sensitive, invested with true vision, can one effectively help Cancer souls. Their reaction is always one of feeling; they live and move in a sea of sensations, thus they will always try to reach others through the feelings and desires. Until Cancer souls free themselves in some degree from their intense feelings, they will limit the light of truth and destroy all hope for vivid vision. Cancer souls, more than those of any other sign of the Zodiac, take on the role of a martyr and feel injured when confronted by the experiences they themselves have brought about. When their personality has entire rule and sway over Cancer souls, emotions envelop their lives and cause prejudices to arise. Cancer people suffer from gastric troubles when they give way to excessive emotion. Music is a fine healer for them. But when they assume the role of a martyr, their false imaginative forces impede their true advancement in evolution.

Whereas Gemini is imitative and takes over ideas from people, places, or books, and elaborates them in ideation, drawing them to a mental focus, Cancer plays the role of a mimic, in fancy feels the part, and livingly dramatizes other people. The power of imaginative feelings brings them so easily to incandescence that members of this sign make the best actors and actresses, and by the same token these are the souls that easily enrobe themselves with complexes of heroism or martyrdom. Cancer being the sign of the soul and of psychic feelings, it is not hard to realize how absorptive this section of the Zodiac is. Knowing this, we see why Cancer people often unconsciously receive into themselves the weal and woe of others; in fact, it is by such osmosis that they become imitative and take on the manner and very intonation of speech of those they contact. This forte to feel the souls of others and absorb their content should serve as a stern warning to Cancer people to be careful in their selection of associates and environment.

Not only is Cancer receptive and absorptive, but in less evolved souls it also calls forth a dominant desire for power over others; sometimes, if not usually, it is a subtle, covert desire to have power over others. Its strong egotism really can brook no leader or teacher and, although seemingly retiring, bashful, and shy, yet it must be in the front and in the swim. Woven in the forces of this sign, there is a strong desire for fame, the will to be right in the front and always to stay there. This desire is an intense urge, and with it is the power of insistence. And, even if these urges may not be open and obvious, they are carried quietly, but none the less firmly, within, for Cancer natives wish to move and mould others, and to this end they use their active feeling forces. This quiet power can be seen at work by those endowed with the sight to see. Only in the evolved Christed soul, in an atmosphere of *freedom* without compulsion, can this power actively aid man and planet evolve better and faster; in the unevolved and evil, this force becomes detrimental to all concerned, but above all to the Cancer soul itself, the victim of its own selfish insistence. For evil, no matter where found or by whom sent out, ever returns, like a boomerang, to its sender.

A paradox of temerity and timidity; blowing hot and cold; being bold, yet bashful; amazingly active, yet apathetic; insistent, yet listless; intense, yet inert; rash, yet reserved; desiring to be first, yet to be last; wanting to wield power over others, yet to be powerless at the same time; sympathetic, yet selfish; giving all, yet personally possessive—such are Cancer souls, caught up in conflicting emotions and moods. These real conflicts are the bane of these souls, until they realize how psychically impressionable they are and then start becoming self-controlled by properly managing both the receptivity and the selectivity so strikingly emphasized in this sign, ruled by the Moon. The Moon is the reflecting light orb, whose psychic astral forces must be controlled by the spiritual light of the Sun. Here the Molten Sea must be cast; the watery Moon and the fiery Sun, the two opposing elements, must be fused into a heavenly harmony.

All Cancer natives incommode themselves and live in self-engendered hurtfulness until they find the light of the Son, from the Sun, and so transmute personality into a suprapersonal spiritual power. Water and fire become compatible only as the wisdom of love lights the soul with solar truth; no other means will fuse these otherwise incompatible elements. Convergence and integration in this sense must take place in this sphere of the Moon, Cancer, for the earthly forces of the physical form come from the Sun by way of the Moon. Practising the difficult art of self-effacing detachment, seeing the real and recognizing the great illusion of the senses and then living in the reality of Spirit—this is the

Great Work for all, but especially for those born in or under the forces of the form-sign Cancer, for Cancer people cling with painfully intense tenacity to the personal and to the outmoded, archaic past. Thus they cannot catch the forces of the future while living in the present, not knowing the true import of the important passing moment, and the pressing, passing, present moment is the Eternal Now.

Although it is well-nigh impossible to teach a Cancer person, because of the predominating physical and psychic forces, yet there is one door still open: the elucidation here set forth, explaining the need for a wise Sun-Moon mergence. Through this searching self-knowledge, this esoteric scrutiny of this feminine, negative, lunar light, the Cancer force, we have recognized the intense unrest, the immense mobility of the Moon. In this psychic, physically formative, etheric-astral sign, two streams of power, the forces of the Moon and of the Sun, must meet and harmonize. The unstable, mobile, and separative lunar force must be controlled and wisely mastered by the fixed, fiery force of the Sun-Son, whose power is the stability of the universe itself. And let it be fully realized that, although the Moon must nourish the children of the Earth, yet the source of life of these children, their sentient and spiritual life, their unborn-deathless life, comes from the Sun. Since mankind has now come of soul age with the descent and entry of the Christ into the Earth, the means to cast the Molten Sea are here for everyone who will use them.

The human body is the temple of God, and the beings of the Spiritual Hierarchies have built it through aeons of time. The spiritual Ego descends into incarnation and clothes itself with the form of the dense physical body, investing this body with its quality of soul and using it as an instrument for its earthly, human activities of growth and progress. The basic structure for the expression and the manifestation of the "I AM" or Ego, the spiritual self, is prepared in this watery, cardinal sign, in which the living organism finds its forces of growth, for it is through the formative forces of the Moon and the help of the Angels—whose sphere is the Moon—that the human being finds his way back into earthly incarnation. This is the ingress into physical life as, conversely, it is also the entrance into the worlds of Spirit.

Thus the Moon is the mother, as it were, of all that is living in a physical form. And yet, as Persephone, she is the queen of the dead, for all beings that take on a physical form must leave that form when it is worn out and done with. It is in this very taking-on of forms at birth and in giving them up at death that the Moon performs this marvelous service, promoting man's evolution and imparting to him that essential newness of life, that renewal which transforms the man, making him "a new creature." In the Moon we find this fecundating, feminine force that carries all beings to higher levels of consciousness, to ever new spirals of evolution by providing them with a physical body.

In this meditation on Cancer, it is my intention to draw out this mood of metamorphosis, this power and function of mutation, the will to effect a change and to bring the new into the Ego's experience, for the Spirit's urge is for ever higher levels of life and for an ever wider expansion of consciousness, in right unfoldment. The driving power of mutation carefully fashions the proper and wise changes in the formative forces of man's life through the ever-recurrent rapid cycle of the Moon, which initiates a new force each month. Thus each New Moon is a new opportunity to the soul to add a fresh impetus to its true growth in God.

Cancer being a sign of transformation, compelling change from the old to the new, the mode of motion and metamorphosis, it is of significant interest to observe that New York, the first city of the New World, where most newcomers arrive, is ruled by the sign Cancer. In New York one has left the Old World for the New, yet many evidences of

Europe are still manifest, and certainly no one has seen or known America who has not lived outside this city which is the connecting link between the old and the new. New York is the sphere where many people change their consciousness, whether they know it or not.

The intense emotionalism of Cancer is frequently brought into play in the exuberant welcome given visiting celebrities and heroes, ranging from the early air conquerors who made successful flights across the ocean, to the most recent astronauts. No other city on earth displays so much abandoned feeling, along with a riotous waste of ticker tape. The Moon's influence is also evident in the business life of the city, involving a rapid turnover. Small profits and quick returns is the forte of Cancer people in business, in virtue of the Moon's rapid course through all twelve signs every month and because of the constant change inherent in Cancer.

Through its astral, lunar quality, there is in Cancer an intense, inner sensitivity that receives and awakens impressions. The soul can thus become subject to psychic stresses and emotional strains that are so intense and inward as to be almost impossible to express outwardly. This may induce morbid peevishness and discontent, which create a mood of contrariness, which in turn may lead to inhibitions or isolation, a withdrawal like that of a crab into its hole, even to the degree of the hermit crab. In their contacts with the outer world, these sensitive souls tend to give way to timidity and fear, and to retreat into themselves, instead of making the leap toward a new, finer, fuller, freer life.

Cancer souls are often devoid of harmony because of their unbalanced urge to live in their feelings and emotions. Sensations or sympathies having forever the effect of throwing them off-balance, they are hurt by a look or by a word, taking for slights and injuries, words or acts never intended to wound. Only as Cancer souls learn to control feeling and, realizing their psychic nature, exercise a proper self-protection against influences from people and places, will they gain a healthy poise and a clearer perspective, for morbid feeling forces collected by these natives invariably color their mood, often giving rise to false notions, suspicion, and fear.

Cancer expresses the paradox of loneliness in the thick of a throng, of isolation that insulates the individual even in the commotion of a city crowd. Cancer seems to say, "Isolation *is*, even though the multitude be about me." The paradox of this nothingness and yet allness in Cancer is the secret of the "come and go" quality of Cancer people—the desire to be right in the limelight and yet to retire at the same time into the wings as far as possible; it accounts also for their apparent contrariness, even though they have no intention of being so.

A flood of feeling surges through all the watery signs; but psychic experience is primarily awakened or touched off in Cancer, much as radio antennae respond to waves of audio-frequency. Thereby feelings become selective and are of every range in this active oscillating sign. In Scorpio, feeling becomes intensified, concentrated, or drawn into a center through the fixed-rhythm action, resulting in rebirth or regeneration. Pisces, on the other hand, offers a vast ocean of feeling and emotion as diffuse as the ocean itself, and as mute as it is moving, sounding out of a silence that only those lighted with the wisdom of love can understand. It should be understood how these three watery signs serve as different fields of feeling-life experience, and how Cancer is the field of open contact with every variety of feeling, so that the Cancer soul learns through the very service of the feeling forces. The wise individual in Cancer will be helped and will make rapid strides forward in evolution as he learns to know his own true nature and raises the quality of his soul, for then true tact, the heavenly touch faculty, will become his own.

There resides in Cancer the retentive memory for the

things of physical life as well as the will to live forever in the past; but true memory power comes of Aquarius, where previous lives and the life before birth may be recalled by the evolved members of that sign. Cancer people, however, often retain things best forgotten, and of some of these natives we may say what was said of the Bourbon kings, "They learned nothing and forgot nothing." This trait may become a clog to progress, for he who cannot forget can never truly move forward. He needs to say with St. Paul, "I die daily," for the native suffers in proportion to his clinging attachment to the past. There is also a clinging attachment to possessions, especially to anything having any sentimental value. Letters received in their youth they often retain far into their old age. Tenacity is a characteristic feature of the Crab.

Yet Cancer is the key to and mode of metamorphosis in evolutionary ascent, the leap from the old to the new. It is Cancer that builds the house of the human body through the Moon's formative forces; here the Ego dwells in the earth-schooling process. Cancer thus provides the physical form for the divine drop of Spirit that is housed in flesh every earthly life. It is the major factor in giving a physical setting for the Spirit, so that the Spirit, in time, through the Christ-mediation, at last makes the very substance of the Earth and the Moon a thing of solar substance, perfected in God through his Christ. Cancer then forms the concrete foundation for the Christed "I AM"-being, the Lord from heaven, who becomes born in flesh when the lessons of the twelve signs of the Zodiac have been learned and the egotistical sense of selfhood has been transmuted into the altruism of the supra-personality. In Cancer the living forces of growth are organized and coordinated into a Christ-whole.

The fault or drawback in Cancer souls still living in their lower Ego is that they are rather unreachable and unteachable because of the element of distrust inherent in this lunar sign. The person is apt to be peevish and discontented, or he may slump too quickly into a sulky mood. Then the Moon inhibits and dims the light; it makes the soul live in, and prefer, darkness rather than the light. The forces of the law of Jehovah, the lunar, racial God, still inhere in many souls, although now the solar Christ has come from the Sun, and man can be born to the Spirit, which is all-embracing and not clannish, feudal, racial, national, or separative. Sorry sourness and ever-smouldering distrust of others will keep Cancer natives unbalanced, incomplete, and in a state of sullen discontent, so long as they continue to live so wholly under the law of the Moon and refuse the unifying, all-embracing love of the Sun. When Cancer people learn to know themselves in their real make-up of soul and spirit, they begin to trust themselves and, with this self-trust, they begin to trust others and to see with true vision in the right perspective.

Sensitivity, receptivity, and selectivity through the psychic forces of feeling make up the very essence of Cancer, for the source and center of the human sentient faculty abides here. Every mood is sensed and sounded in this sign of sensation: the mood of every phase of the Moon, the moods of the whole range of the changing, manifold planetary aspects, and those of the Moon in her monthly and the Sun in his yearly passage through the twelve signs of the Zodiac. As one raises oneself in evolution, a growing union with the whole cosmos is felt and known.

As in Virgo, the extreme contrasts of selfishness and sympathy are active in Cancer, and these qualities are usually centered within the narrow confines of the family, the home sphere; yet Cancer people must learn to love without thought of any return, and this is a hard lesson for them, for although ready to sacrifice all for their own families, few can as yet realize or reach up to the One Christ-Family, the citizenship of the cosmos, for they still live—or, quite often, atrophy— under the lunar law, not having yet grown into the grace

and truth that came by Jesus Christ, the Sun-Son. It is a
matter of growth in God that evokes the solvent of heaven
that brings about the metamorphosis from self-centeredness
to selflessness.

> Man is a Temple, mystic shrine,
> In which doth dwell a God Divine;
> The Holy Temple is defiled
> Till man with God is reconciled.

Leo - The Lion

THE HEART of the Zodiac, its life and fire, is LEO, the Lion, ruled by the Sun, the heart of our solar system. It was in the dim dawn of man's evolution that the sublime spiritual beings—the Seraphim, Cherubim, and Thrones—active in Leo, laid the first foundations of the human heart.

Meditating upon the Zodiac, we are reminded of the simple beauty of the nineteenth Psalm, "The heavens declare the glory of God, and the firmament sheweth his handiwork.

Day unto day uttereth speech [of the passing planets through the signs of the Zodiac], and night unto night sheweth knowledge. There is no speech nor language where their voice is not heard. Their line is gone out through all the earth, and their words to the end of the world. In them hath he set a tabernacle [Zodiac] for the sun, which is as a bridegroom coming out of his chamber, and rejoiceth as a strong man to run a race. His going forth is from the end of the heaven, and his circuit unto the ends of it: and there is nothing hid from the heat thereof. The law of the Lord is perfect, converting [transmuting] the soul. . . ."

The Zodiac is thus a great sounding harp, and the harmonies and dissonances are related to the passing powers of the planets in their ever-changing configurations. Every human being, through his higher Ego and with the help of the Spiritual Hierarchies, selects his own stellar configuration for each entrance into earthly life. The Sun is the dynamic power-center for the forces of the Zodiac and it is also the inner urge and fiery force that gives expression to the "I."

Without the Sun, which is the heart of things, there would be no power to grow and evolve, and there would be no creative living organism. Man exteriorizes his inner Self and is creative and procreative in virtue of the Sun and its sign, Leo; nay, more, it is by their means that he is able to recreate himself in every one of his earthly incarnations. No life descends and enters a flesh body but by the office and power of the Sun, even though the Moon forces must prepare the body, giving physical form to the life.

Leo is the life and power of the Sun, and it gives man his *sense of life.* To learn to know the nature of Leo and of the Sun is to be given the power to embrace the whole living universe pulsing with Christ-etheric radiance throughout the encircling round. "There is no speech nor language where their voice is not heard," for it is in the power of Leo that man can come to hear the sound of the stellar language in the round of the days and the years, as the etheric atmosphere enveloping man and Earth evokes the new life of the Christ, penetrating, active in, and filling all space. Men are becoming Christ-conscious and learning to sense his creative life in the ethers. Thus, more and more men will say, "I *know* that my Redeemer liveth," and they will understand the word of Christ, "Because I live, ye shall live also." Not only the outer but also the inner secrets of space will be revealed through the solar power in this critical period as we approach the next millenium.

Throughout the nearly two millenia since the Christ's descent to, and incarnation on, the Earth, the four fixed signs of the Zodiac—the Man, the Lion, the Bull, and the Eagle—have been used as symbols of the four Gospels: St. Matthew, St. Mark, St. Luke, and St. John, respectively. The spiritual scientific investigator, Dr. Rudolf Steiner, has described how the Gospels are related to the fixed signs.[1] The Lion, indicative of the Gospel of St. Mark, is the symbol for strength, the strength that pulses throughout the world, making all things possible of fulfillment and surging through the world as creative power. The strength and power of the Lion sign derive from the very exalted beings known as Thrones, also called Spirits of Will, who sacrificed their own substance to provide the foundation for man's physical body at the very beginning of mankind's evolution known as the Saturn Period, and this sacrificial gift we still bear within us. The supreme power and strength of the Thrones, channeled through the Christ-Sun-Being, were conveyed to our Earth with the entry of the Christ into Jesus of Nazareth. It is this attribute of Christ Jesus that is described in the Gospel of St. Mark, the "power-filled" Gospel, portraying the cosmic

---

[1] Rudolf Steiner, *Deeper Secrets of Human History* (London: Anthroposophic Press, 1957), chapter I.

will operating in Christ Jesus to bring wisdom and love to fulfillment.

The Sun is the inexhaustible, ever-welling life-giver and, although the planets appear to be the appointed agents as it were, performing their respective office and function, yet all power derives ultimately from the Sun-Son, the Christ. That power, which is fixed and eternal, whose living flame is the very garment of God, is the spiritual Sun that stands behind the physical Sun. As the Sun is the center of our solar system, so in a nativity the Sun is indicative of that eternal deathless being, the individuality, the true Ego, whose power directs and informs the lower, earthly, brain-bound personality, and does so the more man has matured in his evolution. The earthly personality is passing and quite ephemeral, even though its experiences are of vast value to the spiritual individuality, the higher Ego. This heavenly, solar individuality has a life that is eternal and a power that is imperishable; it builds each of the successive earthly personalities.

Leo gives rise and release to the living force known as vitality, as well as to the solar breath of Christ giving life to the Earth and man. With so vast a power of life animating the sign Leo, flooding the world with the radiance of the Sun, its expression in man while he is in a physical body will be contingent upon his soul age, for this radiance of life that veritably riots in this sign of the Sun may manifest as merely intense animal spirits, or as true life of the Spirit. Leo natives have an opulence of life and an overload of strength, stamina, and stability through the vitality which this veritable powerhouse provides. Such souls have an energy that seems effortless, as well as an ability to sustain, manage, and direct, with the capacity to raise and teach, to the degree to which they themselves are refined by their conscious or unconscious contact with the Christ-power.

This sign of the Sun empowers one to express the true individuality of man, the "I AM," the Sun element related to the Christ from the Sun, the Son of God. No sign of the Zodiac can be fully understood without the knowledge of its polar opposite, and this is vital in speaking of Leo, for through this sign and its opposite, Aquarius, man is raised from the dead, which means that he is Christ-born and becomes a Sun-Initiate. The Son of Man, resident in the opposite sign, Aquarius, offers his purified soul to the Son of God. The spiritual divine triad descends from above to meet the purified triune essences—that altar of roses, as it were —from the sentient soul, intellectual soul, and consciousness soul, the work and the fruit of the astral, etheric, and physical bodies, resulting from the activity of the Ego. Thus, the Son of Man, that is, Aquarius, refines and raises its forces to meet the Son of God from the Sun, in Leo. This way came those called in the ancient Mysteries "Sun Heroes," who were capable of uniting themselves with the spiritual forces of the Sun.

Since the coming of Christ, all souls are now eligible to become Christ-conscious—true individuals of the Son, through the sign of the Sun and its connections—each a unique individuality in the body of God. As the physical Sun calls forth the blossoms of the plants, thus the spiritual Christ-Sun develops man's Ego-consciousness to a full "I AM" blossom. The realization of this true "I AM" being, of the nature of the Christ "I AM," is both a self-discovery and a Christ-recovery.

Strength, power, and will are the attributes of this kingly sign, Leo. When others might be weak and be defeated again and again by the various vicissitudes of life, the souls strong in Leo have the strength and the will to meet courageously, intelligently, and in a kingly manner, all of life's difficulties. The power possessed by strong Leo Egos operates for good or ill, according to their soul maturity, producing the despot and arrogant authoritarian, or the creative, benevolent organizer and director, motivated by wisdom and love.

Leo loves aristocracy and royalty, and is, in fact, aristocratic and royal; but anyone negative in this sign sets store by earthly prominence and loves to rule and patronize, is austere, masterful, and condescending, accepts devotion and obedience and expects them as a matter of course, reacting with intense indignation when they are not given. The positive soul, however, aged in Christ-quality through many lives, is known by its works and ways to be truly of the aristocracy of heaven, a king regnant and royal.

As the lion has majesty and dignity, calm composure and poise when at ease, so does the native of the Lion display calm serenity that is lofty and noble. Such gracious dignity must be observed rather than described, for within there resides a radiance that appears to be truly royal. An unafflicted Leo radiates the very joy of life itself; his heart is ardent and as all-embracing as the whole world, and his hospitality is magnificently regal. But, when afflicted, the Leo native will use the same attributes to win approval and praise, so that it might be noted how lavish his largess. Thus the development of the latter will be hindered by his love of honor and adulation. The weak souls will as readily give credence to lies and flattery, to feed their feelings, as they will to truth.

Because of these proclivities, it is often imperative for these natives of the Sun's sign not to be moved or swayed by the opinions or false and flattering appraisals of others, for Leo souls can feed on the lust for honor. They must learn to stand alone and see themselves as they are; otherwise, they might sink in a morass of their own making, through their vain conceit and selfish ambition, as exemplified by the Leo Sun man, Napoleon. No greater, deeper, or more intense selfishness has rise than in this phase of Leo, because so mighty a flame feeds the heart. Every Leo native should know that his greatest and truest accomplishment will be ultimately that wherein he sought not the slightest honor or homage.

And only the soul born to the Spirit can realize such grace of selflessness.

If Leo souls would learn the secret of their sign, they must first cast aside pride, for they will never become the channel for benign spiritual powers, nor the bearers of lofty aspirations fruitful on earth, until pride of place, power, and vanity are forever renounced. The curse of the negative soul in this high sign is the desire for earthly kingship. However, when this negative, self-centered attitude is transmuted by the Christ-born Ego, the radiance of the Sun is realized, and the liberation of this heavenly current, flowing through an ardent heart full of a high and healthy optimism, makes for true service to humanity.

It should be noted that the afflicted Leo souls cannot express harmony and love, the positive properties of this sign. They have no ability to become intimate with others and often they may wall themselves off from others by their cruelty, which is not subtle but open. It is not just Saturn that inhibits and sets fences about souls, but the Sun also, through Leo, may in haughty arrogance cast one away from others, instead of uniting people harmoniously.

The strong force of the Sun through the sign Leo gives to positive souls a large supply of light and love, whereas in the debased the same force turns into lies and lust and pompous egotism. Imperious self-assertion, at times despotic and cruel, is the mark of the man who lives in darkness. In such souls, there is lust for power, an offensive assumption of authority and control which seeks to destroy everything human and everything spiritual. Leo is the fire that is fixed; hence, it ever glows and, with the Sun, it feeds all life. When such a flame is debased, it spreads lusts and destruction in the environment, but to know its real radiance is to emit spiritual light, love, and life.

No sight is worse than that of the bombastic vanity and

the peacock performance of a man gone bad in the sign,
the Lion, as the world witnessed in Mussolini. The dark side
of Leo is as horrible as the light side is glorious. As is true
of Scorpio, there can come out of this sign of the heart,
which emanates heat, either magnanimity or murder, despots
and devils, as well as true divines. All depends upon the
culture and the type of man, contingent upon the direction
and the degree of perfection reached in many lives.

When Leo's royal personality force, during its long evolu-
tionary apprenticeship of many lives, acquires from its op-
posite sign, Aquarius, its democratic universality, then the
soul will refuse to be "lionized" any longer and will be free
from the false and the lying, from all that so deeply debases
and degrades the negative Leo soul. When the patience of
Aquarius is added to the fiery fury of Leo, then comes that
calm that brings to birth the new man of Christ. The purpose
of lives in this sign is to fructify *harmony* within and with-
out. Once this harmony is secured, true love manifests in
the cooperation of the heart with the head. The soul loses
its desire to make itself obnoxious by lording it over others
or demanding their homage; pride and bombast are gone,
as is the vain desire to show off. It is their "dignity" that
disturbs too much the lives of some Leo natives and there
is far too great love of external life. Often, mere appearances
are treasured, rather than the soul-spiritual reality of life.

In the heart of every balanced Leo soul, there is enshrined
the love for those who are truly men of merit, whose worth
is apparent, for, after all, *nobility* is the keystone of this
exalted force of the Sun, which brooks nothing ignoble.

> Lady Clara Vere de Vere,
>   Of me you shall not win renown:
> You thought to break a country heart
>   For pastime, ere you went to town.

❖   ❖   ❖

> Howe'er it be, it seems to me,
>   'Tis only noble to be good.
> Kind hearts are more than coronets,
>   And simple faith than Norman blood.

These lines by Alfred, Lord Tennyson, whose Sun was in Leo, show forth the nobility and faith of this sign of the heart, which prompted him also to write, "A good woman is a wondrous creature, cleaving to the right and the good in all change; lovely in her youthful comeliness, lovely all her life long in comeliness of heart." Tennyson's own warmth of heart and his nobility won him many admiring friends, one of whom said, "What struck one most about him was the union of strength with refinement."

A true Leo man is easily recognized and admired, for the harmony of the Sun pours through his countenance, making him a center of radiance and joyousness that show out as a sunny disposition, whose cheerful presence acts as a healing power. The profound faith of Leo souls is so great that often they are capable of removing the fears and doubts of others at one touch by their counsel and by the vitality they impart. They dispel doubt, fear, and gloom as the Sun overcomes darkness and cold.

There is a warming fire in a true Leo heart, a fire of love that consumes diseased ideas, inverted notions, and feelings that have become fouled through long inertia or for lack of response to the Spirit. The secret of this inner force is a warmth of sympathy so intense that it comprehends another's problems in an embrace that is veritably of the Sun —a solar fiery force. The heart that is healthy in a Leo individual imparts a joyous, free, happy, kindly and yet kingly nature. The driving force expresses itself in dynamic intensity, while the intuition is keen and sensitive in all those who live the life of love and purity. For good or ill, the heart holds the power and the purpose of the man, for in the heart is the focus of the life forces that determine one's status, one's age in evolutionary soul growth. The Psalmist says, "Your heart shall live forever." The fount that feeds and sustains the heart is Leo, along with its ruler, the Sun, the heart of our solar system.

The fury and the fret of Aries, the first fire sign, riotous and out-flying, its vital energies causing chaos and clutter, are brought under control by the fixed-fire sign Leo, and channeled into the harmony of the heart and into true order. Leo is for the fire signs the central coordinating power, blending the forces of all three fire signs. Leo allows the life currents to flow so as to produce stability and strength. Here is done the work of transmutation of consciousness, whereby the fiery feelings of the heart inform the head; and it is in virtue of this warmth and illumination that the power of Christ-kingship becomes possible, and its consummation becomes a verity in soul-aged individuals.

It is the first fiery sign, Aries, the archetypal architect, the hotbed as it were, that springs the creative forces, whose fecundation seems to come from the Moon; yet, the vitality and the expansive power of generation flow from Leo, for the source and center of life are, after all, in Leo and in the Sun. We may say again that Aries is the creative architect, with the power to pioneer, whereas Leo is the creative vitalizing organizer, whose directing idea is divine, the fount from which all things spring; but, the things and systems themselves are developed and brought to execution through Sagittarius. The power to organize is the forte of Leo natives and, through their resources of well-directed energy, truly colossal, their achievements are often made in the world of matter. Witness Henry Ford, whose genius to organize and whose development of the physical resources of the earth were enormous.

It is in this sign of dynamic heart intensity and feeling that every form of creativity and self-expression becomes possible, for it is here that the human being is empowered to be an actor on the earth's stage. Creativity is the character of Leo, and largess and generous giving its forte. All creativity flows from Leo and from the Sun; thus the arts find here their expression and their outlet.

Procreation of our physical children belongs here as well, for life and the child-bearing qualities are derived from the Sun and from the fifth sign, Leo. Man, as actor and performer, creates and makes his entrances onto the stage of the earth through the solar-life sign, Leo. As an actor on this stage, man manifests every gradation, from terrible tyranny to the most marvelous magnanimity. It is here that we must avoid becoming stage-strutters, consumed with colossal egotism. In Leo we may test what we have made of altruism and humility, heavenly exotics still rare in our time.

Leo is both aristocratic and autocratic, the manner is highspirited, and the natural bearing is that of dignified ease, reminiscent of the mysterious gaze of the lion, which never looks at one but sees clear through and beyond the physical man. One should study this marvel in the lion, if one has an opportunity to do so, for "the lion is one of those animals which in a very real sense are Sun-animals; animals in which the Sun develops its own peculiar force." "The lion, more than any other animal, has complete balance between its breathing and its heartbeat. . . . It is all breast organism; it is the animal which, in its outer form and way of living, gives full expression to the rhythmic system and expresses the interplay between heartbeat and respiration in the mutual relationship of the heart and the lungs. . . . If we look for something in man similar to what is found in the lion, it is the human breast where the rhythms meet, the rhythms of circulation and respiration," says Rudolf Steiner.[2]

---

[2] Rudolf Steiner, *Man as Symphony of the Creative Word* (London: Rudolf Steiner Press), chapters I & II.

Steiner further describes deep cosmic connections that stir the heart when understood: how the bird creation, represented by the eagle, on dying, bears spiritualized earth substance to the spiritual world, whereas the ruminants, represented by the cow or bull, through their astral forces, on dying, give spirit substance to the earth. By establishing harmony between the rhythms of breathing and of the blood, the lion holds the balance between spiritual substance and physical substance. Hence, it is the group soul of the lion that maintains the balance between the forces streaming upward and downward, by regulating how many eagles and how many cows are required. The lion is thus truly the king of beasts. In every way is Leo a royal sign.

The character of Leo being conditioned by the heart, which it rules, no one of these natives will be larger or nobler intrinsically than the sum total of his past lives allows, as expressed by the Sun. This expression of the Sun-individuality is, of course, the measure of the man in any nativity, but in Leo it will manifest in the quality of the heart, whether it is cruel or kind, bestial or benign, for the fiery forces of the heart can express both hatred and love, and with no greater power than this mighty fixed-fire sign gives.

When the Leo soul has a heart that uses the will to cooperate with the head, we see one who is individualized and, if spiritually conscious, he or she will become a powerhouse that helps to uplift and redeem people and planet. These positive souls of Leo have a warmth of will that is united to the Father's will and is working as one with him. Their emotions, feelings, desires, and thoughts, working in and through so great a vital power of abundance, produce an aura literally charged with life and, through such radiance, they bring healing balm and benison to all they touch, even as Sunday, the Sun's day, bears a brightness, power, and radiance that may bless the whole week. These souls express love in action.

They are truly magnanimous and dynamic with the Sun's power, and so great is their generative power and the living force of Leo and the Sun that, through their fixed-sign force, they are able to send their thoughts telepathically into the distance as no other sign seems to be able to do.

Leo individuals never lack in decisiveness, for they are always very decided, one way or another, never indifferent, though often they are impulsive; but even when impulsive, they still display their innate generosity. When positive, these souls make their ideals a reality, thus practising the realism of the true and the noble, instead of talking about such virtues. Aries, too, oftentimes weaves a wonderful web of lofty ideals, yet these ideals ever remain in the thought stage. Aries promises far more than it can perform, which sometimes makes the natives appear untruthful, although they would not be so, for Aries is ever straining after the unattainable. But the poised, positive Leo individual, with silent power, may quietly turn his ideals into living realities. In short, Leo fulfills what the Aries native contemplates as a vision. Leo has the inherent faculty of inner will and light that finds the right way and makes the best use of the best. And the more the desires of these souls are spiritualized, the more magnificent is their accomplishment. When their will coincides with God's will, they move mountains and influence large numbers of people for good.

Everyone strong in Leo loves to rule or to teach, and this forte invariably springs from an impulse of the heart. According to the heart's quality through the individual's soul age, so will be the quality of governance or teaching. Great is the life-giving warmth that radiates from the evolved, solarized or Christed Leo soul, acting as balm to heal human hearts; and as great is the suffering, sorrow, and pain that a Leo person may cause if he has turned traitor to true manhood and become despotic.

The warm effulgence of the heart comes to manifestation

in Leo, conferring an exceptionally lavish generosity. This magnanimity is a royal gift that makes of these men and women those we may without falsity call "the magnificent." How glorious is the benign and divine radiance shed by the physical Sun down upon the earth! How that great orb warms and enlivens us all! What could we be without the Sun? There would be no life. Yet, behind the physical Sun there is the spiritual Son, the Christ, now indwelling in our planet and turning this Earth into a Sun itself! Still more, the living Christ Sun-power is specialized in every living soul; every human heart bears the ray of the Christ-Son, who is one with his Father. Thus, we may surmise how profound the connection is of the Mystery of Golgotha, the unique Christ-event, with our *real* life. Not for nought does the old hymn run, "Sun of my soul, my Saviour dear, it is not night when thou art near."

The weakness of Leo souls lies in their desires and feelings, for they are too easily led and played upon, the crafty and the subtle taking advantage of their very warm natures, to lead them into dissipation. I have seen such souls driven to insanity by their descent into a night of lust. Yet, they have been healed because of their true spiritual fire ever burning brightly within. No sign can recover its natives more swiftly after a downfall occasioned by the bestial side of this sign of the Lion through the abuse of the lower nature. In fact, when Leo individuals discern the spiritual light, they find the way of return to God with a facility and force that is truly astounding, making fast progress by their ready response to the Spirit, accentuated by their acute sensitivity. Their whole life is then devoted to doing good, their environment becoming permeated with the quality of so great a faith. They have the power to lift others to the road that leads to the light of love, which is the home and heaven of all, the realm of truth where there lives the wisdom of love.

Leo is a sign of authority and power, conferring nobility

of character and making the natives susceptible to every-
thing lofty; they usually have the ability to govern, rule,
organize, and teach. Their generosity is unbounded and, al-
though ambitious, their ambition is for the most part turned
in the direction of that which perfects the man, to make
for true insight and poised self-control. Their intuition of the
heart is always active and true, consonant with the heart's
quality, the soul age, and type. Leo unites people and holds
them by the power of love, for the destiny and ideal of Leo
is *harmony*. Leo must create harmony both within and with-
out.

The true light of Leo, expressing through the Christ-
consciousness, makes a man a true king, who helps to raise
and refine multitudes of his fellow men, giving his love and
compassion as selflessly as does the Sun its warmth and its
light which shines on all alike.

> I AM the door, the Christ immortal,
> Each soul must pass through my love portal;
> I AM the door, if entered through,
> Come light and love, and life anew.
>
> What is that guidance in my heart
> That makes me not from truth depart?
> I face thy flame's eternal light
> And seek to make my soul all white.
>
> Thou, Christ, art the sublime Sun-being,
> With me alway and ever-seeing;
> From thee, O Lord, I could not hide
> For in thy heart I do abide.

Virgo - The Virgin

VIRGO, the Virgin, is usually pictured as a maiden with several ears of wheat in her hand. The symbol itself will bear a rich yield if one concentrates on it in meditative study, for this is the real way to get at the essence of the stellar script; the fruit of such study lies in its esotericism, in the occult forces and the archetypal fact, the spiritual core within and behind the outer wrapping.

In the symbol of the maiden with the ears of wheat, we

see expressed the idea of virginal purity, the original divine purity—eternally feminine—of the human being before its differentiation in earthly bodies of increasing density, culminating in the present egotistic personality. The soul was then still unsoiled and sinless, without spot or blemish, and free of all impure desire. The ears of wheat symbolize the statement related of the Christ in the sixth chapter of St. John's Gospel, where it says: "He gave them bread from heaven to eat. . . . For the bread of God is he which cometh down from heaven, and giveth life unto the world. . . . And Jesus said unto them, I am the bread of life: he that cometh to me shall never hunger. . . . I am the living bread which came down from heaven; if any man eat of this bread, he shall live forever."

A part of man's astral body is unsoiled and sinless, without spot or blemish. There is another part that must be cleansed, for its evil must be transmuted, as Isaiah says: "Although your sins be as scarlet, they shall be as white as driven snow; though they be red like crimson, they shall be as wool" (1:18).

The sign Virgo connotes such a renewal and cleansing, through the immaculate spiritual birth that takes place in this sign of the Virgin. In Virgo is the revelation of birth brought about by divine creativity which continuously seeks perfection and manifests its urge toward the Infinite. Virgo, therefore, sheds light on the soul's need for catharsis, for cleansing, productive of purity, if one would attain the full consciousness wrought in this sixth sign, for here the Divine Child must be brought to birth within the purified human soul.

Raphael's glorious Sistine Madonna thus becomes a true symbol for Virgo. The veil of the senses is drawn aside to portray the Virgin Mother and the Christ-child, immaculately conceived, born out of the realm of loftiest purity, the divine, angelic realm. It is a true Christian symbol of high magnitude, indicating the purity required for any individual to give birth to the Christ in his own soul. Virgo represents likewise the forces of the soul raised to virginal perfection through purification, or catharsis, that is, a purging of the astral body of all hindering forces, so that it may become harmoniously organized and develop higher organs of perception. In esoteric Christianity, such a cleansed astral body is called the "pure, chaste, wise Virgin Sophia." The highest representative of this was the Mother of Jesus, who could thus receive the illumination of the Holy Spirit and give birth to the child that later, at the Baptism in the Jordan, became the bearer of the Christ. The Deed of Christ provides the Earth and all mankind with those forces that make it possible for every individual who avails himself of them, to transform his astral body, through purification, into a Virgin Sophia, and so to receive spiritual illumination and to achieve the Christing of his Ego.

The sixth beatitude, "Blessed are the pure in heart, for they shall see God," applies to all human souls, but especially so to the Ego whose destiny tasks are strongly influenced by the sixth sign, Virgo, working to attain the Virgin Sophia and then being able to "see God," that is, to rise to the spiritual world and to partake of divinity. Such an Ego can make the Virgo declaration, "I AM the Mother and the Child, I AM God investing a body of matter with the solar Spirit of life." But, whenever matter and selfishness rule in this sign, the brain-bound, earthly view presents a very partial picture and limits the vision to the sense world. Then the Virgo declaration is, "Let matter have rule and reign, my light is the darkness of the brain." Such a person lives wholly in the physical senses, with no knowledge of spiritual realms and values.

Virgo signifies the sublimation of our physical experiences and their transformation into heightened self-consciousness, developing the Ego in its purity and bringing it to ultimate perfection. To achieve this sublimation of true selfhood, one must work for purity on all planes of body and soul. In order to understand Virgo's approach to this task, one needs to know the nature of the thinking, feeling, and willing that are peculiar to Virgo.

Virgo is forever propounding the question, "Why?" Virgo always concentrates on one single question at a time, whereas Gemini asks several questions all at once. Virgo is critical and analytical; Gemini is acceptive and synthetical. Virgo takes in sectional ideas, thoughts, and views. Gemini accepts all ideas and views, as thoughts, and allows the soul to sort out and sift them, the Gemini soul having the power to winnow the true from the false. Both forms of thought power are essential to the development of the soul, for thus it acquires wisdom, coming to know the whole as well as its parts. The Virgo soul colors its thoughts with psychic feelings, whereas the Gemini Ego clothes its feelings with thoughts. From the conjunction of matured thoughts and feelings, there results that rare sublimation called common sense. Virgo analyzes, whereas Gemini synthesizes. Through the resolution of analysis and synthesis, the Ego at last is able to distinguish between, and separate, the three forces of thinking, feeling, and willing, and yet is able to coordinate them. This is the way of truth that leads to initiation. Virgo cannot attain to the truth until the strong, active element of psychic feeling is dissociated from and kept clear of reason, inherent in Mercury, which is quite free of feeling.

Virgo, being a negative Mercurial sign, is not so much creative as constructive, methodical, very orderly and efficient, making excellent planners and designers. These natives are much concerned with details; they know the parts and are in danger of losing sight of the whole; hence, they are apt to strain at gnats and swallow the camel. They are meticulously fastidious, sometimes irritatingly so. Their minds are fast-working, yet often they become narrow and grooved. The chief concern of the Virgo person is detail—statistical and biographical details—and these he loves, uses, and quotes. Through this forte for detail—the parts of the whole—and through the thought inherent in Virgo, this sign produces in its best phase the true servant and ministering angel.

Ever does Virgo seek the reason; it wants to know *why*. Libra, on the contrary, knows why; intuitively it realizes the truth that Virgo wants to know as truth. Virgo, using the brain, requires sight and knowledge as to how one knows why. Virgo says, "Demonstrate to me how you know why!" The intellectual quality tends to be cold, sceptical, and sometimes cynical; hence, demonstration must be made and given to the senses. This is well illustrated by the disciple Thomas, who relied on outer appearance, for he did not have that faith that sees beyond the demonstrable facts. Virgo is the sign of the doubting Thomas.

Virgo is a sign of correction and adjustment. The mind is critical and dissecting, and through such critical analysis Virgo attains to the power of discrimination, for *discrimination* is the one thing needful for Virgo souls. What is discrimination if not the ability to know the true from the false, the essential from the non-essential! Evolved souls in this sign get at the very core, the kernel of the exterior man, as well as to the center of things. No true health or wholeness is possible in man until he attains to this acuteness of judgment and insight of soul, which pierces the darkness of error. In this sixth sign, this acumen must be acquired which shows a high degree of intellectual capacity, at once pointed and comprehensive, plus the intuitive sympathy that plumbs character and situations at a glance. One must arrive at discrimination before the higher faculties can function. The success or failure of Virgo individuals depends upon the discrimination and wisdom they evolve and upon the discrimination and wisdom with which they give themselves in constructive, loving service.

In Virgo one sits in judgment upon oneself, for it is in this sign that judgment is passed, and not only upon oneself, but on all creative activities in life. It is because of this self-scrutiny so searching, this intense, serious, critical analysis of oneself and of all things that Virgo is designated as the sign of self-judgment and of adjustment. Yet, this inner need for correction and rectification arises only as the soul develops the positive quality of true discrimination, the power to discern the truth or falsity of a thing, idea, person, place, or whatever else it may be. Flooding feelings and sympathies too often swamp the soul, so that the findings of pure reason are distorted and judgment is falsified. Susceptibility to sympathy, in this sign, and the coloration of thinking by such sympathy or feeling, is apt to destroy the higher touch that tells the truth; but as thinking is separated from feeling, then the light of the Spirit can operate. Discrimination must be applied to the feelings no less than to the thoughts, in this sign of minute details.

To attain to the needed power of discrimination, the Virgo soul must learn to conquer the habit, or tendency, to be cynical, worldly-wise, and clever, and to be a master in destructive criticism. He who dissects with dissension destroys the truth he would behold, and the folly of ever finding fault and splitting hairs repels more than it reveals the archetypal essence, the true clue and key he seeks, and he makes himself obnoxious with his dissection. Virgo must learn to use constructively its natural power of analysis, thus becoming truly discriminative.

Virgo brings essential lessons of incessant repetition, myriads of impacts of repeated operations or actions, through years and through lives, in order to vitalize and build the time element and the rhythm of the etheric body, which forms the forces and the matrix for man's physical body. Man will continue to have what the world calls "a bad time," until he acquires in his etheric body a finer sense of true time and attunement to the cosmic rhythms. The etheric within and behind the earthly personality assumes special importance in this intensely sensitive sign, which rules the *sense of movement.* The repetition evident in this sign of rhythm may become senseless and servile, turning into the unintelligent response of an automaton, or it may lead to the parroting of ideas, as to right or wrong, the true or the false; or, it may, when positive, give birth to, and bear the high power of, a fine, stabilized personality endowed with a spiritualized will.

In Virgo the Ego should rise to its purest development, but in many Virgo souls today it is introverted. Pain and conflict, soul strife and mental torment, arise from the attempt to manifest and make conscious in the personality that which lies concealed in the inner being. This is the root of the inferiority complex peculiar to Virgo natives, which after all is Ego-consciousness or even egotism, smothered and suppressed. Because of their inferiority complex and its often accompanying subservience, souls strong in Virgo make their lives a misery by dwelling on unwholesome, morbid, and false thoughts and feelings.

Virgo is a sign so psychic yet intellectual that individuals not yet balanced in it exhibit qualities both negative in feeling and very erratic in thought. The solar plexus being often more active than the brain, with the brain not lighted by the brain-free forces of Spirit, they carry untruth within themselves, which makes them not only deceive themselves, but also badly misjudge others. As constructive criticism in Virgo leads to wise discrimination as well as to deep discernment, thus right appraisal of the self leads to a healthy adjustment of the Ego, and wise analysis leads to wisdom; but,

failure to bring this wisdom to fruition damages the soul
and makes the witless weakling without will.

Although the forces of sympathy and service are inherent
in this sign, the element of friendship is not in it. Few friends
are made when the nativity shows definite Virgo qualities
without the support of other sign factors. They do not show
much of themselves, not even to their intimate friends. Virgo
individuals are rarely understood at first meeting, for they
are naturally shy and reserved, but when friends are made,
they treat them well. Many a Virgo person separates himself
from others and becomes solitary because of his critical na-
ture. Through his acute analysis of microscopic kind, he often
creates animus rather than amity. It is this fact, in connection
with the invariable inferiority complex in this sign of work
and service, that sets up a wall between Virgo souls and
their intimate friends and brethren, a wide gulf often exist-
ing between parents and child.

In the practical affairs and experiences of everyday life
—banking, business, trade, or industry, usually involving
constant repetition—Virgo souls learn their largest lessons.
Yet hard lessons often come through marriage, and they are
deeply affected by this relationship, the union itself depend-
ing more upon the purity of the partner than upon any other
quality. The primness and the spinster quality of this sign
conduce sometimes to a preference for celibacy, or to an
aversion to marriage.

The great mystery of sex and love is inherent in Scorpio,
Libra, and Virgo, ruled respectively by Mars, Venus, and
Mercury. Mars is the most passionate, Venus refines the feel-
ings, whereas Mercury lifts the relationship to realms of
thought. Purity is the first purpose of Virgo, the sign of the
Mother of Jesus and of the immaculate conception. When
man awakens spiritually to the plan of God, then does he
become animated with the power to drive out the dross and

purify his personality. Then can matter and Spirit merge through the mediating Christ-quality.

Every Virgo person, whatever his or her soul age, is a stickler for physical purity and cleanliness. Science and hygiene are much loved, and hygiene particularly is overworked, as are the bathrooms. Soap and sanitation for maintaining physical purity are more than mere foibles with Virgo natives; they are almost a fetish with them.

Virgo and the sixth house of the nativity rule health, and the natives of this sign, when responding positively, never seem to grow old. Consistently they maintain good health. But those that are negative are obsessed by an incessant fear of ailment and often imagine they are ill, therefore the mere idea of ill health should never be suggested by their friends or even mentioned as an inquiry. The purity of the body depends largely on the elimination of waste products by the intestines, which are ruled by Virgo. The worrying propensity of Virgo natives acts readily on this cleansing organ. There is often a dread of blood, so that they cannot bear the sight of it, but if this is conquered, Virgo people make the best nurses. They exhibit a fine sympathy for those who suffer or are in trouble, and they are happy in the healing of wounds. It is not by chance that Virgo indicates purity and health, both of soul and body, for health depends on the purity of the blood; and pure thoughts and desires, as well as pure food, maintain the purity of the blood.

No sign is more sensitive to mental, psychic, and atmospheric conditions than Virgo. Their bodies act as barometers, and they sense the change in wind and weather before it occurs. They are so sensitive to their surroundings that people and places, as well as the weather, affect them for good or ill much more than they know. All atmospheres of mind, feeling, soul, and spirit affect the Virgo souls, therefore they will be wise to create in themselves the power of self-protection, so as to avoid future hurt. The growing purity of their soul will increasingly demand purer surroundings and associates. Even what they read has a decided effect upon them; hence, if they would avoid being harmed, they should exercise discrimination and make a wise selection in what they read, especially before eating and before going to sleep.

As a result of their concern for detail and their wish to be discriminative, Virgo individuals, striving for purity and health, often become food fanatics. Without becoming fanatics, however, they can use their insight, supported by statistical data of which they are so fond, in rendering a vital service to mankind in the sense of pure food and purity of air, for devitalized food and polluted air are becoming ever greater menaces to good health.

Only when Virgo's love of cleanliness reaches out to a higher level than that of the body and is raised to the level of the soul, may we say that cleanliness is next to godliness, for the hygiene of the soul is a decided impetus and help in our approach to the spirit of truth. It becomes a heavenly hygiene, the purity that tells of *truth*, that instant spiritual cognition symbolized by the wise virgin with the "oil" of Christ-soul-growth, the only illuminant. All souls have lamps, but not all have oil in them.

We may gain a finer portrait, a more vivid insight into the nature of Virgo as we reflect upon the woman named Martha in St. Luke's Gospel. In chapter ten, we read how Jesus was received in Martha's house: "And she had a sister called Mary, which also sat at Jesus' feet and heard his word. But Martha was cumbered about much serving, and came to him and said, Lord, dost thou not care that my sister hath left me to serve alone? Bid her therefore that she help me." No words are more valuable in valid appraisal of this sixth sign—so sensitive and psychic, yet also often selfish in its sympathies, unwise in its compassion, and lacking in true discernment and proper discrimination—than the words addressed to Martha by Christ Jesus, "Martha, Martha, thou art careful and troubled about many things; but one thing is needful and Mary hath chosen that good part, which shall not be taken away from her."

Mary is one of those wise virgins who received the light of the Lord and thus secured the essential oil for her lamp. Here we see the evidence of the positive power at work in the soul to produce individuality. People like Martha become burdened with detail and earthly concerns, "careful and troubled about many things," but not about the "*one* thing needful," which requires the will of positive vision and compassion born of love. Not until thinking is concentrated and its force is made continuous in application and meditation, can the vision be gained to build the will and thereby gain control over the otherwise elusive and fluidic Mercurial forces of this psychic sign. Martha evinces dissatisfaction, discontent, and criticism, through her unwise and wrong analysis; she is the bearer of an erroneous attitude, lacking the light of vision. So long as one remains in the Martha-category, one will be overanxious about material concerns.

Virgo feels the connection between matter and Spirit well enough, yet the Mercurial splitting and scattering renders the spiritual cognition inert, destroys devotion, and negates conviction. Virgo has the power of spiritual discernment, and its natives can take the greatest interest in spiritual activities, but their dexterity with detail, devoted to petty concerns, makes them lose sight of the over-all plan and principle of *life*. Because Virgo receives only small sectional views, unlike Libra which sees the whole, Virgo souls can achieve far more effective work when they are under the direction or guidance of individuals strong in cardinal signs, unless cardinal or fixed signs are strong in their own nativity. The perfection of perspective is the result of work done in Virgo, even though that perfection may not be in evidence until the next sign, Libra, is reached. But no perspective can be gained until the weaknesses of subservience and selfishness are transmuted. When spiritual discernment at last lights the mind of the Virgo native, then true sympathy will make the soul active in *service*, the forte of this sign.

Leo Tolstoy, who had many planets as well as his Sun in Virgo, has said, "The happiness of man consists in life, and life is in labor. . . . The vocation of every man and woman is in serving other people." Where work is concerned, Virgo individuals often prefer using their wits rather than their hands; they prefer the exercise of their ingenuity to hard work, although they are by no means lazy or afraid of work. They do try, however, to evade whatever they find unpleasant or disturbing. Virgo is the sign of the subordinate, those who work or serve, the working classes and the so-called inferiors, that is, all those under the charge and direction of others; but they sometimes serve in a high capacity.

Truckling servility is sometimes the vice of Virgo, although it is not so obnoxious as the servility found too often in the fawning, negative Capricorn, which is of the Uriah Heep type. All work or thought can be dignified in virtue of the divine in us. No stigma can be attached to any true servant in any serving capacity, whether as a shoe shiner or the president of a nation. No work or office is so low or so menial that it cannot be dignified by the Christ-attitude. Not only did Christ Jesus say, "He who would be the greatest among you, let him be the servant of all," but he also demonstrated it in action by washing the feet of his disciples, thus humbly showing how the higher, or the more evolved, are dependent on the less evolved. St. Paul says with truth, "Let this mind be in you, which was also in Christ Jesus: who, being in the form of God, thought it not robbery to be equal with God, but made himself of no reputation, and took upon him the form of a servant, and was made in the likeness of men" (Philippians 2: 5-7). This servant quality pre-eminently inheres in Virgo. Sensible, sound, and sympathetic service is essential for Virgo, and those go farthest and fastest forward in evolution who realize this and give of their effort and mental energies to this end, even reflecting the quality of sacrifice indicated in its complementary sign, Pisces, the Fishes. Humble gratitude should be ours for the privilege of serving. No one can command until he has learned to obey, and obedience is learned through service and proper subordination, but this has in it nothing of servility.

Virgo natives are often connected with concrete, practical affairs and callings of life. They usually display a ready adaptability for business and industry, banking and trade. At the same time, there is in this earthy and mental, yet psychic sign, that mood which makes the artist who portrays exquisitely delicate detail—detail of gossamer fineness. In painting and music, super-refinement and most delicate tracery are characteristic of Virgo. It manifests in the music of that master of refinement, Chopin, with the second decanate of Virgo rising and the Sun in Pisces, as it does in the music of Mendelssohn, with his Moon in Virgo, and particularly in that of Mozart, who had Virgo rising at birth. Likewise, the artist, Dürer, an excellent engraver and painter, had Virgo rising, with his Sun and Moon in Gemini. The literary genius and expert scientist—though this is as yet rarely recognized—also practical statesman, Goethe, had his Sun in Virgo. The spiritually awakened Virgo individual looks upon and uses his art and knowledge only for the welfare of the world—to serve others. If one looks for refinement and exquisite detail in art, one should look for common signs in general and for Virgo in particular. Thought power as well as the most delicate artistic quality come out of this reserved sign, even though this is not always apparent nor always cultivated by the natives of this sign.

Virgo individuals who are spiritually awakened will give themselves in dynamic action in service to mankind; those unawakened certainly serve themselves, as they mistakenly think, working for mere dollars, which some of them never cease counting. Their lives are wholly devoted to acquisition, until at last they discover how subversive and detrimental this pursuit is, and they realize that their physical forces and the blinding brain block their road and bar their vision into heaven, delaying the soul's perfecting.

One of the worst vices of this psychic-thought sign is selfishness, sometimes coupled with a fastidious, exacting nature and a critical attitude that is destructive and prevents the critic's own soul growth. Subtle craftiness is often there, too. The term "vixen" is then well applicable to this sign in its negative phase. The positive Virgo individual, however, applies this subtle power in proper constructive fashion in addressing himself to the finding of right answers to urgent, impelling questions. He then exercises constructive criticism, developing the faculty of true, logical purpose and, the purer the motive, the finer his etheric body and astral body become. Thus knowledge and wisdom are flowered.

Virgo, like Gemini, is a sign of cognition, but Virgo natives stand between the "devil" of selfishness and the "deep sea" of unwise sympathy, both of which are inherent in the psychic nature of this sign. A balance must be sought through the light which only wisdom allows, and this wisdom must be worked for by acquiring the faculty for instant, inner discernment, the result of a progressive power of discrimination. The secret of developing these faculties lies hidden in the love that Virgo natives must awaken and make fruitful. So long as the Virgo person remains the victim of his senses, he must perforce be restricted by his intensely utilitarian views.

Virgo is a sign that brings psychic experiences, but too many persons confuse psychic forces with soul growth and spiritual attainment. There is a vast difference between the sensitivity to the atmosphere of the astral world on the one hand, and on the other, the purity and love that are needed before one may safely enter the spiritual realms in virtue of one's own power and self-direction. The former is usually a relic of atavistic or instinctive clairvoyance, whereas the second is true initiate-consciousness. However, many an individual in this time of materialism would have no interest in the teachings of spiritual science, were it not for his or her own firsthand psychic experience. Virgo individuals are capable of making excellent progress in soul growth and spiritual achievement when they seek the chastity and purity symbolized by this sign of the Virgin.

Through Virgo come severe self-examination and continuous close questioning. The inner life centers on very diligent dissection. Thus, thinking serves the soul to bring out the faculty of discrimination, and in doing so, no detail, however minute, is missed. In the highly evolved individual, this intense mental activity leads to such a sublimation that thought becomes spiritualized to the point where the soul seeks the divine ideation of God, as the one directing Idea, and the Father's will. Right mental activity at last leads to right spiritual thought and direction. Virgo natives must sublimate thinking by incessant seeking, sorting of ideas, and arriving at right and true answers to all their questions.

One thing more than others that must be transmuted in Virgo is the habit of worrying, particularly over insignificant trifles. Mercury seems to have Virgo people ever on edge, and thus they fritter and fling away much of their best force. They must guard also against criticizing destructively and seek, instead, to transmute their urge to condemn. It is quite all right to analyze constructively, but Virgo natives so often shift to the negative side, becoming destructive in their thinking and cynical in their attitudes. Through their avarice and cynicism, some estrange themselves from the very idea of God and forget all compassion.

It should be the aim and purpose of the Virgo person to make continuous adjustments which carry the Ego to new stages and create fresh attitudes toward the experiences of life. He must eradicate the soul-destroying element of destructive criticism while still retaining the power of right and wise analysis, learning at the same time to curb purposeless prolixity and to avoid the digression and waste of mere verbosity. Controlled continuity of thoughts must become the watchword. With the control of thinking comes a conservation of speech and action, and growth in wisdom—a desideratum for the evolving Ego.

The unevolved Ego is so exacting and self-sufficient as to be intolerant of other people's ideas, views, or teachings; it undervalues or dismisses any judgment but its own. This attitude is the result of the sectional, separative brain-thinking, the "darkness" in which the unevolved member of this sign lives. He lives in the little things of life, the parts and bits, rather than in the comprehensive over-all view. It is this limitation that makes these souls purblind and exacting —a mood they carry in themselves and try to induce in others, and it is the root of the fastidious attitude of the over-particular, to which can be traced most of their disturbance and distress, with the exception of the psychic susceptibility inherent in this sign. No man becomes benign or beautiful of soul or truly tolerant until he consciously acknowledges his own faults and failings. Such a recognition, coupled with a growing self-knowledge, will impart a powerful impulse to overcome the undesirable Virgo habit of indulging in dissecting, destructive criticism, which the unevolved in this sign carry as constant function.

It is the task of Virgo natives to discern and dissect, to analyze and evaluate, in order to be wisely discriminating. Discrimination enables one to see the guiding principles amid details, to hold on to the essential, and to be wisely compassionate. The Virgo person sits in judgment upon himself and on all things; thus he subjects his life to continuous adjustment. So long as he remains in the darkness of his brain-bound intellect, he maintains a utilitarian outlook often clothed with a vigorous materialism, but the moment he sees the light within, none gives finer or greater service and none shows a larger growth of soul. Such Egos have become genuinely constructive in outlook and in criticism, and they are then able to help others by their decided acumen in seeing and serving.

The fear to which Virgo natives are frequently subject is the direct result of living in the darkness of the earthbound intellect. The mood of matter is too dominant; the Spirit must much more illuminate matter. Virgo souls become soiled as they sell themselves out to matter and neglect the Spirit. When they succeed, however, in getting rid of their materialistic and egotistic impulses, their power to purify themselves makes them radiate gloriously their innate divinity. Virgo souls who have become aware of the truth of the wisdom of love, seek to live in the chaste purity of this sign of the Virgin Sophia, most mightily represented by the one for whom St. John uses no name but refers to as "the mother of Jesus."

When Virgo is dominant in a nativity, there is an urgent need for purity and purification. Although these souls are often fanatics in so far as personal cleanliness and hygiene are concerned, such cleanliness alone is not enough; it must not stop there but should be extended to a hygiene of the soul, to one's thoughts and feelings, to a heavenly hygiene, working alchemically to cleanse the soul with a will that works in wisdom. It is this discriminating wisdom that is "the one thing needful," for these are the souls who must work to win a balance between a sordid selfishness and a sloppy sympathy, gracefully detaching themselves from a desire to be served and finding their own inner forte to serve others, for the weakness of Virgo is selfishness, its glory is glad service to others. Individuals born in the sign of the Virgin gain true satisfaction in life and make real advancement when they gladly offer themselves in wise service to others.

O turn thy thoughts to cosmic life,
Embrace the world beyond the strife,
Take in the view within the light,
Beyond the senses, Spirit-bright.

O cleanse thy soul and understand
The movement of the Spirit-band,
The Elohim, and living whole,
The Christ himself, who feeds thy soul.

Get wise to life, ennobled be,
Serve God and man, and live as free;
The body's barrier, woven tight,
Must loosened be to see the light.

A second man must come to birth
Within the person on the Earth;
If man will live the life, and love,
He brings to birth the Lord above.

Libra - The Balance

LIBRA, the Balance, or Scales, is the seventh sign of the Zodiac, of the airy element, and cardinal in quality. Its archetype evokes *balance*, and thus persons strong in Libra ever strive to realize in themselves the maintenance of balance, from the tightrope walker to the judge dispensing justice. The scales must always be balanced. Constantly are Libra souls weighed and ever do they weigh themselves, to see what is lacking, in order to maintain harmony and poise. No harmony can exist in man without constantly producing balance; nor could the physical organism exist without the kidneys, which are ruled by Libra, along with the waist or loins, the central portion of the body.

Inner and outer balance results in *wholeness*—the *union* of the threefold being of man, made up of body, soul, and spirit. As love is the secret of life, so is this process of integration within man the secret of God, who is love. And, as God is impartial power, giving to all creation his exquisite *equilibrium* that sustains the cosmos, with worlds and systems self-ordered and self-acting, so does man work and at last win this power and realize his divine estate as a Son of God; and thus experiencing the Christ in himself, he achieves balance and harmony.

Figuratively, we may speak of Libra, this central, sacred, sabbatical sign, as the flywheel of the Zodiac, for as power and motion are maintained on an appointed course in proportion to the balance supplied, stability being given by the gyroscopic balancing force, so does man elevate himself on the spiralling course of evolution as he acquires an increasing harmony of balance. To become balanced is to become whole, and wholeness results only from a union or integration of forces. This wholeness is secured through the Christ working in the soul, relating the soul to the spirit in full Ego-consciousness.

No proper comprehension of the signs of the Zodiac is possible without a growing working knowledge of the meaning of the Christ. This fact becomes vital when we examine the seventh sign, for this sign has for its office the power of crucifixion. When the Sun enters Libra, it changes its course from the northern to the southern hemisphere; there is a crossing over the equator. Day and night are equal in length, light and darkness are balanced. Thus the quality of balance is realized when the Sun reaches the equator, midway between the Tropic of Cancer and the Tropic of Capricorn.

When Libra is dominant at birth, there manifests in the life a change-over, a cross-ification or crucifixion of the man and, through this crucifixion in Libra, man achieves a true balance and finds the peace which "passeth understanding," the unconditioned joy which only the Christ can give.

Venus, the ruler of Libra, rules not only the venous blood circulation, but also Friday; and the Crucifixion occurred on Friday. The esoteric student will note that natives of this sign pass through the Good Friday spell as an actual experience. St. Paul says, "They that are Christ's have crucified the flesh with the affections and lusts" (Galatians 5:24). The degree and power of such a crucifixion will accord with the status of the soul. Libra persons, especially, must sacrifice the flesh to the Spirit, so that the soul may be refined. Thus do they rise out of sufferings and sorrow, which occasion intense thought about their experiences in feeling, until a balance of the head and heart is achieved through the will. Only in this wise is that wholeness acquired that makes for wholesomeness and equanimity.

"What crucifixions are in love," says Herrick. Love is literally the life of Libra; those born in or under this Venus sign are crucified in the flesh through their desires and feelings, until purification thoroughly refines the soul and brings it to a state of poise and peace. All earthly marriages are but a shadow of the heavenly pattern. After one has experienced the divine marriage conjoining the lower self to the higher, this sign with all its sufferings leads at last, by way of Golgotha, to the crown of Christ. Then is heard the voice which removes the last sting of pain with the words, "Peace I leave with you, my peace I give unto you, not as the world giveth, give I unto you. Let not your heart be troubled, neither let it be afraid" (St. John 14:27).

As we meditate further upon Libra as the central sign of the Zodiac, we gain a clearer idea of its flywheel, balancing force and thus of its power to coordinate the threefold soul forces of thinking, feeling, and willing, resulting in greater equilibrium. Only those who have lived in Libra intensely can say much about its force, and then it has warrant only if they have lived in all the other signs of the Zodiac so positively that they are now illuminated by the higher intuitional consciousness. It is spiritual work, along with suffering in the flesh, that awakens man and brings him into contact with the Christ within.

Of the three signs, Virgo, Libra, and Scorpio, the central sign, Libra, seeks to distill the qualities of the three, taking the pure essence of each and bringing all three into harmony, creating a true balance and thus peace. When this harmony is won by overcoming the fierce onslaught of inner conflict and by suffering trials in the flesh, the riot of desires finally having been brought under full control, then do we behold a man filled with true compassion for humanity. Libra evokes a passion for peace and brings peace through passion, for in this sign harmony is achieved through conflict. This sounds paradoxical, but how else could peace be attained, except through that mighty war that engages the flesh with the Spirit!

In Libra, illumination comes through the intuition as the soul refines the desires and mediates between the lower and the higher self. In Virgo, the soul must achieve discrimination through a process of dissection and elimination, thus learning right discernment in thinking and in feeling that undergoes purification in this psychic-mental sign. This process is further intensified by the sublimation of feelings and desires in the sign Scorpio. The result is a distillate of pure consciousness, which attunes the soul to the world of harmony and unity.

So do we see all souls at some time, in some life, become refined in this sign of crucifixion, until the lower self of the senses is brought into equilibrium with the higher self by balancing the heart and the head through the sovereign will.

Thus re-formed, man gains that refinement which creates positive soul forces, and this is important to know, for it is this Christ-consciousness that we come to the Earth to secure.

In examining Libra, it is helpful to look at a pair of scales, for Libra is the sign of the Scales, the Balance. The scale pans stand for thought and feeling, the head and the heart. The two pans should have exactly equal weight and thus be balanced. The point of suspension of the scale beam, the fulcrum, symbolizes the will. Meditation on this symbol of Libra soon shows that it is a triad related to the Trinity.

Libra souls desire perfect harmony arising from the balanced threefold man whose thinking, feeling, and willing here become separate, free, and independent, yet are harmonized and are under the control of the Ego. Christ-concord is true peace, but this peace cannot possibly be established in the human personality until the progress in concentration and meditation releases equally and independently the forces of thinking, feeling, and willing. Christ-concord, that brings surcease to troubled hearts filled with fear, comes to man as he uses his will in spiritual activity, to exact in himself a just balance, a perfect equilibrium.

He who would attain to this state of Sabbath rest, which makes the soul ever more active consciously, must achieve this inner balanced power. The threefold forces of thinking, feeling, and willing must be equalized as the triune symbol of Libra, the Scales, indicates. Mankind is in the process of developing into a Hierarchy known as "The Spirits of Freedom and Love." Freedom and love are qualities that we must evolve here in the flesh on Earth. As our conscious Ego becomes spiritually active by willed thinking, we become increasingly free. And as we bring thinking into our life of will, we perfect our actions and attain to greater deeds of love. In Libra, we see how souls are given opportunities to test their soul quality and so secure balance, sometimes bringing to resolution a series of past earthly lives. This sign of rest, this sabbatical sign, comes to mind with the invitation, "Come unto me, all ye that labour and are heavy laden, and I will give you rest" (Matthew 11:28). No one can achieve this rest, this Christ-concord consciousness, the balance that brings peace, until equilibrium is secured, for this is the one thing needful if man would rid himself of fear, earthly errors, and worries.

Just as the scales ever strive toward equilibrium, so do Libra-lighted souls always long for and cherish the attainment of inner balance. They know that such a state of poised power, effected by equilibrium, would free them from all anxiety. With such balance acquired, the light of a higher world would shine down into the earthly man. Intuitively do Librans find the way to the higher consciousness. In Libra, souls can achieve success in all spheres of life as they realize the inner peace and "rest" which this balancing sign confers.

Creative balancing power manifests in the free forces of cooperation in the cosmos, without which the planets and the constellations would never maintain their courses. The planets turn on their axes, move on their orbits, and maintain all their other motions in virtue of the investing grace of God, thus creating the harmony of the spheres, the symphony of sounding balance and concord of the cosmos which, being true music, is the voice of God. Likewise, man, the microcosm within the macrocosm, must seek in Libra to approach the Christ Mystery which will harmonize him and make him a cosmic cooperator, enabling him to keep his course forever ascending on the solar spiral of evolution toward the revelation of new truth.

In Libra, the light of the world moves man to find the harbor of heavenly harmony, through whose sounding tone the soul perfects its balance and acquires the equilibrium of love and peace. Libra says, "I AM the soul of peace and love, the embodiment of music, the ecstatic essence of fair thoughts wedded to fine feelings expressive of courageous deed." This is the essence of blended thought, feeling, and will, yet with these three soul forces rendered independent of each other. The perfected symphony of the man become supra-personal, the soul mediating between the personality and the spiritual Ego in true poise, is effected in this sign of music, which leads to the octave; then all life is known to be set to music and is essentially musical, no matter how dull and drab the world may have become.

The stars all cycle and spiral in their courses to the accompaniment of the music they create; every force in the universe, be it the most minute or the very mightiest, sounds forth a sacred song, and this is the Word, which was "in the beginning." Were not the Word of the Christ-life still sounding, only a void would exist and not life. Man is made creative and active through the sounding tone and word in the world, even though he knows it not.

Yet man's life today is rendered colorless, abstract, empty, and even disastrous because he is no longer conscious of the world of the Word, because of his ignorant intellectual opposition to and rejection of the spiritual worlds and beings. The madness of materialism has made man deaf to the Word. Although it was necessary that man be plunged into materialism, in order to achieve Ego-consciousness and freedom, now is the time to regain the higher consciousness. To do so, man must conquer the dragon of materialism. In this sign of justice and balance, Libra, man meets this satanic dragon opposed to the Christ, for this is the foil of evil set against the Christ, and some time, in some life, a choice of paths must be made here. Wise is he who chooses the Michael Path to the Christ, for he who would correlate and communicate with the Christ can do so through Michael, who is the Countenance of the Christ now. In 1879, Michael entered the Earth sphere of spiritual activity and became regent of all those who seek the beneficial forces essential for their right development and healthy progress. The time of Libra is the time of Michaelmas, September 29th. The Sun's passage through Libra each autumn is the season of Michael, who slays the dragon of the Ahrimanic death-dealing forces of earthly intellectualism that seeks to negate the Spirit. Now man has the choice of becoming either the helper of Michael or the servant of the Ahrimanic hosts.

Man, at this time, cannot yet discern the divine design nor hear the Christing-tones sounding in the heavenly harmonies, even though day and night he himself is giving forth his own sound, good or evil, delightful or discordant, according with his state and quality in evolution. In short, musical sound underlies all life, and it is in the equalizing measures of Libra that man is ever refined and raised to higher harmony, for in Libra, balance is to be attained, and the divine beings who made man in their image brood over his destiny, seeking to perfect man in the poise of true peace, the balancing of the scales. Until this ability of finding balance is gained, the Comforter is not found, nor will that peace come which the Christ gives, a power not of this world. Man is filled with fear and troubled much until he finds his balance in the sign of the heavenly harmonies and music, the sign of justice and concord, in which all men are weighed, life after life, until they achieve a true and effective equilibrium and equanimity.

There is much more to music than its earthly tones, for behind the sounding element conveyed by the chemical ether there is its spiritual essence, whether man knows it or not. This spiritual essence, the heavenly soul of the tone, is separated by the ear from the earthly sound. Likewise, there is much more to man than the physical body that stands before us, for concealed within man and beyond the gaze of physical eyes, there live the soul and the spirit, although men who identify themselves with the physical body are not conscious today of their existence. By the power of Libra's light we can grow to envisage this part of man, his soul-spiritual life now veiled from our gaze.

The power of sounding music surges through Libra, relating sensitive souls to the Divine Musician. When great symphonies are being played by orchestras, the musicians are inspired by the heavenly lords of music through this sounding seventh sign of the Zodiac, Libra. If one could truly see with spirit eyes, there above the performers could be seen the surging, serried ranks of music-creating beings who sound out the tone and color in pure complementation.

There is no finer road into the spiritual worlds than that by way of the musical sounding tone through Libra. Here we find shapes of joyous beauty, the consonance of myriad colors blending into a symphony of sound upon the wings of which we raise our souls to the heights of sublimest rapture, transported into the ecstasy of the Christ-life. It is in this sounding power so mighty that we attune ourselves to the love that pervades the entire Earth. Love is the secret of life, and its power manifests in music, in the sounding song of God. What once the priesthood accomplished in the temple rites now is achieved through music. Today the true musician is the hierophant of the Mysteries, seeking to raise humanity through tone to the heightened power of the Spirit.

True beauty of love comes into being through the harmony which the love of God imparts through his Christ. The essense of the Christ is found in all forms which love creates, and there lives the light of Libra, as it does in all those souls who seek to serve the souls of men, to protect the weak, the insulted, the injured races, the ailing and the pitiful, whose light is dim or dulled by the sweat of cruel cadences of pain. Out of the harmony which is love, all things are made, and in the same mighty music shall all be refined and at last resolved. This love is not sentiment, but a dynamic power that weaves through all things and provides everything needed by all for the perfect unfoldment of consciousness.

Man's task on Earth is not only to become aware of the law of love but also to realize himself as this very love and to outstream its radiance. Then will the lower nature become spiritualized by the higher man, the Lord from heaven. As man comes into this higher consciousness, all his creations, on all planes and in all realms, take on a growing beauty and perfection. The Ego uses the forces of the soul to create, be it in the making of a dress, house, ship, song, or poem. Librans often express love and harmony in color and in tone. Even if one is not creative, Libra gives an intensified feeling for, and appreciation of, beauty, especially in art and music.

He who would find the beauty of love and achieve peace, must realize the light that leads to union through the operative wholeness of the sign Libra. The Christ says he came to those who needed a physician, for he would make men whole. To be whole is to be healed by him who redeems the earthly man immersed in matter. Libra represents the supra-personal, the spiritual self that is the opposite of the personal self, the earthly Ego, represented by Aries, its complementary sign. Those who open their hearts to love align their souls with the pure light of Libra, the air sign which unites, as in one atmosphere, the soul forces of all it contacts. The marked power of Libra is *union*, its characteristic is conjugality and true marriage.

So it is that the quality of fusion, the longing for union with others inheres in Libra, for this is the sign of association, soul assimilation, and amalgamation, the sign not only of marriage but also of attraction in a social and associative manner. He who is strong in Libra and holds aloof from others denies himself his best evolutionary development and negates the very purpose of this airy sign, which fosters companionship with others, partnerships, but in particular marriage. Libra leads to marriage, but when severely afflicted, it may cause annulment or denial of marriage. It brings people together or it separates them, depending on their bent or stage of evolution. The vice of Libra is to hold aloof, not realizing the sense of wholeness which it could attain through companionship. Only the negative response to Libra leads one to avoid people, and if an isolation from others is maintained, one nullifies opportunities for expanded life and growth.

Human relationships may be brought to the point of a *fine art* in Libra. The quality of conjugality, or the power to fuse in a true union, manifests on the personal plane as the desire to please others or even to sacrifice for them; in its inner, higher aspect it manifests as spiritual devotion. The power of sex manifests the universal, cosmic urge that ever seeks to balance the pairs of opposites in every field and phase of life. To blend and merge, to unify the twain into one perfection, achieving true marriage and union, is the ideal of Libra. In the welding power of wedded association can the higher Christ-life be made animate, and such true marriage may be achieved in Libra, for it is in Libra that balance and harmony become consummate. Those who remain isolated and refuse to associate themselves never approach the union of true marriage which is companionship with the Christ-life.

The "power of detachment, this psychic freedom, this capacity to feel deeply interested in the fate of others even at a moment when the sense of union with the beloved is present in great intensity, is characteristic of human love in its most spiritual aspect. Love may vary infinitely in degree, range, and intensity: but the quality of love, whether the tension be high or low, is always 'rest.' This is what distinguishes it from passion, straining perpetually in unrest," writes D. E. Faulkner Jones in the remarkable book, *The English Spirit.*[1]

---

[1] D. E. Faulkner Jones, *The English Spirit* (London: Anthroposophical Publishing Company, 1935), pages 118, 102-104.

The further description of love applies perfectly to Libra:
"Love between two human beings reaches its highest perfection when they are equal, though different, in power, for then is achieved that perfect equipoise born of two equal forces, mutually supporting each other in space: the image of the material earth itself. Spencer describes it thus:

'For love is a celestial harmony
Of likely hearts, composed of stars' concent,
Which join together in sweet sympathy,
To work each other's joy and true content,
Which they have harboured since their first descent
Out of their heavenly bowers, where they did see
And know each other here beloved to be.'

"Gray's description of Venus [the ruler of Libra], suggests a being whose essence is 'poise,' who moves freely in space because she has achieved perfect balance.

'Slow, melting strains their queen's approach declare:
Where'er she turns, the Graces homage pay;
With arms sublime, that float upon the air,
In gliding state she wins her easy way.'

Power to move freely in space comes only from a perfect balance of physical forces, whether these are in a human body, or incorporated into the principles of a machine. Human love, at its highest, gives to those who achieve it the same kind of freedom in the psychic and spiritual planes of existence that physical balance gives in the material universe. It gives spiritual and psychic 'poise,' and a sense of inner power akin to that which fills the athlete when he feels body and mind working in perfect harmony. . . .

"Rudolf Steiner speaks of 'Two' as the number of manifestation on the material plane. Human love comes into being subjectively whenever a man or woman brings thought, feeling and will into a state of balance, and directs them outwards, in devotion, but it can only become manifest in creative earth-activity when two such outpouring forces meet and bring each other to rest, in mutual balance.

"Christ Himself cannot work creatively on earth except so far as the outpouring of his Divine Love can be 'held' and made manifest by an outpouring force of love from man towards Him. The extent to which Christ can work with power on earth depends on the extent to which human beings can love. When the isolated individual turns in love to Christ, He can work subjectively in that man's being, but the full power of earth-love only becomes manifest from the inter-action of human beings in mutual love. When the inter-locked love-force of two or more human beings can flow out towards the Christ, then can begin not only a subjective working of Christ in the individual, but an objective manifestation of his power on earth. 'Where two or three are gathered together in My name, there am I in the midst of them.' "

Although Libra is the sign of equilibrium, poise, peace, and rest, it is none the less intensely mobile and all-permeating, taking on the quality of fulness, filling all things. In this sign, we find a force that is volatile and so all-pervasive as to diffuse itself as the very air, to permeate the whole soul of man and not just a part of his consciousness. Through this power to permeate, forces are engendered that impart the radiance of a still higher consciousness, which descends as it were from heaven. In the evolved Libra individual, the forces of the soul are used, not just the brain, as in most, and it is in virtue of this power to discern and unify that there arise such perfect perception and intuition. The thinking is separated from the senses, and brain-free messages come by way of the mediating soul. Thus we see why

Libra-lighted individuals have such innate, instant intuition, a teaching from within.

All air signs impart the quality of intuition as well as the power of reasoning. They develop spiritual cognition that transcends the physical forces of the brain. In Libra, the sign of soul, man is individualized and brought to a state of poise and harmony through the illumination bestowed on him by the super-conscious Christ-contact. As the fire signs impart directive dynamic action and energy, and the water signs incessant change and the transforming force of feeling and sensation, so the air signs merge man with the world of thought and mental-life experience.

Like all cardinal signs, Libra marks the beginning of a new mode of motion, a movement that separates thinking from the senses, holding the respective expressions of consciousness—the lower man over against the higher self—in exact equilibrium, the subjective and objective being balanced. Such a balance causes one to become effectively creative by comparing and weighing of things, ideas, men, and everything else, bringing to manifestation the quality of justice.

Only if we still our sense perceptions can we become aware of and unite with those realms of rarefied thought wherein all ideas exist that find expression in the physical world. This is the archetypal region where all originating elemental forces are found as living centers and here is the true source of all life. Therefore, as we deliberately control our feeling forces and our thinking forces through our will, we can come to the harmony of balance, and this Libra brings about when the physical is shut out and we behold the heavenly facts and forces; hence the intuitive, perceptive power of Libra natives. Without this sense-free power of controlled detachment from the body and brain in utter calm, with feeling and thought balancing the scales, there cannot be heard those messages from the soul which are the true tuition from within. This is a marked power of all air signs, for they are intuitional.

Man has a brain and a sensory system; he has also a mind-soul of a still higher degree, yet beyond these, there stands his spirit. Most persons use only the brain; they are intellectual and remain spiritually ignorant. But man becomes aware of his higher being as a soul and spirit only as he directs his soul-forces to the supersensible. Man's spiritual ignorance today is the result of this lack of balance. It was a wise man who said, "A false balance is an abomination to the Lord, but a just weight is his delight" (Proverbs 11:1), and again, "Divers weights are an abomination unto the Lord, and a false balance is not good" (Proverbs 20:23). Although this may refer to balance in commercial dealings, the principle applies equally well to man's consciousness, as is obvious in "The Lord weigheth the spirits" (Proverbs 16:2). At the present long removal from these timely utterances, it is evident that most people cheat themselves by their unknowing lack of balance. The air signs bring about a restoration, Libra providing the pivotal power of balance. Libra stands essentially for the union of the soul with the higher self as well as with the personality.

Individualization through the Christ in man is to be achieved in earthly life, and this divine force is at work within all men, to spiritualize the personality. Man's personality is merely what the name says, for *persona* in Latin means a mask, and most men believe they are well hidden behind such masks; but they are not hidden from those who have evolved that spiritual intelligence that confers the faculty of intuition, for intuition instantly distinguishes the false from the true with unfailing precision. If the light of Libra can so see the real man—and it can if it will—what is this faculty if not the pure power of the supra-personality, and what is this supra-personality if not another guise for that name and power which is the Christ. Thus the Libra soul knows without resorting to ordinary thinking once it has become aware of the soul-spiritual and of that ocean of the all-pervasive, all-permeating Christ-current flowing through all life.

And, speaking of this intuitive power, let us distinguish it from that other faculty that is psychic and of the astral feelings, for intuition, while not identical with ordinary thinking, is derived with the help of thinking by the permeation of thinking with supersensible reality, with the higher, spiritual realms. Facts are often faulty in psychic perception, due to illusion and distortion, and because of the impurity of the seer; but facts perceived by the intuition of a purified soul are never faulty—they are true and are gained in virtue of purity and balance.

This intuition is a cognitive faculty akin to clairvoyant thought, for the perception of Libra is not merely the ability to apprehend objects by means of the senses; rather, it is that forte possessed by all true poets, that facile force which indicates and declares, nay, which speaks of the spiritual fact, idea, or being behind the thing, thought, or person. This faculty is thus more than just cognition of sense phenomena, for joined to this power to perceive there is the ability to conceive; thus, percept and concept the object and the idea back of the object—become linked, providing an immediate understanding of the object perceived, without reflection but solely in virtue of intuition, which Libra imparts innately. Of course, this light of Libra is the higher and finer as the soul has been made "pure as He is pure." Thus the status in evolution marks off the man or woman having residence in this sign, which plays so large a part in the Christing of the individual.

We are weighed in the balance when we are natives of the sign of the Scales, for Librans have been given much, and much will be required of them. A Libra life is a life of readjustment and new direction, for a series of past lives is now up for correction and consolidation upon new lines, through a balancing that makes for a new departure in life. A higher spiral of life and a heightened consciousness must arise. The lower self and the higher self are being weighed, and the scales must be equalized through the Christ-fulcrum, the pivotal point on the scale beam. This is the source of the power and of the consciousness that is intuitional.

Balancing is a continuous process. One fails in this sign if he rests on past laurels and refuses to break new ground beyond the acquired powers of the past. And those negative in this sign do so often fail in this respect, even though they are gifted; they waste and scatter their forces, become superficial and smattering, are inconstant in their ideas and relations, postpone their duties and lose precious opportunities. Perseverance pays true dividends here, just as the habit of postponement bankrupts the soul and wastes valuable earthly time. The difficulty consists in attaining self-mastery, that is, becoming one's own master, avoiding all extremes, maintaining the golden mean, using one's gifts and talents wisely, arranging times for work, rest, and recuperation, thus becoming an integrated individual. It is the part of wisdom for Librans to be themselves and not to pose in a role. The unevolved Ego, however, fails to make the spiritual contact that wisely directs by means of truth.

Libra souls are keenly perceptive, with marked powers of comparison, and in virtue of this faculty of instant insight and cognition, they have a natural faculty to assess and appraise, to weigh and to judge, and a power to give and take that no other sign possesses. They have this unerring judgment and such a fine power of comparison as a result of an impartiality that stems from their ability to detach themselves from their own person; standing aside as it were, they are open to inspiration from the spiritual realms. It is through this gift that Librans have the inner means of expounding and teaching the occult facts that declare the nature and being of man and of the Christ. It is because they have this inner, higher light that they accept, and work with, the forces of destiny with finer effect. This is the result of their right attitude, for they know the exact justice of destiny and of things as they are, and not as they appear to be. It is not enough to say Librans have a love of justice, but rather that justice is their love, and for this love of balanced being, this harmony of justice, will they work; and they are impelled and accelerated by the very experiences of life to attain that poise which is peace.

When Libra souls are negative, their desire to please degenerates into a docility so plastic as to make them injuriously amenable to the desires of others. Such a state of passive docility makes a man neither hot nor cold, a person without spine, indifferent to the reality and purpose of earthly life and disloyal to the Christ within. The one aim should be to please the Christ within, who speaks as intuition. This higher wisdom or inner voice one possesses in quality and available accuracy only in proportion to one's power of coordination —Libra's forte and force—which makes for wholeness, in virtue of the coordination of body, soul, and spirit.

The positive Libra force welds into oneness. The negative Libra force, on the other hand, disintegrates, scatters, and separates. Negative natives in Libra scatter their soul powers, love to please others in a personal sense, or merely to gain from others their approbation; if they sink into their senses and live therein, they crucify Christ the more in this sign of crucifixion. Yet Libra holds the power to unify and make one, so that the soul may be raised from the deadening mood of matter to the life of the Spirit.

In Libra comes consummate knowledge of suffering through love, for this positive sign of Venus is also the exaltation for Saturn; and, Venus and Saturn sublimated and merged produce stability in feeling and thought. "Whom the Lord loveth he chasteneth" and much purification is wrought in this sign, for the suffering is invariably the fruit of feelings in the marital relation, an agony of soul created by choices that are compelled and successively presented, until escape becomes impossible and the native, out of his very pain, stands free at last from the great illusion which the astral world and the senses present to the brain-bound personality. Thus man finds release from the conventional glamor as he evolves in this sign. Libra, therefore, calls forth experiences engendered by marriage, and no harder lessons are to be found nor worked through than those that eventuate here, nor is there a finer field to refine love and to establish the essential poise and the unperturbed equanimity and power that knows and understands.

Generally, the experience of Libra natives is that they are not happy living alone, and so they seek until they find or earn the harmony and balanced life they crave. Their desire for harmony is so great, and the soul's sensitivity so intensely acute that the slightest disharmony, false or wrong note, is instantly felt and experienced as a wound. In virtue of this same faculty, Librans are not happy listening to many of the special renditions of the great composers' works as they are given by the various orchestras; each departure from the master's original version is easily noted and deplored.

When one is evolved in Libra, then a definite effort is made to unify not only himself but also those in his environment or out in the world. Napoleon, with Libra rising, was a classical example, yet he failed as he projected personal ambition into his endeavors. The general destiny of Libra brings free association with others and with the public. It calls for companionship and communion of soul as an inner urgent need and on levels of equality and among peers, for in the intensely ideal sense Librans are seeking union of soul with likeminded kindred souls. Yet, Librans are seldom proud or overbearing; they are kindly and impartial, no matter what one's station in life. Their friendly feeling and affability awakens a friendly feeling in others, loosening tension and tautness in human relationships. Highly evolved Librans are love personified.

Libra should lead us to meditate upon and realize fully that all mankind is now weaving, consciously or unconsciously, the "wedding garment." This work must be done on Earth in a body of flesh and form; it is the result of the activity of the Ego in and on the threefold body of man, the interaction producing soul forces. Through Libra balance, the true Christ-correction, man is enabled to fashion the "white robe" spoken of in Revelation. The enquiry of one of the elders, "What are these who are arrayed in white robes, and whence come they?" drew forth the answer, "These are they which came out of the great tribulation and have washed their robes and made them white in the blood of the Lamb" (Revelation 7: 13,14). The robe of the soul is made white by the veritable life of the Christ in all. The divine alchemy of the Spirit within man, working out as tribulations in the earth-school, engenders pure harmony, contentment, and equanimity through Christ-correction in the sign of crucifixion, the sign of soul and of balance—Libra.

Contentment and *equanimity* are our most urgent need in this century of constant crisis. Equanimity is no passive quality; it requires incessant balancing between two opposite tendencies. The one tendency leads to passion, pride, egotism, selfish isolation, and to an other-worldliness of bliss and beauty in a cloud realm apart from the earth. The other tendency plunges us into earthly error, materialism, mechanization, and standardization; it keeps us ignorant of the Spirit and enslaves us to matter.

No longer does it suffice to conceive of good and evil as merely two opposite poles; evil itself has two opposing poles and it is the function of the good to maintain the balance between the two extremes. In the first quarter of our century, the eminent spiritual scientist, Dr. Rudolf Steiner, whose Moon was in Libra, not only repeatedly spoke of a Triad, but expressed this concept also in a monumental work of art —a large statue carved in wood, located in Dornach, Switzerland. There is a duality of polar powers: the one, Lucifer, induces spirituality and also beauty, but a spirituality that lives in the clouds, unrelated to practical earthly life; the other, Ahriman, seeks to chain man to the earth, keeping his thinking brain-bound, unlighted by the Spirit. The Christ, however, a being of cosmic purpose and outstreaming love, stands perfectly poised, his feet firmly on the earth, as the Representative of Man, maintaining the balance between the two powers, one pulling upward and the other downward.

This Triad is present in every human soul. In the West, Ahriman tips the scales, enslaving man to matter and producing a culture that carefully omits, if it does not directly deny, the Spirit. In the East, Lucifer weights the scales—or did so, until Western influences prevailed—estranging and alienating man from earthly life. However, in the West there are innumerable isms and drugs that draw souls as into clouds of illusion or other-worldliness undervaluing earth-realities and blinding them to the existence of the darker, the Ahrimanic, side of earthly experience, so that they see only the beauty of the illusory light of Lucifer; or else, they hold on to a spirituality that was right for earlier centuries but, lacking spiritual intelligence, is not effective in dealing with modern materialism.

In the midst of the chaos and conflict of our time, we need the Libra light of a higher consciousness, the intuition and the selfless supra-personality of the Christ, in order to remain poised and balanced between the false light and lust of Lucifer and the darkness and error of Ahriman—between senseless rapture and rigidity.

Thus, Libra may shed light on the resolution of the most

relevant present-day problems. It promises no easy peace, but equanimity achieved through a constant process of Christ-balance. And in this process there is flowered the soul of divine love.

THE COSMIC SYMPHONY

God's *love*, God's *life*, eternity,
The *light* of heaven—Holy Three!
Sweet efflorescence which doth bear
These myriad blossoms everywhere.

Where'er I look I see thy soul,
Thy living essence, ever whole!
Behind, within the core of everything
God's archetype doth always sing.

Beyond the Earth in finer sphere
There doth thy handiwork appear;
From Highest Hierarch to the gnome,
Thou art their "rest," thy life their home.

Scorpio - Scorpion & Eagle

SCORPIO, the eighth sign of the Zodiac, is a sign of great intensity and of extremes as different as are its two symbols, the *Scorpion* and the *Eagle*. Each sign of the Zodiac has its positive and its negative side. All too often, uninformed persons judge a sign by its negative aspects only and thus dislike the sign. Unfortunately, Scorpio is disliked more than any other sign. It was, however, this mighty sector of the Zodiac that early in man's evolution stimulated life forces and roused matter to life; and this very same sign later killed the living creation in order to prepare for a new planetary existence that would carry evolution forward to a higher octave. Thus, the constellation of the Eagle became also the Scorpion, bearing the sting of death.

In its lower phase, Scorpio debases and stings the man, sometimes to the death, so that man may be aroused and awakened to the light of truth, and it is through such transmutation that Scorpio is the Eagle. In this higher phase of the Eagle, we see the man of powerful thought and ultra-keen insight into people and things. The regenerative function is thus seen to reside in this magical sign, which rules death, the dead, and the raising from the dead—raising from the scorpion to the eagle that soars above the mountain tops and whose flight has more to do with the heavens than with the earth. Scorpio has to do with occult science, but especially with those phases of it that are related to regeneration, to the nature of death, to those who have died, to our relation with the dead, and to how death leads to life on a higher level. Magical forces and vast regenerative powers here have their rise. The strong will in the lower, unevolved man simply serves the selfish and unbridled lower appetites and desires, whereas in the advanced soul it can manifest as healing power and as fruitful, positive, constructive deeds. Thus, two kinds of power may be found here, which act as vast driving forces, extremes as different from one another as the two symbols, the Scorpion and the Eagle.

Eight begins a new octave. It is the number of evolution, and so this eighth sign is of vital importance in this respect, because here is the field of feeling and desire, that mighty battlefield where lower desires related to the senses and the lower nature struggle with incessant intensity, until at last divine desires win the victory, as win they must if evolutionary advance is to be made. Each triplicity has a central focusing sign which intensifies its forces. Scorpio is the central or fixing sign for the watery triplicity. As a result, feelings and sensations are intensified in this sign to their highest power, becoming desires that produce either heaven or hell, depending on the soul's quality and status. Invariably, there is a mixture of both, for this sign of astral energy or soul force causes an experience of extremes, which work silently within, to restore and rehabilitate the soul through what St. Paul calls "the washing of regeneration." The forte of Scorpio is to raise old forces and faculties to a higher octave of power or condition.

No pain is more poignant and no ecstasy more exquisite than that provided by this sign of a fixed-watery combination. Here is a field of force that holds veritably the vice of Saul and the virtue of St. Paul. The first is blind to truth and is murderous, whereas the second, a man of heaven, twice-born, is profound, compassionate, and a zealous exponent of the Christ. Such is the range of extremes, of powerful contrasts inherent in this highly occult sign, which cleanses and corrects the forces of feeling, so that higher, holier desires, and spiritualized thinking may result. Neither extreme is weak; both are intense and strong-willed.

Often the soul of the Scorpio individual is most active in his feelings. Not much intelligent spiritual thought is active yet; thus his feelings hold him enthralled and these correlate with the astral or soul world, the world of desires ranging from the lowest sphere of feeling to the very loftiest. These divergent feelings will relate either to the Moon or to the Sun; therefore, feelings will be either psychic, watery, emotional, and of the lower nature, or they will be fiery and of the heart—respectively from below or from above the diaphragm.

In no other sign do we find such intense impulses for good or ill. In the unregenerate, they work in the lower desire nature and selfish personality with incessant insistence. Small wonder then that Scorpio provides pronounced difficulties for the neophyte, for he who would not yield to the seductions of Kundry, and so become a Parsifal, must have dealt with the ugly serpent that lies in the swamps of the lower nature, the monstrous nine-headed Hydra, symbolic of unregenerate, passionate man. Its heads cannot be cut off, for if this were done, two new heads would replace each head lost, unless it were cauterized. This means that feelings and desires cannot be repressed with safety; they must be transmuted, regenerating the man and engendering self-control. No proper passage with safety upon the path of return to God is possible unless this lower scorpion of self is not merely repressed but entirely transmuted.

The virtue of this sign, then, is not merely death and birth—it does hold the secret of both—but more: *regeneration*, or better, *rebirth*, for out of the amniotic waters of Scorpio there comes just this rebirth. Thus Christ declared in truth, "Except a man be born of water [Moon-personality] and of the Spirit [Sun-Son-Christ-Self], he cannot enter into the kingdom of God. That which is born of the flesh is flesh; and that which is born of the Spirit is spirit. Marvel not that I said unto thee, Ye must be born again" (St. John 3: 5-7). Only thus is it possible to become one of those who have "gotten the victory over the beast," as St. John says in Revelation 15:2. The test of Scorpio is so difficult and dangerous an experience for most people, because so many cannot lift themselves clear of its lower phase and mount up into the sky on eagle's wings, which is the promise and provision of Scorpio's regenerated forces.

The spiritualizing power of the stellar script can be properly understood only through concentration and meditation upon the informing forces of the Zodiac and the planets, for these are the Spiritual Hierarchies who carry out the plan of God. Thought, deep and sustained, upon the idea and being of God and his Christ, informs our soul to liberate at last his Spirit in us through the mediation of "the Lord from heaven," the Christ-soul within. Only after prolonged and profound thought can we realize that it was divine desire and design that created not only our solar system with our Earth, but also our physical bodies, which we now wear and use or abuse. Thus are we indeed the temples of God.

Desire that is divine is at one with the will of God; it is directive in idea and creative in imaginative scope as well as in physical fact. As worlds and systems are born of God's divine desire, so the creations of men, God's children, are likewise the fruit of desire; it becomes divine as man becomes purified and illuminated by the presence of the one priceless ingredient—the Son, the soul of God within, the Christ. Desire in man must become transmuted to meet the need of an age of new truth when love shall rule, an age when the immaculate conception will be no longer looked upon as a myth or a miracle but as a calm, planned, beautiful reality, as practical as it is perfect, for the children of the New Age— individuals of far higher sensitivity and purity—will need physical bodies that will be conceived in loving harmony and truth.

Since Scorpio is the sign of the *warrior* and the battle-ground of the desires and of the soul world, where man must fight to become the victor, this statement identifying divine desire with the will of God becomes essential if we would evaluate Scorpio esoterically. Here is the fixed force creative of desire that is ever urgent and intense. According to the age of soul and the accrued debts from the past will be the assault of suffering and mighty conflict, lies and lust pressing it upon man till such burning in hell makes him at last exchange his lies and lust for truth and love. This is the light and direction of desire become divine. So again do we see the magnitude of this magical sign of driving force, regeneration, and new birth.

As there are lines of force in water which transform it into the solid form of ice at a certain temperature, so there is a force in the sign Scorpio which transmutes feelings into the form of "solid" desires which are intense. It is not enough to say that this sign intensifies or fixes feeling, rather, we should realize that through Scorpio's peculiar mode of motion, which is rotary or serpentine, feelings become charged and changed into active, dynamic desires. Latent feelings live in the receptive, fluid, fecund Moon's sign, Cancer, as psychic seed as it were, but they are brought to objective fruition only when they become driving desire in Scorpio.

With this occult fact in mind, and knowing that negative desires destroy the soul, whereas constructive, divine desires actually create positive will, which augments soul growth, we should understand Scorpio as that field of dynamism where Cancer feelings and sensations are transformed and become tangible. Thus, generation becomes either degeneration or regeneration, according to the vice or virtue of the soul, for these forces inhere in this revolutionary-revelationary sign. Realizing how strong the desire element inheres in Scorpio, we see why it is called the sign of the warrior, for the "I AM" has to do battle in Scorpio and should in time emerge triumphant from that truly greatest of all wars, and not like Judas Iscariot betray the Christ or higher man. Those who live on the lower levels grope in darkness. Death and deception, the falsities of the brain-bound intellect flourish in the lush weeds of the desire world. The Scorpio warrior has to deal with and work in this desire world, the great empire of error, until he fights his way to the light of truth in the sweated blood of his own agony and through just such suffering he emerges triumphant from the realm of death into the dawn of truth, the state of great joy.

It is incumbent on Scorpio persons to dissolve or transmute their personal limitations and inhibitions, learning to manage and control their very intense emotions and their secret life of feelings and desires held as a mighty magazine within, ever seeking to enlarge their views by gaining lofty eagle elevation. Having reached the new altitude, they can divest themselves of the old, hindering personality conditions, for Scorpio signifies the raising of any faculty to a higher octave. It speaks of death and dissolution, then regeneration and a new birth. Everything in creation that makes the grade is incessantly raised to higher octaves of life and power, and the sign force that effects this elevation in consciousness is the dynamic, creative Scorpio, the power of the Eagle Spirits. Often Scorpio proves to be a scourge to raise the man from the scorpion sting of death, so that he may be possessor of a higher new life.

In this fixed watery sign, old attitudes must be transformed. By rising to a new altitude, one attains to a new attitude. This conversion and elevation occurs usually through the office of much pain, and such pain is known to be benign, for the egotistic personality can be raised to higher expression only through the application of this very salutary prime mover—pain. Hereby we see why Scorpio in its negative phase is correlated with purgatory, for one actually burns in hell when grappling with one's desires, conquering them by generating will. In this sign, vices such as jealousy, love of revenge and of argument, the urge to oppose and to fight, to be obstinate and to hate, must be reversed through the use of the will and, since Scorpio holds the power of immense driving force, no other sign is better designed to dissolve such demoralizing habits and confer supersensible powers in occultism and in healing, if one works with and loves the Spirit.

In this mightiest of alchemical signs, the colossal intensity and pressure—and often utter degradation—bring elevation in evolution through "the washing of regeneration." The first seven verses of chapter three of St. Paul's Epistle to Titus is written as though for Scorpio souls: "Put them in mind . . . to speak evil of no man, to be no brawlers, but gentle, shewing all meekness unto all men. For we ourselves also were sometimes foolish, disobedient, deceived, serving divers lusts and pleasures, living in malice and envy, hateful, and hating one another. But after that the kindness and love of God our Saviour toward man appeared, not by works of righteousness which we have done, but according to his mercy he saved us, by the washing of regeneration, and renewing of the Holy Ghost; which he shed on us abundantly through Jesus Christ our Saviour; that being justified by his grace, we should be made heirs according to the hope of eternal life."

Heirs of eternal life! What a heritage! Yet one to which less thought is given than to temporal earthly inheritances. Scorpio has rule not only over death and discarnate souls, but also over the goods of the dead; hence, legacies come under its domain. In addition to ruling over those of a material nature, it has to do with our soul-spiritual legacies that we bring with us from past earthly lives as our own rightful individual inheritance, accruing to our own eternal spiritual Ego. At present, we are writing as it were our will and testament for our next incarnation. Invariably we fall heir to the results of our own deeds.

Many persons are prejudiced against various signs, but against Scorpio most of all, which, of course, is a wrong attitude. The element of evil is often attributed to this sign; yet all human beings, whatever their zodiacal sign influences, have some error or evil to correct and transmute in their earthly life. Only from the misuse and abuse of sign forces, from their negation, comes depravity. Strength and healing power are the very essence of Scorpio, the dynamic octave sign of evolution and regeneration. Inherent in it is that power which lifts the consciousness to a higher octave. Therefore, one should ever point out the high privilege and purpose of all persons whose zodiacal configurations connect them with this marvelous, magical sign, for when the dark forces are dissolved through the white-magic side of Scorpio, the soul comes into a high reward as a true healer and helper of humanity.

He who would live in truth and preach its gospel must be devoted, and such devotion is the force of this sign. There would have been no Reformation in Europe without Martin Luther, and there would have been no Martin Luther without Scorpio, the sign that gave him the positive militancy to change the course of church history. In the unevolved and weak, Scorpio becomes debased, making the man depraved through lust, whereas in its highest Eagle phase it becomes the lofty light of the initiate. The initiate, Goethe, had Scorpio rising with Saturn therein. He is best known for his literary genius, especially for his *Faust*, showing the struggle of the soul in attaining peace; but the time is yet to come when the world will recognize the comprehensiveness of the spiritual and scientific world-conception of this creative scientist and philosopher. The very great spiritual scientist and high initiate, Rudolf Steiner, likewise had Scorpio rising; his range of research in supersensible realms and his description of the cosmos, along with the practical application of spiritual science in all departments of life, are extraordinarily far-reaching, from farming to the Christ-Mystery.

No matter how malicious the man or how magnanimous, how sunk the sinner or exalted the saint, how foul the murderer or fine the martyr—all these extremes are found in Scorpio—there is at the same time an active, transforming fixed force that produces stability in the soul. It takes strength to sin, such strength as comes out of this powerful fixed sign of desire and attachment; but, in time, sin will throw a man down hard, the reversal rousing repentance. And who is there in flesh who was not at some time a prodigal son, for all those who come to Earth are prodigal sons, and all souls will at some time suddenly remember their Father's home and then and there decide to return. They become tired of feeding on husks of flesh and form, and yearn for the Spirit and the life. Such remembrance and return is invariably made under the direction of this mighty regenerator and prompter of God, Scorpio. One thing is certain: no path of return to God can be trod until the battle is fought and won in this battlefield of the great illusion, the senses and unbridled desires whose forces are concealed in this occult sign where so much lies latent. It offers the road of return, and often it leads through sex, for the sex organs are ruled by Scorpio. This return is marked by the stability, the calm command and constructive control of desires resulting from the competent management of feeling and the directive power of spiritualized thinking.

There is nothing lukewarm about people strong in Scorpio; it is all or nothing with them. This fixed sign of intensity gives very decided likes and dislikes, sympathies and antipathies. Its natives do not attempt to hide their opinions; they are outspoken, emphatic, strong, and unyielding. They tread firmly on their heels and have often a pronounced lower jaw (and sometimes a prominent or "eagle-beaked" nose; Scorpio rules the sense of *smell*). They are warriors or champions for evil or for good. They have fine constructive ability, intense power of working force, and they do things with such celerity and dispatch that they have the job done while others are still thinking about it. Instability is the mark of the man who is inert and indifferent. There might be applied to this kind of real "won't-work," whose numbers make so much deadweight on the body of humanity, the words of the Christ: "I know thy works, that thou art neither cold nor hot: I would thou wert cold or hot. So then because thou art lukewarm, and neither cold nor hot, I will spue thee out of my mouth" (Revelation 3: 15, 16). When such souls come fully under the influence of Scorpio, they cannot be lukewarm; they are compelled into action that at last energizes

experiences that bring stability, that silent inner Eagle
power, which commanded, allows the soul to soar into the
skies and move in heaven.

He who would solve the mystery of life and death, he who
would know why man must perforce make so many entrances
and exits upon the stage of our earthly theater, must earn
the right to go backstage and there mingle with the director
of the great drama. When this auspicious moment occurs,
man must have gained a conscious control over all the soul
forces of thinking, feeling, and willing, which makes him a
conscious cooperator in the great drama with the otherwise
unseen directors of destiny. No other force is more excel-
lently designed to make man independent of time and space
or to make him a fine helper of humanity than the marvelous
occult power concealed in Scorpio. Truly, it is a storehouse
of hidden power, which is not revealed to the profane or
vicious, the impure or impious, the perverted or polluted, the
licentious or lewd; all these heads of the Hydra, the snake
of the lower self, must be cauterized through right transmu-
tation before the secrets of life and death can be revealed
and realized in this sign of generation, degeneration, and re-
generation.

Scorpio ruling the organs of generation, man has been led
by this serpent force into degeneration, the resulting lust
flinging him down into the dust, to crawl as the snake must,
yet with added writhings of agony, the impurity and iniq-
uity at last inducing effectual reversal and regeneration. Thus,
in this sign of threefold power, through generation, degenera-
tion, and regeneration, there works the magic that makes
the Scorpio man more than man. And then we realize the
truth of St. Paul's words: "So when this corruptible shall have
put on incorruption, and this mortal shall have put on im-
mortality, then shall be brought to pass the saying that is
written, Death is swallowed·up in victory. O death, where is

thy sting? O grave, where is thy victory?" (I Corinthians
15: 54,55).

The gates of death and of regeneration are opened by
Scorpio. It deals with death as a true Christ-dower, for death
performs an important function in giving entrance to the
spiritual worlds. Those born in or under Scorpio are always
connected in some manner with death or the dead, those
human beings without their physical bodies who live in the
soul and spirit worlds, spheres of life closer to us than our
hands or feet, right in our midst, where beings unseen affect
the lives of those who live on the Earth, for good or ill, accord-
ing to their quality, while we, in turn, harm or help them by
our attitudes.

> Although the earthly body die,
> The soul and spirit death defy
> And are in contact much the same
> With loved ones who on Earth remain.
>
> For worlds of soul and Spirit are
> Not bound by space, they are not far,
> Our soul and spirit in them live,
> Our love to loved ones we still give.
>
> The welfare of humanity
> Is thus promoted endlessly;
> The sense of loneliness is gone
> As love flows freely on and on.
>
> B.J.

Scorpio reigns over the soul world, over death, and the
after-death states. Heaven and hell are those realms where
hopes and wishes of earthly kind are, after death, fructified,
frustrated, or finished with. When every trace of the earthly is
overcome, the soul is given over to the soul world, and the

spirit is then free and unfettered to pursue its journey through the spiritland, after which it returns through the soul world to a new incarnation. The soul world is a sphere of mighty contrasts whose range includes devils and divines, sinners and saints, the most devoted and the most destructive, those who have not conquered the dragon of debased desire and error, and those who lived the higher life—the Scorpio phase and the Eagle phase—with the neutral people intermediate. Here is the judgment seat referred to by St. Paul, "For we must all appear before the judgment seat of Christ; that every one may receive the things done in his body, according to that he hath done, whether it be good or bad" (II Corinthians 5:10). The soul world is the clearing house for the Ego.

By misusing Scorpio's forces, man has degraded the sexual function and brought disease, debility, and death to the Earth, under which load of lust he still groans. The negative forces of Scorpio have debased man's thought power and also his speech forces, inducing him to use dissembling words called diplomatic or tactful—crafty and subtle words, spoken, written, and thought. When annoyed or aroused, the unevolved give sharp, stinging replies and are not too choice with language, yet no finer souls exist than Scorpio natives following the positive path. The Christ makes it clear that words and thoughts are real and creative, and that every word must be accounted for and will come up for judgment.

As Scorpio rules over death and the after-death experiences, it is relevant to state that the soul world, also called the astral or desire world, is divided into seven main regions. The three lower ones are called purgatory, hell, or Hades. In these regions the soul is cleansed of error and evil in a true burning in hell, for there the soul's desires are frustrated, having no physical body for their fulfillment. At length, through this painful though salutary service, the lower desires burn out, sympathy overcomes antipathy, and wishes become unselfish. The three higher regions of the soul world are correlated with the triune forces of soul light, soul power, and soul life. In these spheres, man receives his reward for all his good thoughts and his constructive, loving actions done while in the body; here all good desires become fructified and nothing but sympathy with the soul world prevails. But there is a fourth sphere, a midway and neutral region, a state of consciousness to which the Egos of all those men gravitate in whose souls scientific materialism had predominated and who had identified themselves solely with their physical bodies. This is an awful, colorless sphere, indeed. The souls who come here are too good for hell but not good enough for heaven. They believed that death ended everything, and here they live in terrible, grievous emptiness and boredom, until they free themselves from their attachment to the physical and unite their soul forces in sympathy with the surrounding soul world.

It is in the forces of the soul world, existent on the Earth and in the after-death state, that man must conquer completely his selfish desires and his antipathies, and it is in this sign of the warrior and of serpent wisdom, Scorpio, that man must contest and conquer desire. In this conquest, the destruction of desire is not intended but rather the *transmutation* of desires to make them divine. In this transmutation, man strengthens his force of will, with which sovereign power he is at last able consciously to direct his destiny and to "rule his stars."

Only when the sting of the scorpion is extracted can the wisdom of the serpent be secured and positive progress be made through the other signs of the Zodiac. After the balance is turned in Libra, then comes the eighth sign, Scorpio, the sign of the octave and of that field of force wherein man must secure his spiritual power through sublimation and spiritualization. All those who failed in the preceding sign of Balance, Libra, tend to become depraved in Scorpio, whereas those who succeeded in Libra become individuals who can transmute the sting of the scorpion, master its mystery, and mount upon eagle's wings to soar into the face of the Sun. The scorpion crawls on the ground, but when the sting of the scorpion is transmuted, the wings of the eagle unfold, empowering the soul to soar to the mountain top.

These hints explain why this sign holds souls of such contrasting extremes as those of Dr. Rudolf Steiner and Josef Stalin, both with Scorpio rising. We see how selfish feeling and desire drag the soul downward into the anarchy of habitual hatred, jealousy, pride, secretiveness, vicious vindictiveness, malice, instant action ever inciting to strike through heart or head or hand, and a personality that is a detestable nuisance to itself as much as it is to others, until the very experiences of life, through their tumult and evil power, bring at last suffering in sufficient degree to bring release to a higher level of consciousness. Thus does Scorpio become the power *par excellence* to effect regeneration. The soul then ceases to look downward through the eyes of feeling and desire, but on the contrary it begins to look upward and becomes more and more sublimated, its gaze directed to God, knowing at last that those who "wait upon the Lord shall renew their strength and shall mount up with wings as eagles."

In Scorpio, one can indeed mount in thought to the mountain tops or, in a moment of passion and uncontrolled anger, one can become completely bereft of thought. Feeling is so intense and so overpowering, so intensely and instantly active, so ready to strike with the sting of the scorpion, that in the undeveloped, such action actually annihilates thinking altogether. In the moment of incitation, usually proceeding from the lower realms of the soul world or from discarnate human beings—the so-called dead—thinking is swept out and aside, and murder or other violent crimes are committed. All Scorpio souls need to exercise *patience* in order to prevent such a momentary loss of self-control and sanity, and to gain insight and understanding.

Once I corresponded with a man born in Scorpio, who was imprisoned in the largest prison in America. He suffered his days there in the remorse of a hell that only Scorpio could create and suffer. In a drunken brawl, this man gave vent to his feelings and, helped by invisible evil beings, he became bereft of reason and killed his wife. Luckily for him and for the state, he was not put to death by the state as a scarecrow to other would-be murderers; he lived in a very real hell, in a remorse so intense that it was like true burning fire, and no remorse compares with that experienced by a Scorpio native, for he suffers as no other can for wrongdoing.

Remorse for wrong done is exemplified by the suicide of Judas Iscariot after his betrayal of the Christ. Judas comes under the influence of this sign of the betrayer, and Leonardo da Vinci, in his Last Supper, placed him as the eighth from the right, not counting the central figure of the Christ. The Christ is like the Sun, and Leonardo in one of his sketches related the twelve disciples to the twelve signs of the Zodiac. As the Zodiac would be incomplete without Scorpio, so would the twelve months of the year be incomplete without November, and the twelve disciples incomplete without Judas Iscariot. It was Judas who gave the kiss that led to death. By November, all plants have died; from Scorpio come those forces which needs must be death-dealing, so that new life may emerge again and evolution move forward and upward. Even the greatest crime ever committed, the Crucifixion, the death of Christ Jesus, the Son of God, on the cross, led to the Resurrection and to the permeation of our planet with the sublime Sun-Spirit, whose continued life here enables the Earth to evolve through all cycles of time to come.

Lucifer, the "serpent" of Genesis, tempted woman, then came death and division, the agony of sex suffering, the loss of our spiritual vision and of our touch with the divine beings, and the separation of mankind into various races and nations. All this prepared the way for Ahriman and our present civilization with its intense, vigorous materialism, culminating in two world wars in the first half of the twentieth century and in our failure to establish genuine peace. Even though our planet is known as the sorrowful star, the sphere of suffering, yet it is known also that the Earth has for its keynote joy, the utter antithesis of sorrow. To know fully the sunshine of joy, we must know its opposite, the shadow of sorrow, and the deeper the shadow, the brighter the sunshine. The perfection of man and planet will be achieved through polarity, the pairs of opposites at work in Scorpio to bring to man his crown and consummation, converting, as St. Paul says, the earthly man into the celestial man.

Only as the solar Christ-light, the light of the world, illumines the earthly personal man, and Scorpio regenerates him and brings him rebirth, can it be said of man that he has become wholly and truly practical. With this practicality attained, then does division cease, at-one-ment or union of body, soul, and spirit is achieved, and there stands the practical man of purpose and power with spiritual prestige won through Christ. Thence comes full sanity in the realm of humanity. In the forge of the fiery element it is easy to weld and shape metals, and many are the consummate artists, but this is not so when the perfect, priceless gem has to be cast. Yet, so intense are will and desire in Scorpio souls that, awakened, theirs is the strength to furnish that furiously intense power that creates the philosopher's stone, the pearl without price.

In Parsifal's quest for the Holy Grail, we read of Amfortas, who ruled the castle of the knights with power, until one day he yielded to temptation, lost the sacred spear, and received a wound that would not heal. From that moment he lost his spiritual prestige and his power, and he lay agonized with the wound. When Parsifal came, he saw the sad state of Amfortas and was stupefied with compassion. He left Amfortas and passed through intense sufferings and trials, until he was able to return with acquired Christ-power, the full insignia of the Grail. With the sacred spear he touched Amfortas' wound, which healed immediately, and thereafter he took charge of the Grail castle. Here we see how dangerous the serpent power of Scorpio may become, unless we pass the test that raises the spiritual forces in man, as can be done in this mighty magical sign. May all those having this sign force, who read this, realize their privilege to work and make themselves holy, so that they may bring themselves up into the ken of the One who heals all wounds. And these will be the ones with the gift to heal others.

In the soul of every individual there resides the harvest of all his good and all his evil, as an essence. This is the sum total or quintessence of all his earthly lives. When a man leaves the ways of the world, walks upon the path of return to God, and undergoes the necessary training for the attainment of higher knowledge, the fruits embody themselves into a shape that is spiritually visible. All evil thoughts and actions that have been committed but not atoned for will, when the aspirant seeks conscious entrance into the higher worlds, face him in the shape of a demoniacal form called the Guardian or the Dweller on the Threshold. Those aspirants who have trod the upward path, whose hearts have long expressed love, will have nothing to fear at this time. It is only those filled with pride and hatred, who have refused to face themselves as they are, that are likely to collapse in palsied fear and terror at this meeting. All those who have cultivated the wisdom of love, with its reverence and humility that give the quality of teachability, have faced the Dweller through many a life.

The Dweller on the Threshold is the result of all unredeemed evil, and today we see mankind as a whole facing its Dweller. This is an astral entity; it feeds upon the foul food of the lower regions of the desire or soul world with its murderous desires. The lies and lusts of the past, all that is left over, must now be redeemed. Mankind as a whole now faces the consequences of its hatred, greed, and ignorance. This synthesis of sin comes from the crawling, stinging lower phase of the sign Scorpio, and before we can move on to the higher, new life cycle, which the Eagle, the higher phase of this sign, brings, we must have faced this demon and dissolved its evil force. This dissolution would not be possible save for the sum of all our good forces and that Greater Guardian of the Threshold who emerges as the embodiment of all that is glorious and grace-filled. The power given to us by this beautiful, benign being, the embodiment of all our good and truthful thoughts, feelings, and acts as well as of all that we may yet become, allows us to face the fiendish Dweller on the Threshold and to dissolve it wholly.

Standing between the place of Crucifixion in Libra and the Mount of Ascension, which is the virtue of the higher Eagle phase of Scorpio, there remains to be dissolved this Dweller on the Threshold comprehended in the lower phase of Scorpio, the sting of evil, "the adder on the path," spoken of in the Bible. "Dan shall be a serpent by the way, an adder in the path [of return to God], that biteth the horse heels, so that his rider shall fall backward." This statement aptly refers to Scorpio. Also, "Dan shall judge his people," and "I have waited for thy salvation, O Lord" (Genesis 49: 16-18).

Only as we redeem the sting of the adder on the path with the antidote of Christ-love and truth, can we cease feeding on low and base desires and feelings, and through their regeneration raise ourselves on Eagle's wings, to soar and to see into the face of the Sun. When we meditate upon this sublimation and perfection of the man, let us think of this eighth sign of octave and evolutionary Eagle power. Note well how Scorpio correlates with the law of spiralling evolution, from the lowest to the loftiest. All who would dissolve the evil Dweller, who would meet his challenge and pass the barrier that prevents premature entrance into the spiritual realms, must burn this barrier away with love and selfless devotion. For it is only those who rise from the lower life of lust and lies, the great human ignorance, and hatred, who earn the wings of the Eagle to mount and soar to heavenly heights.

Once the Eagle phase begins to manifest, secret sources of life become available, leading sometimes even to initiation. When Scorpio's intensity and dynamic power are combined with insight, one may gain a deeper vision and achieve much, both in exoteric activities and in esoteric studies. Through "soul X-ray" insight into people and things, this sign confers an acute faculty for detection, which manifests on various levels, from the detective to the spiritual researcher. Its penetrating vision sees clear through the souls of others. This penetration and insight serve also the diagnostician. Doctors are almost invariably strong in Scorpio. This sign makes the best surgeons, with a steady hand, unswerving and skillful.

One of the chief characteristics of this sign of hidden and secret things is secretiveness. I remember one born in Scorpio who often used to say, "Never let the left hand know what the right hand is doing," with no knowledge or idea of the real meaning of this phrase, but simply in the light of the secretiveness common to this sign. Yet, there is nothing hidden that shall not be revealed at some time, sooner or later, in this life or in future incarnations. This applies, too, to every supposedly secret thought, be it good or evil. What we sow in thought, feeling, and deed, that also we shall reap.

As the eighth and octave sign of the Zodiac, Scorpio is concerned with evolution, and evolution is a process of an unfolding, spiralling ascent whose circling scrolls would never mature and bring forth new life by fostering the growth of consciousness were it not for the process of sowing and reaping. Evolution is the very life of God in pulséd beats of in- and outgoing breath whose measure conditions time and space, seasons and ages and, through the Christ, creates the conditions of destiny by the effective working of cause and effect. Thus the perfect Word speaks and constructs the cosmos, and the harmony of the spheres voices the order that is divine, in virtue of which the law of correspondences in time will bring it to pass that the will of God is done on earth as it is in heaven.

Just as we must climb the highest mountain to obtain the finest and farthest view, so must we go to the greatest of the Gospels to get the most profound view of God's plan for man and planet. This view we find in the Gospel of St. John, the Gospel· for which the symbol is the Eagle of the sign Scorpio. In no other of the Gospels do we find such sublime, all-embracing, transforming, transcendental, eternal ideas that hover and circle like the eagle in the heights far above the everyday events on the earthly plane. These transcendental ideas are the wings that carry us to the heights of eternal, divine wisdom in the Eagle realm of the wisdom-filled Cherubim of Scorpio.

This divine wisdom was embodied in the divine, cosmic man, Christ Jesus. The *Word*, known to the Greeks as the *Logos* and to the Persians as *Honover*, the "meaning-filled tone" proceeding from the sublime light-being, the Spirit of the Sun, this Word, which was "in the beginning," created all things and "was made flesh" in Jesus of Nazareth, revealing the fullness of God's grace and truth. This Word makes the water taste like wine, cleanses the temple, makes it possible to be born again, born of the Spirit, gives eternal life, is the well of water springing up eternally, so that man need never thirst, heals the nobleman's son and the infirm man, and says: "I AM the bread from heaven—man need never hunger; I AM the living water; I AM the *light of the world*, the Spirit-light that streams down upon, irradiates, and weaves through all existence and gives sight to the blind; I AM the Good Shepherd who gives his life for the sheep; and I AM the resurrection and the life."

Every human "I" is a part of the divine "I" that encompasses all the wisdom of the universe as it was, is, and shall be. From the Gospel of St. John flows to us this eternal wisdom; therefore, this Gospel has in it the power needed for the continuance of the Earth's existence and further evolution, and the power that every human "I" needs for the achievement of the transformation of the sting of the Scorpion into the soaring wings of the Eagle.

THE FIERCEST WAR THAT MAN DOTH WAGE

No value have the things of earth
Save as they serve to bring to birth
Within the person of the man
A fruitful knowledge of God's plan.
The fiercest war that man doth wage
Takes place within his earthly cage,
From this he has to free his soul
To bring to birth the Christ, his goal.

All contest comes to Christ the man,
All fiery forces are but fan
To fuse the Spirit with the Earth
Till God's own Son is brought to birth.
The Lord from heaven builds the flesh,
His Spirit doth it full enmesh,
Then doth his alchemy divine
Transmute the base, the gold refine.

When once we are become of God,
Alive are we to light the clod—

Those souls so sunk by matter stark
Who take the light to be the dark.
These blinded mortals hinder much,
As souls diseased we treat as such,
The Earth today is hampered by
These darkened ones who Christ belie.

No other will but God's be done,
No other race but his we run,
We are not clay but God's own kin,
Only the touch with earth brought sin.
Yet shall the Earth be made pure white
By love and life of Christ, the light;
Our sins although they scarlet be
Are wiped away because of Thee.

Sagittarius - The Archer

SAGITTARIUS, the Archer, is the sign that beckons to higher places and to higher realms. It produces experts at adventure and ardent aspirants to the Spirit of truth. To Sagittarians, life opens out as a journey—a journey toward a distant though definite goal. This ninth sign of the Zodiac is the third and last of the fiery triplicity, giving fiery enthusiasm. In this third common sign, as in the other three com-

mon signs, there takes place the development of thought,
for use in this life or in a future incarnation.

Sagittarius is aptly symbolized by a figure that is half
horse and half man, the man aiming his arrow toward the
sky. This indicates the man who is not only rising above and
transmuting his animal-like physical nature, but one who is
aiming to reach divinity; his goal is heaven-high. This
image symbolizes also the link of the spiritual consciousness,
which is brain-free and supra-physical, with the lower con-
sciousness represented·by the horse, the symbol for the intel-
lect, the mode of consciousness dependent on the physical
brain. Ideas and ideals are forged in this fiery sign of mental
light and are made ready for reception by the intellect,
creating spiritual intelligence, thence to flow into daily living.

As a result, the evolved Sagittarian realizes the illumina-
tion of the intellect by the light of the Spirit, and in this
fact the time-space function of the brain becomes lighted
by the Christ-forces of truth and love. Thereby the body,
soul, and spirit of man are coordinated in the Sagittarian to
such a degree that the intellect translates the heavenly light,
so that the normal life of these natives is one of joyous,
buoyant, *aspiration* and perennial *optimism*. They have what
might be called "soul bounce." Through this they are able to
inspire others with good will and cheer, sparing no pains to
bring healing and hope. They are completely confident, as
was St. Paul, that "all things work together for good to them
that love God" (Romans 8:28).

The symbol denotes the Ego emerging from its animal-like
state, taking on the shape of a noble form and erect posture,
feeling the forces of the "I AM" flowing through it and
directing its aspiration toward the stars. The sign is a dual
one, as are all the common, mental signs, and in its best
expression it exhibits the delight of devotion, aspiring to live
on the earth with consciousness of the spiritual world, which
vivid dreams and sometimes actual vision have made valid.

When man has conquered or transmuted his desires, his life of feelings and emotions, as a result of his life in the preceding sign, Scorpio, there can sound out of his soul the power of truth, for Sagittarius stands for the Spirit of truth.

In his Epistle to the Romans, chapter 8: 5-9, St. Paul wrote about two kinds of mind:

> They that are after the flesh do mind the things of the flesh; but they that are after the Spirit, the things of the Spirit.
> For to be carnally minded is death; but to be spiritually minded is life and peace.
> Because the carnal mind is enmity against God: for it is not subject to the law of God, neither indeed can be.
> So then they that are in the flesh cannot please God.
> But ye are not in the flesh, but in the Spirit, if so be that the Spirit of God dwell in you. Now if any man have not the Spirit of Christ, he is none of his.

The ideal is to spiritualize the earthly, physical personality, which is prone to materialism, and so to realize the work of Scorpio in its regenerative action; then to attain the goal of God through the Spirit of truth. The Spirit-mind of Sagittarius is the mind of Christ-truth. This very sensitive sign of the Zodiac, along with the ninth house, indicates acute sensitivity and receptivity to states of spiritual cognition, whereby Sagittarians get the elevation and perspective which is cosmic or Christ-centered.

All men at some time must reach the status of a Christed soul, and this occurs as man takes on the mind of Christ-truth and translates in his body and brain the light of heavenly realms. This is the sign *par excellence* for this marvelous convergence of all types of consciousness to lift and light the soul and make the man not only more than an animal but also more than an average human being.

When the Christ-mind lights the soul, we see in some phase and degree the manifestation of superior powers, for the bridge has been built between the earthly, physical, brain-bound man and the brain-free spiritual Ego in touch with truth. Body, soul, and spirit are coordinated in the man who lives in the Spirit-mind phase of Sagittarius; hence, some element of creativity flowers, as well as the power of prophecy. Scorpio gives *in*cisive *in*sight; Sagittarius, expansiveness and *fore*sight. Let us impress forcefully on our minds the fact that, until the intellect becomes illuminated and made spiritually intelligent, man remains bound to his Moon-moulded brain, which is selfish and separative; thus darkness reigns in varying degrees. It is Jupiter that prepares the soul to take in and use the Christ-mind light, for Jupiter is the planet of cosmic thoughts and divine wisdom, and it is the ruler of Sagittarius. When we have first brought clear thought to bear on a problem and have worked on it patiently, then Jupiter beings help us during sleep, so that on waking we find a solution or grasp a new truth.

If there is a sign calculated to take on the Spirit-mind of truth, it is indeed this ninth sign of the Zodiac. The Archer is the path of pure thinking; hence that acute mental, spiritual acumen possessed by all evolved souls in this sign, which is extremely volatile. So extremely volatile is Sagittarius as a spiritual, mental force, and so vast its velocity that, whenever these natives still live in the lower phase of this sign, they become addicted to physical speed, and they make the high-speed records, in athletics, in automobile racing, and in the air. In movement, the Sagittarians dart like an arrow and are fleet of foot. Especially when this sign is on the eastern horizon of the nativity are they fast, sprightly walkers, fond of hiking and mountain climbing. Sagittarius rules the thighs and the pelvic region, especially the hips and the sciatic nerve, and some say the muscular system, all of which have much to do in propelling the body through space.

When we understand the acute spiritual sensitivity of this ninth sign and the ninth house, we can see that few can make the grade demanded by its highest phase, for it shows the man become free of his lower nature, with the personality being used for Christ's sake. When the personal side is still stressed, the Archer is given over to excessive activity and ruinous restlessness that can break down the physical body not accustomed to bear the higher mental-spiritual currents. It is those who have not yet made their way to the domain of the Spirit that resort to mere physical speed and seek to make and to break records. The spiritual urge is diverted to physical use, instead of being made to express the Spirit mind. In any case, there must ever be ascension and new peaks to climb.

In connection with Sagittarius, we must observe the great love for the out-of-doors and for outdoor sports, which it gives. Incidentally, we may note that it is primarily in the field of sports that the fine factor of fair play is known. This fact, that the concept of fair play should prevail in sports and not in other departments of life, deserves being pondered. Were fair play introduced into all human affairs, then we would have brotherhood much sooner. The idea of fair play and its realization emanate from this Jupiter-ruled sign. Although it extends now only to sports, it will increasingly reach out to all human affairs—to industrial, racial, governmental, national, and international relationships.

Like Aries and Leo, the other fire signs, Sagittarius has extraordinary vitality. In Aries, it is as dynamic as Mars; in Leo, it is the very life of the Sun. In Saggitarius, ruled by Jupiter, it is often sustained by one's spiritual being; hence Sagittarians continue on their way when many others have fallen by the wayside and dropped out of the race. That

which is "vital" speaks of life—it connotes the "liver"—and
no one could be a liver of life, or move or think in a physical
body, without the warm arterial blood and the liver, which
are ruled by Jupiter. What a vast network the arteries are,
extending throughout the entire organism, providing chan-
nels of nourishment! As the blood makes its extensive journey
through the arterial system, so the Sagittarian feels at home
on all the highways of the world. No place is too remote for
this great adventurer. Assimilation, physical and spiritual
growth could not take place without this benign planet of
spiritual being, Jupiter, and its sensitive sign, Sagittarius.

Those persons who are the most pleasant, with buoyancy
of soul, the most sane, with true optimism and joy ungush-
ing and real, are balanced Sagittarians. The reason for this
buoyancy is that Jupiter also rules the two adrenal glands,
which may be called "poise producers." They turn the tide
of flooding, morbid feelings and emotions, which have rise in
the Moon, or in the forceful, discordant Mars, or the gloomy,
melancholic, and inhibitive Saturn. The action of the adren-
als, through Jupiter's rule, pours power into the heart, to
maintain the blood stream against all such insidious nega-
tion.

Although Sagittarius is not the ruler of the heart, which is
Leo's domain, it holds the key and secret to that organ of
love, for Jupiter furnishes the vital arterial blood to the heart,
and we know that "blood is a very peculiar essence." No life
is possible for man without the blood, a spiritual substance
in which the Christ has vantage. Just as an engine without
steam or gasoline remains inert and useless, or an electric
motor dead without current, so man's heart would be lifeless
without the blood supply, for the heart is not a pump
as is commonly supposed. Thus there is a valid vital rela-
tion of the heart and Leo to the blood and Sagittarius.

In the sphere of consciousness, Jupiter represents the divine mind and cosmic wisdom. To approach this wisdom, the intellect alone is inadequate, regardless of how indispensable it is in ordinary earthly life and regardless of the marvelous advance it has wrought in the achievements of civilization. The Jupiter qualities of *devotion* and *reverence* are prerequisites if one is to advance toward an understanding of cosmic wisdom, thereby becoming spiritually intelligent. It is in the sensitive sign of the Centaur, the Archer, that man transcends the light of the mere intellect and reaches out beyond the senses. When the illusory appearance of material existence is pierced, the truth is found that makes man free. Rightly does St. Paul say: "Be not conformed to this world: but be ye transformed by the renewing of your mind, that ye may prove what is that good, and acceptable, and perfect will of God" (Romans 12:2).

With the advent of the radio, there arose a new art, that of tuning in and listening in. This allusion to listening in on the radio is apt for the sign Sagittarius, for it is in this power of the renewed mind, the Christ-mind, that man, consciously or unconsciously, listens in to his higher spiritual being. To listen in, in this wise, means no longer to conform to the world, but to be transformed by renewing one's mind, which then knows the will of God and attunes to the consciousness of the Christ, whose divine mind transcends one's intellect and informs one truthfully. Thus, as we grow in soul evolution, we may take from Sagittarius this gift of God, which is true spiritual intelligence and the Christ-consciousness, whose light is the spirit of truth and the wisdom of love. Then man's intellect no longer swamps him with error, fear, and falsity. This spiritual intelligence is the result of the intellect attuning itself and listening in to the Spirit-mind, the Christ-mind. When this is achieved, man realizes the plan of God for mankind and for himself, and he treads the Path; he now travels *consciously* on the long, arduous evolutionary journey to ultimate Christhood. Indeed, Sagittarius beckons to higher goals, and the highest is complete Christhood.

Human beings must grow in soul quality if they would evolve and grow in the sense of the Spirit, for it is not merely a process of listening in that is involved but right attunement and selection. Not all persons can take in the light which Sagittarius supplies to those who love God with deep devotion. Some are reckless and yield to the Centaur's vice, which is rebelliousness, like that of the wild horse, and sometimes lawlessness, even to discarding all ethics. Others support and expound erroneous ideas and teachings. The sorry thing today is that many people still listen in to the false promptings of the lower realms of the desire or soul world; thus they live and move in selfishness and perpetuate systems that serve "the prince of this world" and not the Lord of love.

As the first sign, Aries, allows one to say *I am*, and the fixed, second fire sign, Leo, allows one to say *I will*, so the building, thought-maturing, mutable third fire sign, Sagittarius, allows one to say "*I see* the way that leads to a conscious goal." Sagittarius serves human evolution through the power of the renewed mind. Its exoteric keyword is "*I seek for food*," whereas the esoteric keyword is "*I see the goal*." Thus the Sagittarian must seek for food and, through various vicissitudes, come to a place where he can see the goal. One difference between Sagittarius and Gemini is this: Gemini knows not for certain where its many activities may lead, whereas Sagittarius has the inspiration and the inner confidence of a definite aim and goal that prompts him to action. The Archer ever keeps his eyes on the goal.

Without his thinking faculty, man remains animal-like. So long, however, as thinking is limited to materialistic concepts, it remains grounded; man does not see his divine goal, and he does not attain to that elevation that extends his horizons to include Spirit realms with their cosmic perspective. Observe the truth of these words, taken from *The Old Commentary*, and how they relate to Sagittarius: "The Sons of God shot forth like arrows from the bow. The forms received the impulse [of mind] and lo! a God was born. The tiny babe knew not the great event." Few as yet know of the cosmic goal that lies ahead of man's long future evolutionary journey. Those who see the goal know that man himself is to become a cosmic being, not in the materialistic sense of space travel as an astronaut, but as a cosmic creator in the spiritual process of world-becoming.

Not until a sufficient number of people come to know the mightiness of mind illumined by the higher Christ-mind light, will mankind find its true place and will fear be banished. A flood of feeling swamps people in times of crisis, yet out of the very sorrows of the Earth is the new orientation taking place that makes men and women see the real and approach the truth. This meditation is written with one major purpose in view—to contribute to a new orientation of mind and soul, so that those who read might realize the boundless potential of the renewed mind, the Spirit-mind, that attunes one to the "good, acceptable, and perfect will of God" (Romans 12:2), the directing idea in the evolution of man and Earth. Once the Spirit-mind is known and active in the soul, the flooding force of fear or feeling, and the pain, become neutralized or cancelled. The Christ-mind can never be fear-filled; it can "never be found wanting in presence of mind or in calm penetration of all situations of life." [1] Without some degree of this Christ-mind, there is bound to be in man an immense imbalance, which amounts to what may be called insanity. Without this Christ-mind, man journeys through life without proper direction and lacks the divine goal that the Archer confers.

---

[1] Rudolf Steiner, *Knowledge of the Higher Worlds and Its Attainment* (New York: Anthroposophic Press, 1961), end of chapter VIII.

Let us look at Sagittarius in the light of the law of the Lord; then we shall see why few can express its positive power so high and holy. Most souls are not by any means clear of the subtle and often loathsome toils of their insidious personalities. To seek the higher life and not to surrender the personality wholly to the law of God, which is one's destiny as duty, is to court danger of no mean kind, for when spiritual and occult work is commenced without purity of purpose, the lower forces are stirred up in the person, and he can with ease descend along the left-hand path.

When one obeys the call and command of his own destiny without hate, heat, sorrow, or resentment, then that soul is truly philosophical. Sagittarius produces a mind given to philosophy. Not all Sagittarians are devoted; yet, when this quality of devotion is joined to philosophy, we observe that beautiful phenomenon of a man truly religious, an individual in love with love and literally embodying in himself and in his daily deeds the law or will of God. Would that there were many more such souls on Earth today, to raise it sooner to Christ-height!

One such soul was Abraham Lincoln, who had Sagittarius rising, with Saturn and Neptune conjunct the Ascendant. True vision that makes a man a seer and prophet comes out of a soul that loves truth and honesty—marked traits of Abraham Lincoln, who earned for himself the sobriquet "Honest Abe." His apt anecdotes, always on tap, clearly reveal that he was a Sagittarian philosopher. Another strong influence of this sign manifested in his ability to dream true dreams. Thus did he foresee his own death.

Sagittarius, like Gemini, is strong in speech but weak in silence or listening. The Sagittarian, having what amounts to clairvoyant thought, is loathe to hear one through to the end of the sentence or statement, for he knows beforehand what the speaker has in mind. So would he spare and cut short the speech of others, even though this often annoys.

It is because of this clairvoyant-thought faculty, along with a free, frank, outspoken, and straightforward expression—in contrast to Scorpio's secretiveness—and a large sense of detachment, the result of an unconscious sense of the universal, that the Sagittarian so often uses words as darts, hitting what is false and weak in others. He knows the vulnerable spots in the human character and exposes them, which as often disturbs or destroys the dignity of people who live only in their personalities. So detached, and yet attached to a sense of truth, are Sagittarians that they actually intend no hurt in their outspokenness, exposing what is false in others. It is done simply to unmask the little personal lives of others, so that the light of Spirit-truth and the level of the universal might be sought and secured. Thus they instinctively search for and espouse the truth and easily detect lies and errors calling for adjustment, much as water seeks its own level.

Although the Archer never misses his mark, because of the clairvoyant quality of his thought, no one is more sensitive than he is to harsh words, which wound him far more severely than physical blows. And no more righteous indignation is seen than that exploded by Sagittarians in a veritable torrential velocity. Well do I remember one whom I had made conversant with the truth that the spirit of man is eternal—it exists before birth and after death—and that reincarnation is a reality. She gave vent to fiery indignation because the church to which she had always belonged did not teach this truth about the reincarnating Ego.

The souls of most Sagittarians are moved in an unconscious, if not conscious, manner by the intuitional forces of the light of truth that is beyond and above the brain organism. As a result, idealism is constantly carried as a current. Because of this lofty quality of mind and ideals, Sagittarians not only resent innuendoes and accusations that would not cause a ripple of comment from other sign members; they are aroused to a fury of righteous anger in the degree in which their ideals have been degraded.

As the natives of the fixed bestial signs, Taurus and Scorpio, ruling the creative voice forces and the generative organs, tend to abuse the sex function and to squander sex forces, so that they must seek to transmute their desires, so do the natives of the two signs following these fixed signs —the common signs, Gemini and Sagittarius—wantonly waste their vocal forces in irrelevant and incessant speech, often mere garrulous chatter. To those intimate with the forces of the Zodiac it is seen that the natives of these two mental signs must seek to conserve and control the forces of speech, so that the innate wisdom of love may flower. Sagittarians are fond of all forms of racing and need to be on their guard lest their tongue, too, run a race. One of the chief exercises they should set for themselves is to bridle or *control the tongue,* thus making speech a feeling for truth.

Not until one dimly realizes the speed of the Spirit—or, better, the all-permeability of the Spirit—can one understand the immense mutability and indefatigable activity of Sagittarius, which often leads to ruinous restlessness in the undeveloped souls in this sign, for it produces an inner speed that presses the body on beyond endurance. It is the spiritual pressure within that makes these natives "seek for food" and, after seeking, "see the goal," for they have an innate hunger for the spiritual worlds, unless they live wholly in their personality—the carnal mind—and are moved by selfish ambition rather than by aspiration. It is this pressure bearing down on the personality that produces love for travel, especially for long journeys and voyages, which are ruled by this sign, as well as for cosmopolitan concepts and an interest in foreign countries and peoples, from whom they usually gain great benefits.

Snobbery is not the vice of these open-minded, free, expansive individuals, even though they are fully aware of enormous inequalities in evolutionary progress. Although they are tolerant, they have little patience with narrow-minded views. Sagittarius must be realized in the sense of its vast expansiveness, for it is as wide as the world and needs plenty of space for its activities. It gives a will to conquer new worlds, to open new areas of thought, and to acquire an ever-expanding consciousness. With a consciousness as universal as that conferred by this sign, it is small wonder that Sagittarians show such a large sense of freedom and independence. This is also the result of the expansive Jupiter.

In the soul of the Sagittarian there dwells, either consciously or unconsciously, the innate realization of his sonship with God, and this idea, dream, or vision, no matter how vague, is carried within as a constant craving to be at some time satisfied. This sign rules religion, hence Sagittarians have a natural sense of religious intelligence and are for the most part the pillars of the church. Ministers are often strong in the Archer, whose upward-directed arrow symbolizes aspiration to divine purpose. As Sagittarius rules the *sense of taste,* its natives will be moved to manifest a compassion in the degree in which they have "tasted of the Lord."

In a world built up by critical, egotistic, and separative forces, criticism is condoned and accepted. However, all those spiritually aware and serving the Christ, thereby making the lunar forces serve the solar light, know what a vice gossip is, and how it is made worse by the press that panders to it. Were the world to cease worrying and cease holding spite and malice through gossiping, and were it no more to have curiosity about the concerns of others, then friendship would flourish. In virtue of their love of fair play and their world-wide interests, evolved Sagittarians are not addicted to worrying, nor concerned about other people's affairs in the sense of curiosity or of purveying malicious talk or gossip. With the unevolved, it may be otherwise.

To know the forces of every sign of the Zodiac and thus to be all things to all men, to know how to abound and how to be abased in the manner of St. Paul, implies a close intimacy with the plan of God, and one establishes this knowledge of soul and spirit through the variety and vicissitudes of many lives. Many secretly or openly declare their wish to be teachers, but only those devoted to God in heart, in mind, and in soul, who have taken the impress and impulse of Jupiter through the sign Sagittarius, can ever hope to be true teachers of men, no matter whether their present nativities show planets in this sign or not, for to be fit and able to teach in the sense of the Christ, the teacher at some time must have acquired the touch and the wisdom provided by Jupiter.

The Sagittarian or Jupiterian teacher is much desired, for he has that inborn empathy that knows the individual need of the pupil. He does not teach by telling; he is the true educator because he educes—draws out—answers from the pupil, who thereby learns to think for himself; he educes the teacher within the pupil. Moreover, the teachers in this sign lack the prejudice that is all too common in teachers, and with such a rare fragrance—for perfume it is to be without such fault—a rapport can be readily established between teacher and pupil. This is essential if teaching is to have an educative effect. All those who would serve the world and themselves in true redemption, and thus salvage souls, must have the expansive, all-embracing forces of Jupiter.

Each triplicity of the Zodiac gives flow and force to some quality of consciousness. There are four triplicities and four elements: earth, water, air, and fire. The earth signs call out that condition of consciousness that is connected with physical reality. The perfection of physical experiences is the result of wise life in these signs. The water signs bring man the realization of the consciousness concerned with the feelings and sensations, so that the imaginative forces become perfected and made amenable to the Spirit. The air signs bring about an expansion of consciousness through thought and mental forces, so that the human being as a soul is seen apart and distinct from the sensual, physical, personal man. In air signs, man comes to consolidate thinking and, through concentration in thinking, he brings to maturity the wisdom that may lead to a knowledge of God. The design of man's divinity is realized through the avenue of the air signs. The fire signs confer the kind of consciousness that affects the will to be and that makes man say, "I am that I am." Out of the fire signs comes the dynamic directing idea.

In the first fire sign, Aries, man's consciousness is riotous, unless it is given direction. Its marked feature is rash, wild, outflying impulse, and a mind instinctive with spontaneity. Riotous rapidity that leads to excess is the mode of Aries whenever there is no fully self-directive consciousness. In the fixed fire sign, Leo, the power of will accompanies the self-consciousness. The characteristic consciousness of Aries is transmuted and matured in Leo till harmony and stability result, head and heart being balanced and cooperating. The power that nourishes and sustains the soul stems from the vital generative forces of Leo. As man's consciousness is differentiated in Aries and brought into a state of harmony in Leo, these forces are resolved into that distillate of mental force in Sagittarius that brings release to the light of heaven. In this sign of the Spirit-mind—where the only guide and the one Teacher may be found, the Christ, who is the law and its fulfillment—there takes place the sublimation of consciousness and the perfection, which are the fruit of right transmutation.

Evolution provides the power to progress by ever taking on the new. Sagittarius promotes the sublimation of the soul by correlating the intellect with the Spirit-mind and, through this union and transmutation, a bridge is built from the brain-bound personality, living in its physical form, to the higher spiritual being and to that spiritual realm that is the source of all ideas.

Thus the Sagittarian is a prophet, and these souls, when evolved and Christ-elect, may reach into the realms of real religion, art, truth, and tone, where the poetry of the one philosophy eternally pulses in the divine rhythm of God. Through such artistic creativity Beethoven set down his symphonies, for he had his Sun, Moon, and Mercury in Sagittarius. His contemporary, Joseph Haydn, another master composer, had Sagittarius rising, with Uranus therein, and also the dynamic Mars. The marked features of the Sagittarian may be discerned in the last of that long line of musicians, Carl Maria von Weber, who so brilliantly expressed in tone the ethereal of the fairy world and what the world calls romantiscism, in his *Oberon, Der Freischütz,* and other works, especially in his *Invitation to the Dance.*

In this freedom-loving, fiery sign of the seer, we see the marked mode of the Spirit-mind consciousness that connects one with truth through the mind of Christ, and this in the degree provided by the soul's purity, aspiration, and devotion. The Spirit-mind manifests through the higher being called by St. Paul, "the Lord from heaven," which then expresses in the personality; but not till the personality is subordinated and consecrated to God, can the Christ-mind appear. For most people, to acquire the mind which was in Christ Jesus, the lessons are long and the journey arduous.

The Sagittarian is the seer of the goal, and his is the elevation that forever allows a further expansion of consciousness and the vision of still more distant goals. Once a goal is reached, another is seen. In fact, this is the sign wherein the forces of relationship move upward in evolutionary expansion, for Sagittarius relates one to the Christ-truth and the teacher within, working as a leaven, to realize the onward advance, the soul-progressive journey. This occurs as a result of a right relationship—the linking of the intellect with

the sense-free Spirit working in the soul. It has been truly
said by a prophet, "Where there is no vision, the people per-
ish." The quality of true vision animates the Sagittarian who
is mature, balanced, and evolved, as was Abraham Lincoln.

The evolved Sagittarian strives for perfect perspective by
securing views that portray the widest possible picture,
floodlighted by the Spirit. He may spend years of his life in
reaching a goal, only to see another, for truth is infinite and
moves one forever forward and upward. Thus we see why
Sagittarius gives inspiration and aspiration—an eternal
spiralling journey—and why those who are negative in this
sign move simply in vicious circles, rather than in ascending
spirals of an ever forward and upward evolution.

> Let food be sought the sheep to feed,
> Who would be pastor knows the need,
> Who would God's highest riches reap
> Lives in the light and feeds his sheep.
>
> How few have yet truth realized,
> Engrossed, enamored, hypnotized
> By earthly forces and the form
> Which separate and bring the storm.
>
> To love the truth is Christ to know,
> His is the life and way to go;
> If you would know the truth that frees,
> Then learn of him, he holds the keys.
>
> All those who *seek* shall find the way
> Which brings return upon the ray
> Of Christ who is the loving whole,
> For all mankind the *living goal*.

Capricorn - The Goat

THE SIGNIFICANCE of each sign of the Zodiac can be secured by deep thought and meditation upon the symbology of the sign as portrayed in the pictorial representation apart from the written word. Especially is this true of the most meditative sign, Capricorn—whence comes the constant call to delve more deeply into every subject—although the symbols of all signs must be studied to grasp their deeper content. The more occult-minded one is, the richer the rewards in true gold of God, for God and the Zodiac are inseparable. The tenth sign of the Zodiac is so mighty in its import that we can do no more than hint at its subtle importance, its sublime magnitude, and its major effect to individualize man, making him a soul quickened by the Spirit, one of a great whole, yet with a distinct sense of individuality.

Capricorn has several symbols. The best known is the *Goat*, a thrifty animal that climbs high up the mountain, cautiously moving from crag to crag, seeking the summit. Capricorn looks for the topmost position. Consciously or unconsciously, the inner motive is *ambition*, which may be used for good or ill. All too often it is used to exercise authority over others and, with patience or with cunning, to secure prestige and power. Therefore, it can readily be seen that the quality and the direction of the soul—allied only with the body, or also making contact with the Spirit—count for more in this sign than in any other, except Scorpio, which is likewise a sign of extremes. Capricorn may not be as murderous as the lower phase of the Scorpion, but it can be cold, calculating, crafty, servile, utterly selfish, and unscrupulous. The extremes range from the black magician to the most selfless, reverential priest or high initiate; from the hardest, most conniving politician or cruel, power-loving dictator to the completely dedicated statesman serving his nation or the world.

The various symbols of Capricorn help to elucidate these vast differences. One is the *Crocodile*, an amphibious creature, aquatic and terrestrial. Another is the *Fish-goat*, whose rear is shaped like a fish, its front like a goat. Like the crocodile, the fish-goat is amphibious, as much at home in the water as on land. Both have the faculty to swim in the depths, but on land the crocodile stays near the shore, often in the mud, whereas the goat can climb to the loftiest mountain top. Here is symbolized man's power to sink into a sea of selfish desires and egotism, or to conquer the lure of the desire world and, realizing truth by transcending the five senses and physical reality, to rise up into the mountain range of spiritual reality. The dualism of Capricorn manifests in the symbology of the amphibious creatures, whose dual attributes portray the physical and spiritual nature of man.

In ancient days, Capricorn was linked with *Makara*, the Pentagram. H. P. Blavatsky says in the *Secret Doctrine*: "The FIFTH ORDER is a very mysterious one, as it is connected with the Microcosmic Pentagon (sic), the five-pointed star, representing man. In India and Egypt, these Dhyānis were connected with the Crocodile, and their abode is in Capricornus." With his arms extended to the sides and his feet apart, man forms the five-pointed star. In the same stanza, there is a direct reference to the dual office of Capricorn: "The Fifth Group of Celestial Beings is supposed to contain in itself the dual attributes of both the spiritual and physical aspects of the Universe; the two poles, so to say, of Mahat, the Universal Intelligence, and the dual nature of man, the spiritual and the physical. Hence the number Five, doubled and made into Ten, connecting it with Makara, the tenth sign of the Zodiac." [1]

The tenth sign of the Zodiac is Capricorn, and ten is the number of completion. The constellation comprises a group of stars that forms the figure of a goat. Interestingly, there are twenty-eight stars there, a number whose digits add up to make ten, twice the number five. Although Gemini rules the hands, we may never too often look at our ten fingers, five on each hand, complementing each other and giving us the power of accomplishment. It is only when the physical and the spiritual in man complement each other that the

---

[1] H. P. Blavatsky, *The Secret Doctrine* (Adyar, Madras, India, The Theosophical Publishing House, 1962), Vol. 1, Stanza 7: l f, pages 266 and 268.

Capricorn individual's accomplishments reflect his completion as a whole human being. Capricorn people, who use only the head and seem to have no heart, are the hard type of selfishly ambitious Egos, whereas the completed ones have balanced the functioning of the head and the heart.

Still another symbol for Capricorn, as yet seldom known, is the *Unicorn*, a triumphant being, victor in all strenuous tests. It symbolizes the highest phase of this sign of initiation and of the world Savior.

It would seem that in referring to this marvelous, mighty sign of the Christ brought to birth—this Christmas sign, Capricorn—one is presumptuous and is stepping in where Angels fear to tread, yet one must not hold back, for the time is come to speak of the mysteries of God to those who have ears to hear. No man can become a Christ-man, thereby reaching completion as a perfected being, unless he learns to correlate with the forces of Saturn through Capricorn, because the cradle of the Christ is in this animal sign; hence he was brought to birth in a manger with animals about him. Although many people still express the animal attributes of this sign, do not for a moment think that only animal forces inhere in Capricorn, for there is a side to it so lofty that few save initiates—those who know at firsthand —know of it. What is known exoterically is that Christmas always falls on December 25th, when the Sun is in Capricorn and human hearts are warmed with the fine feeling of good will and love that prevails at this season of the year.

Through the birth of Christ, a new impulse was given to the Earth. Every year, after the entry of the Sun into Capricorn, there is a renewal of this impulse. The esoteric understanding must now become exoteric, the understanding that Christmas is the season of spiritual birth and the most propitious period for initiation into the mysteries of life; for during the Thirteen Holy Nights from December 24th to January 6th, the Christ-etheric forces reach their greatest intensity and amplitude within the Earth. One of the key sayings for Capricorn is, "Let the door stand wide." At Christmas time, the door from the Earth to the spiritual world stands open wider than in summer. Cancer represents the door to physical birth; Capricorn, the door to spiritual birth, to initiation.

Cancer and the Moon are the Mother-forces; Capricorn, with Saturn, its ruler, are the Father-forces. They confer wise counsel to the human father-principle. In their loftiest expression, Capricorn is the sign and Saturn the planet that stand for the Father-God, who is the foundation of heavenly and earthly existence—a being, almighty, yet related as a Father to his creatures. It was Christ who revealed God as the Father, saying, "I and my Father are one," and "I am in the Father, and ye in me, and I in you." Here a great mystery is elucidated when we are able to see beyond the lower phase of Capricorn and, piercing the illusions of the senses, reach up into the realm of spiritual reality, which underlies as a foundation, though not physically visible, both the heavens and the earth.

A most effective statement is found in the first chapter of Revelation, "I am Alpha and Omega, the beginning and the ending, saith the Lord, which is, and which was, and which is to come, the Almighty"—the archetype of all archetypes. Only as one clearly realizes that Saturn is the force of the "first and last," the beginning and the end, can one know the plan and power of the Father. The lowest and the highest forces in us, the physical body and the Spirit-man with which the physical body is correlated, are powers of God himself. This lowest and highest—this physical body and its Father-force above, the Spirit-man; this human and divine man—have reign and representation through this mighty sign Capricorn and its ruler, Saturn. It was in the Saturn Period, the first of the seven great periods of evolution—of which our Earth is the fourth—that there were laid the beginnings of man's physical body and the germinal forces for the sense organs, the sense of *vision* coordinating with Capricorn. It will be in the last period, the seventh, that the Spirit-man will be perfected.

Since the Christ is one with the Father, no man becomes a Christ-man unless he has taken the chastening yet loving Father-forces of Saturn and Capricorn that instill strength of will and power to endure. The pedagogy of pain, about which most men complain, has a high purpose. Elevation in evolution is secured only at the price of pain. Freedom from the thrall of the senses is gained through the apprenticeship received from Capricorn and Saturn, the forces of the double five. In meditation on this sign—this Father-force—keep ever in mind this pair of fives, which represent the lower, physical, earthly man on the one hand, and on the other, his overshadowing yet resident Father in heaven, above yet within, the highest part of the triune higher self, which is the true, real being. As you utter the words, "Our Father which art in heaven," in the most highly occult prayer ever given, strive to gain a growing knowledge of the Godhead power to which you are related as a son, through the glory of his Son, the Christ, remembering always, "I and my Father are one." Apply these mighty truths to your own soul and learn with growing grace of the presence of the Father and the Son—the divine being of the Godhead—in you.

Through the lower, negative phase of this Saturnine sign are men seduced into a love of power and place. Although intense egotism marks our era, all mankind is in the Christ-crucible of a cleansing that tends to merge the physical with the spiritual in mankind, for the light now shines more incandescently into the darkness, so that the darkness may be dissolved. This is the time to overcome the vast egotism and intellectualism that are creative of the worldly-wise men and our modern civilization, which now produce much chaos, but out of which Christ-unity and order will arise.

In the lower phase of Saturn-Capricorn the soul is seduced through the selfish desires in which nearly all mankind lives to some degree, and through the senses and the brain-bound intellectual forces, the darkness that limits and blocks the light from above. Out of the Luciferic selfish desires comes man's immense egotism that produces dictators in every sphere of life, from personal relationships to heads of nations; and out of the Ahrimanic darkness comes the seduction of mankind through materialism that produces the vast inertia and inanition of spiritual life and spiritual activity among the masses. This darkness, however, is the darkness before dawn.

Saturn and Capricorn in their lower aspect thus deceive through the senses and give to the undeveloped a distorted sense of values that makes personal ambition and a consuming lust for power the main motivating force of their lives, which may take on a tinge of black magic, as evidenced in some modes of advertising and salesmanship. This tendency to wield power over others was markedly manifest in Napoleon, who had the Moon in Capricorn and Saturn in Cancer at the Midheaven. We see in the German Chancellor, Bismarck, the blindness of egotism and personal ambition; his Moon was in Capricorn, as was the Moon of his twentieth century successor, the dictator Adolf Hitler, who had, in addition, Saturn elevated in Leo at his Midheaven, ill-aspecting Mars and Venus. These examples illustrate the maniacal lust for power and for national supremacy that motivates such men, who, however, do a certain cosmic work. Capricorn functioned, too, in the fanatical religious fervor of Oliver Cromwell, Lord Protector of England, who had Capricorn rising.

It is in Capricorn's negative manifestation that this thirst for power is so pronounced. Out of it there has arisen our competitive spirit and economic system. In this Saturnine sign is the seat and source of the idea of separateness. Mankind, for the most part, lives and dies in this great illusion of separation; however, it is by development through separation, selfishness, and materialism that man attains to freedom and finally to a true selfhood, an Ego-consciousness that is divine and benign. Man's apprenticeship must be served in the deceptive light and in the darkness spoken of in Revelation 12: 9, 12, 13: "And the great dragon was cast out, that old serpent, called the Devil [Lucifer, the false light], and Satan [the darkness of materialism], which deceiveth the whole world . . . the devil is come down unto you, having great wrath, because he knoweth that he hath but a short time. And when the dragon saw that he was cast unto the earth, he persecuted the woman which brought forth the man child."

In the lower phase of Capricorn exists the force of selfish desire that is served by the use of the brain, which by itself cannot conceive spiritual reality. Man for the most part lives in this great illusion, and he lives there even after death, the victim of the experiences of his earthly life and thought, filled with the same old desires and thoughts. "The devil" and "the dragon" blind the mass of mankind through the blinding false light of egotism and the darkness of the earthly brain. Those souls that are in or under Capricorn but not yet in touch with this sign's higher phase are unyielding and impervious to firsthand knowledge of spiritual truth. Although many still do not live in the light of the world—the Christ, hid with the Father in the world and in man—be it remembered well that, in the positive phase of Capricorn, there dwells the Father-God, the highest aspect of the Trinity.

These considerations show us how the lower part, the fish-tail, or the crocodile element of this sign, takes the soul into selfish isolation and the darkness of materialism, there to make that conquest that at last brings a knowledge of the truth—and this knowledge of truth about God, man, and the world comes through the Saturnine pedagogy of pain, unless it is accepted voluntarily. No matter the pain that comes from Capricorn and Saturn, that pain has a true and beneficent purpose. For the aspirant on the path that leads to God and home, Saturn's pedagogy forms the field of victory over the senses. With this truth our own, in full clear title, we can truly appraise and appreciate pain. We cease to be woebegone and world-weary because of the incessant impacts of grief, ingratitude, and lack of understanding. We see the ineptitude of man, yet also the promise and the power to express his godhead-forces in a body of flesh. All these things we see and more, and as a result we cease to waste further forces on the desire for personal position and comfort. Knowing the plan God has for man, we begin to cooperate with that plan. Thus the false light of Lucifer and the darkness of Ahriman—the devil and the dragon—are of service in developing man through selfishness, separation, and materiality, to a sense of the "I" and freedom.

Men do not behold the world in its physical-spiritual reality until the Christ is born in them. When one's heart has been sufficiently crushed with grief and suffering, then does the light within reveal the light without. No one has the power to know the way or exemplify the way until the light in the head connects with the heart and so gives the radiance that enables one to respond to the higher phases of this sign. Then a light-bearer and world-server is born.

From these reflections, we may get a more comprehensive, deeper idea of this sign of the Father and of the inestimable service of Saturn, whom most people take as a thorn in the side because of his pedagogy of pain. Anticipating the fruit of Christ-freedom that such pain produces, we realize that in this or a future incarnation we shall cease to be the prisoners of our physical senses and of the lies and errors of earthly life in which there is little if any conscious radiance of the Spirit. Through disciplined work, we set our souls free from the deception of flesh and blood, and from the darkness of the intellect unlighted by the Christ-consciousness. We learn from Saturn and take from him those forces that would give us the power to pierce the delusion of the senses and of the brain.

Today the world dwells largely in the luring Luciferic light of the lower egotistical self and in the Ahrimanic darkness of the intellect unlighted by Spirit-truth. Out of this chaos there will be resolved cosmos, the divine order of God. The forces of chaos will be reduced through the light that now shines in the darkness. As we search at firsthand into the majestic God-man sign, Capricorn—the sign that enables man to use his body for the sake of his Christ-soul and lift these to the Spirit, usually through the pedagogy of pain—can every one of us become effective leaven to help the Lord of our planet to leaven the lump. Then do we share his burdens and become light-bearers; we no longer despise pain or recoil from it, but allow pain and sorrow to speak, for they have a message that lights the path for us. We should suffer our souls to understand, so that our intellect may be informed of the truth.

To realize the sooner the truth that brings freedom, we must direct our feet toward the path that leads to reality. This physical world is not the realm of truth, but the scene of the senses, the world of form, which is illusory. Within every human being there is present a power that lights the way to walk. This power is the light of the solar man, the Christ-born man; and this sign, Capricorn, brings him to birth, after the vast travail in and through its lower phase of egotism and materialism. When egotism is expended and materialism is overcome, then altruism and spiritual intelligence may manifest. Egotism is the King Herod who seeks to kill all infants, so that the Christ-child might be slain. No force is more effective in thwarting the growth of Christ-soul than personal ambition, the egotism of a negative Capricorn. Aquarian altruism makes it possible for the Christ-child to grow and mature. Yet must this child come to birth out of the pain and pressure of the earthly senses in the animal-related body—stalled in a manger, of a truth. The Christ is born and cradled in this sign of the Father, Capricorn, even though he matures and becomes "all things to all men" in the next sign, Aquarius. As we transmute egotism into altruism, we create, with growing force, a sovereign power, which is the divine will of the Father. Those who have found the way know the divine will through the power of a positive Saturn.

Saturn, as Chronos, is Father Time, the Guardian of Time. As the Cosmic Recorder, it is the planet of cosmic memory. The Saturn-beings have recorded everything that has happened since "in the beginning," the Saturn Period, when human evolution began. Saturn imparts to man retentive memory. It is also the producer of a silent power, the fruit of patience through many lives of helpful hindrance.

Saturn can be hard and sinister, cold and calculating, power-loving and intensely ambitious as well as servile. It can, moreover, be very diplomatic and often dissembling, which is often the right name for diplomacy, for no true tact or touch faculty comes out of lies and errors born of egotism. It becomes a different Saturn when matured in the positive phase of Capricorn and watered spiritually in the next sign, Aquarius. Such a process produces a wholehearted outgoing love for all mankind, without an iota of exclusiveness, through the union of will with truth, to bring the wisdom of love of the Christ. Those who have touched these potent powers of the Father and the Son, can declare the acceptable year of the Lord and proclaim that a New Day is near when the devices of the devil and the old dragon shall have been pierced and their lies and errors, the fruit of egotism and cold intellectualism, will be recognized. Mankind will be lighted with the torch of truth, which brings spiritual intelligence and makes the dedicated, responsible server, ranging from the devoted father of a family to the president of a nation.

Consciously or unconsciously, Capricorn natives have within them a power of authority over others, and it is this mode of mastery that brings them to a place of power or responsibility, onerous or otherwise, in the family, community, nation, or the world. The sense of power, authority, duty, and responsibility in Capricorn becomes admirable only in proportion to the actual amount of Christ-consciousness manifesting in the individual. The greater this power, the finer and better the success, at least spiritually and eventually practically, for it should be etched on the mind that the dual factors of practicality and spirituality inhere in Capricorn in a marked degree.

Capricorn endows its natives with the quality attributed to the goat: the ability to climb cautiously from crag to crag and from summit to summit, ever ascending, the mountain peaks being their happiest habitat. Although Capricorn confers the powerful inner impulse to progress both materially and spiritually, there is in its negative phase a social ambition to place and power that demands satisfaction and impels one to seek its realization in obsequious conduct. This may descend to downright servile fawning, a cringing quality feigning utter humility, such as Dickens depicted in the character of Uriah Heep, who ever washed his hands with an invisible soap, unctuously commenting, "I am so humble." But only the weak, undeveloped persons in this sign stoop to such abject fawning to curry favors from others.

The weakness of Capricorn persons is their thirst for power, fame, honor, admiration, and the desire to be known by the so-called great. Christ Jesus referred to them as Pharisees who love the uppermost place at feasts, the chief seats in the synagogues, greetings in the markets, and to be called of men, "Master, Master." Ideas of place, power, prestige, and personality are strongest in Capricorn, which inclines toward snobbery and love of mere fleshly form and exterior conditions. This sign often denotes a person animated by strong ambition and egotism. The power of the Father-force is inherent in Capricorn, but when the darkness of the brain is strong, this sign manifests an intense desire to wield power that brooks no competitor in its field of action.

True enduring power comes to Capricorn Egos in proportion to their moral and spiritual growth. As the intellect becomes lighted by spiritual understanding, they cease to react to the gall of jealousy, covetousness, and the fearsome suspicion that someone is about to steal their place, power, or prestige. As they overcome the darkness by the growing radiance of the Christ-light, which shines in that darkness, they gain positive power and make proper progress.

The paradox of Capricorn is the paradox of Scorpio, for heaven and hell, light and darkness inhere in both signs in their opposing extremes. A negative Capricorn person lacks the power to perceive the spiritual Christ-light that shines in the darkness; he cannot discern spiritual reality, and in his egotism and self-sufficiency he believes his ideas and views are the only right ones, the only truth. So strong is the force of form in this Saturn sign that the Spirit often remains untapped and unknown. Such a state of spiritual dearth, if accompanied by ambition for personal place or power, makes some of the wealthy men of finance. If wealth disappears or if prestige is lost, it is the negative Saturn-type of Capricorn-person that resorts to suicide. If the soul has indeed been sold to the devil, there might be tendencies that border on black magic. A compelling power to cheat oneself or others issues from Saturn's darkness. This is not reversed until the light of the truth of Spirit reveals to man that there are other worlds than the physical world, that back of the form, of which he is informed by the senses, there is the life that builds and sustains the form, and that it can be perceived only by developing latent higher powers. Salvation and immediate progress come as the Christ-light breaks through into the brain-bound personality. Not till then will Capricorn individuals become self-effacing and thus true servers, be it in industry, finance, government, or religion.

The mighty power of the Father-force in Capricorn is only tapped and expressed when the native of this sign realizes the light that shines in the darkness, for once this light is comprehended, the highest attainments are achieved through the action of the Christ within, who is all-wise, all-loving, and all-intelligent. As our era passes, the master men of Saturn will come with their selfless executive-directive forces to make life worth living, whereas at present selfish Saturn souls seek to gain power over the soul and substance of myriads of men. When the humanitarianism of Aquarius is added to the patient persistence of Capricorn, Christ-altruism is added to the Father-force. Then, as Christ said, "I and the Father are one."

Egotism changes to altruism as the Capricorn native is lighted in the head and heart. The secret of Saturn and Capricorn is that one acquires virtues and takes on the soul of a sage only after one has passed through the tests, the hindering restrictions, which this sign provides. One realizes the weight and worth of Saturn after passing through the Job initiation.

Whereas Sagittarius is expansive, Capricorn is contractive and cohering. The idealism of Sagittarius is brought to concrete action in Capricorn in virtue of the power of persistence and the genius of concentration. The high altitude that allows the spiritual attitude of Sagittarius to manifest can be made concrete and truly practical in the highest positive expression of the Saturnine sign, Capricorn. It may be stated that nothing truly practical exists save as soul and spirit manifest in the forces of form. Just as this sign can render a soul impervious to the Spirit, so can it shed on it the highest spiritual light, depending upon the stage or degree of the soul's evolution. Most souls born in or under Capricorn remain blind and deaf to the Spirit, because their intense ambition is turned earthward by way of their genius in the purveyance of goods, or in political life.

Conversely, it should be noted that one may err in clinging solely to the spirituality of this lofty sign, without planting one's feet firmly upon the earth. In India, which is ruled by Capricorn, the meditative mood prevails, and physical reality is regarded as *maya*, illusion. The one-sided Capricorn-force prevents the Indian from attaining completion as a personality and from gaining mastery over the natural resources of the earth. Moreover, the Capricorn concept of disparity in social standing reaches its extreme application in the Indian caste system. Distinctions between a "superior" and an "inferior," however, are maintained throughout the world, snobbery being characteristic of Capricorn people everywhere, along with their struggle for place and power.

The real need of Capricorn souls is for moral and spiritual growth; they must cease striving for worldly place and power. They must become superior inside, throwing off all fawning and snobbery, that pride that thrives on the external values of life, on power, worldly distinction, and pomp. They are prone to regard their ideas as the only truth, and it is this tendency that creates the condition of loneliness and isolation, for a steel-gray shell forms itself about these souls, and in this incrustation they remain, impervious to the spirit of truth and the warming expansiveness of love.

This tenth sign of the Zodiac corresponds to the tenth house, which, in a map of the heavens, is the Midheaven, the vital point indicative of one's integrity, one's honor, which predicates one's worldly standing and prestige, one's good name among men, and one's true spiritual name with God. Capricorn improves the true status of its natives as they improve their moral and spiritual quality. When their destiny is affected by the growth of the soul from within outwards, they become powerful organizers for good and rise far above the difficulties of their early environment and those connected with the parents, almost invariably involving either some distinct painful disharmony, or fateful separation.

Someone unaware of the zodiacal forces may get the impression of reticence, if not of aloofness, which is, however, the way self-restraint manifests in Capricorn, when it is not animated by the next sign, Aquarius. Capricorn has an uncommon capacity and love for work, spurred on by immense ambition. Capricorn Egos will work for their own interests without stint or stop. They are apt to stumble on the rock of trying to keep up with the Joneses. In the unevolved phase, self-interest and the secret desire to gain and wield power are great; we see these traits exemplified in politicians, businessmen, financiers, and all those who are opportunists and "use" others, that is, those whose moral and spiritual growth is not commensurate with their vast ambitions.

Whenever ambition is turned toward earthly, personal ends, it becomes dangerous for Capricorn souls; they are toppled, as was Napoleon. Even Woodrow Wilson, with his Sun and Mercury in Capricorn, his Moon on the cusp of Capricorn-Aquarius, and Saturn at the Midheaven in Cancer, failed to achieve his ideals which, as time will prove, were more Jehovistic than Christ-Aquarian, for they fostered separatism, notwithstanding the external organization of nations within the League. All Capricorn natives become positively endowed with permanent place and power as they align themselves with the Christ, as the spiritual side of their nature blossoms, leading them to transmute their egotism and separateness. No sign is more earnest or steadfast than Capricorn, none more inclined to meditation, the soul diving ever deeper for food and facts, none more rigid in self-discipline and the fulfillment of duty and responsibility. This rigidity and stability, however, which are an asset in some domains, may become a hindrance in situations requiring change. It is a poor boast to say, "You will always find me the same." We are on Earth to make progress, and Capricorn natives make progress through incessant perseverance. Their development is advanced as they sacrifice their interests and personality to the Spirit within, saying, "Father, not my will, but thine, be done."

One of the most notable geniuses of all time was Michelangelo, who had Capricorn rising. As an architect, sculptor, painter, and poet, his creativity was stupendous. Architecture as a human art is possible because man bears within him the cosmic memories of the ancient Saturn Period, when divine beings impressed the laws of Saturn upon the primeval, spiritual form of the physical body, which was to become an organism in space. The architect has the power, possessed by the ancient Greeks in an especially high degree, to liberate the spatial forces which are within him, and to externalize them.

Some well-known men born with the Sun in Capricorn are: Benjamin Franklin, Sir Isaac Newton, and Rudyard Kipling. William Gladstone, for so long the Prime Minister of England, had the Sun and Mercury rising in Capricorn. In the field of finance and business, Andrew Carnegie and John Wanamaker stand out as Capricorn-Sun natives. The musician Robert Schumann had Capricorn rising. Louis Pasteur had six planets, including the Sun, in this Saturnine sign, all in the third house, and as a result of his investigations, people now fear bacteria as much as in the Middle Ages they feared ghosts. The very fear of bacteria produces the most fertile soil in which the germs can breed.

Not until Capricorn souls overcome their fear can they achieve true health. Among the most characteristic negative qualities of Capricorn and Saturn are fear, gloom, pessimism, depression, and melancholy. Light and darkness pervade these souls. When they ride high, they are jolly, but when depressed, none are more gloomy in mind and soul. They should exert every effort to gain an even balance. When melancholia and morbid states of mind and feeling saturate and sink these souls, they are prone to numerous ailments, such as sclerotic conditions, digestive disorders, colds, and diseases of the skin and joints. One ruse often resorted to by Capricorn persons is threat of suicide if they cannot immediately have their own way. Their worst enemy is despondency; the lack of buoyancy is in direct contrast to the optimism of Sagittarius, which is ruled by Jupiter. For this reason, it is important that they be informed of the science of the Spirit, which elucidates life and gives it profound and rich meaning, purpose, and value. They should know, too, of the very real presence of discarnate earthbound, ignorant human souls who try to impress their own wretched state of consciousness upon those who are negative and despondent, so that they become enshrouded in deep depression or wish to commit suicide.

The mind of a person strong in Capricorn is so searchingly scrutinizing, in a gaze incessantly turned inward, that, if at all negative, it inclines to morose moods and gloomy brooding, whereas in positive persons it leads to fruitful meditation and eventually to an elevation of consciousness and to evolution, which discloses the light that was ever shining in the darkness. Out of the inevitable destiny that this sign invariably confers—oppression, limitations, frustrations, delays, and denials—out of the darkness of this formative, soul-building force, there comes at last the light of the loving, living Christ.

For the northern hemisphere, the Sun stands lowest on entering Capricorn, and then it begins its ascent at Christmas. It signals the birth of the Christ, the Spirit of our Earth, who is spiritualizing the planet and all it holds. The Moon, however, has its "fall" here. The reflected light of the Moon wanes, so that the true light, the spiritual light of the Sun-Son may shine once more with raising, refining power. If we concentrate our thoughts on these facts, we come to see the true meaning of matter in relation to the Spirit. The form, and the life behind the form, become manifest.

No one is so keenly aware of formality, ceremony, and appearances as a Capricorn person. To live wholly in the outer, physical activities is to drown the voice of truth; and this often happens to Capricorn natives. They live in the social and legal framework of life but ignore, or are oblivious of, the truth of Spirit; they love the formal rather than the free expression. Here are the keel and bulwark of the social organism, just as in this sign are also the keel and bulwark of the physical body, that is, the skeleton and the skin.

Capricorn rules the skeleton and all joints, especially the *knees*, endowing the body with stability and flexibility. This framework, a thing of marvelous wisdom, was built through aeons of time by the beings of the Spiritual Hierarchies. Without the skeleton and the wonderful joints of the knees, men would have no stance, no stability, and no power to move and to act. Every time we walk, we walk in virtue of the divine beings and know it not! On the other hand, the bony skeleton is the hardest, most solid, mineralized substance in the body, and it is the symbol of death. Thus we see why too many of the Capricorn natives become ossified, lose resilience, are dead to truth and to the life of the Spirit. They incline to custom and take to politics, business, law, worldly routine, and the established way of life, averse to change. In its higher activity, however, Capricorn makes the true priest and wise administrator; then worldly ambition and the desire to rule others are replaced by a spiritual vision innate in this stabilizing and service sign.

Cowardice, a characteristic of uncontrolled Capricorn

forces, is aptly indicated by the expression "weak-kneed," and this sign's arrogance and egotism are brought out by the saying that they "refuse to bend the knee." The really lofty natures in this, or any other sign, humbly bend the knee and bow to the Father whom this service sign represents.

Individuals strong in Capricorn and Saturn progress in evolutionary development in the earth-school as they learn to take on true humility and reverence. Then are egotism, self-centered ambition, and disbelief overcome. If they are not overcome, however, the more Capricorn natives flourish outwardly, the more are they apt to wither inwardly. It is through the forces of flesh and form, the outer ceremony and show, the material, external values, that they become bankrupt in the sense of the Spirit. As they give the Spirit the right place in their lives and realize its power, then do they become light-bearers and true "doers of the word," for executive, directive, and organizing skill is found in this sign to a high degree. As they rid themselves of the negative force of competition, they become highly cooperative, capable, and self-sacrificing servers. With their admirable courage and sense of responsibility, individually and collectively, one can say of them what Christ said as recorded in St. Matthew 20: 25-28.

Ye know that the princes of the Gentiles exercise dominion over them, and they that are great exercise authority upon them.

But it shall not be so among you; but whosoever will be great among you, let him be your minister;

And whosoever will be chief among you, let him be your servant:

Even as the Son of man came not to be ministered unto, but to minister, and to give his life a ransom for many.

All human beings, be they strong in Capricorn or not, may

apply the maxim given by Rudolf Steiner as an exercise for the month of January, when the Sun is in Capricorn: "*Courage* becomes the power to redeem."

A SATURN SONG

Man suffers most from what he fears;
He dreads the most what ne'er appears;
Thus does he often bear far more
Than God for him did hold in store.

ADDENDUM

It is in keeping with Capricorn that there be presented here a summarizing paragraph dictated by the author at the very close of his earthly life, twenty years after this book was written. Age had taken its toll, the thread of life was tenuous, but he spoke with the simplicity of one standing at the threshold of the spiritual world, surveying the harvest of his life's experiences:

Capricorn, on the higher level, is the sign of the statesman, and on the lower level, of the politician. It is both influential and affluential. It makes for the rich merchant, the company promoter, the very astute businessman, wealthy on the one hand, and, sometimes, stingy on the other. Capricorn is characterized by the grave and the serious. All serious work must be done by the agency of this sign. It calls out earnest endeavors and looks to the elderly person for any assistance needed. A long period of waiting is required by these souls. Capricorn is a culmination of destiny forces one cannot dodge, especially those demanding patience to endure delays. Souls strong in this sign wish to set their house in order and to keep it in order; and they excel in organizing. They are always ready with wise counsel. Age, maturity, and wisdom are representative of the father-principle. The highest business of this sign is that of being about the Father's business.

Aquarius - The Waterman

AQUARIUS, the Waterman, is symbolized by *The Man* who bears a water pitcher out of which there flows the water that revitalizes the Earth, dried up for want of the spirit of truth and the wisdom of love. This water of life rejuvenates humanity, parched for lack of truth and love. As an object of meditation, this symbol is immensely rich, especially in this day of dearth of the Spirit, on the threshold of the Aquarian Age. In this sign of the Son of Man, the matured man becomes more than man—a man Christed with the help of the Angel in man, a man become all things to all men, a "Perfect Man." Awakened response to this Angel-Man sign deals with the individual, yet in the sense of the Christ-universal; hence it fosters friendship and brotherhood. The Waterman is bound up with the human and the humane; it embraces all humanity, and its characteristic feature is its love of human beings, a feeling of cosmic kinship with all mankind.

As man's physical form is the mould that some time must receive the higher birth, the spiritual birth of the Christ, so Aquarius is the matrix sign that receives, synthesizes, and balances the forces of all the other zodiacal signs. The centering powers of the Zodiac are the four fixed signs, each fixed sign having two companion-signs, as it were, one on each side. *Taurus*, the Bull, is the fixed, centering force between Aries and Gemini; *Leo*, the Lion, between Cancer and Virgo; *Scorpio*, the Eagle, between Libra and Sagittarius; *Aquarius*, the Man, between Capricorn and Pisces. The eagle, representative of the bird creation, bears in its whole body specialized forces that correlate with those of the human head. The lion is largely a rhythmic system. The bull is predominantly a digestive organism. Man combines and harmonizes these three elements of the eagle, the lion, and the bull head system, rhythmic system, and metabolic-limb system—in a balanced manner. Thus Aquarius, the *Man*, is the sign of signs, the synthesis of the four fixed signs, which in turn are the synthesis of all of the twelve signs of the Zodiac. It is understandable, therefore, that Aquarius should rule the science of the stars.

In Aquarius, the highly evolved individual matures into a spiritualized being, the "perfect man" of Christ, described by St. Paul in Ephesians 4:13, "Till we all come in the unity of the faith, and of the knowledge of the Son of God, unto a perfect man, unto the measure of the stature of the fulness of Christ." This describes the balanced Aquarian, one who has come of soul age by making independent, though co-ordinated, the soul forces of thinking, feeling, and willing, correlated, respectively, with the head and nerve-system, the rhythmic system, and the metabolic-limb system.

Today, most Aquarians are as yet far from being perfect men. No man takes the lofty love and light of Aquarius, nor becomes a member of that brotherhood of initiates fitted to take the love of heaven and earth and to transmute the hate received from the reactionary and retarded people, nor becomes worthy to serve as a leader and spokesman for mankind, unless he has met, and is moved by, his higher self, the Christ-Angel within, called by St. Paul "the Lord from heaven." Highly evolved souls, responding to the mighty mood of Aquarius, become conscious of the Spirit in the Earth, the Cosmic Christ, as well as conscious of the guiding eternal being, the spiritual self within. These awakened ones become conscious cooperators with the Christ in the evolution of the cosmos. The Aquarian Age, the age of altruism and brotherhood—when the Sun by precession of the equinox will be in Aquarius for 2160 years—will not properly prevail until the Sixth Post-Atlantean Civilization, which will

---

[1] In approximately five hundred years, the vernal equinox will be in Aquarius. Our present Fifth Post-Atlantean Civilization will continue into the fourth millennium. Meanwhile, two other factors should be considered, which have an influence similar to that of Aquarius. One is the transition at the turn of the last century, from the Dark or Iron Age, which had lasted for five thousand years, to the *Age of Light*. The other factor is the advent of the *New Age of MICHAEL*, which began in 1879 and will last for about three to four hundred years.

Seven Archangels—the Six Planetary Intelligences and the Sun Intelligence, Michael—in regularity of rotation serve as regents, directing and guiding the evolution of mankind by determining the fundamental character of successive minor ages. Gabriel, the Moon Intelligence, introduced during his regency, which came to an end in 1879, the impulses that entered strongly into the physical bodily nature of man and centered man's attention on physical heredity, natural science, and nationalism. In contrast to

follow our present one. For brotherhood to blossom then, preparation must be made now.[1] The preparers are those awakened ones who respond to the spiritual call of this Angel-Man sign, as did John the Baptist, the preparer for the Christ.

In John the Baptist there lived an Angel who had to go before to announce the approach of the Christ-Ego that would live in Jesus of Nazareth as *the* Lord from heaven. John the Baptist, who baptized Jesus in the Jordan, was able to be the bearer of this Angel because he had taken his initiation in the sign Aquarius, the sign of the Angel or the perfectly balanced Man. In virtue of John's baptism with water, there was brought about a loosening of the etheric body from the physical body during the immersion. At that moment, the baptized were made incisively aware of the significance of the impending Mystery of Golgotha, the great world-historic Event and Deed of Christ.

He who receives a solar initiation in the Waterman acquires a special power of effecting in human souls a higher birth, a changed consciousness, so that the soul forces of thinking, feeling, and willing become subject to the higher

---

the forces of Gabriel, those of Michael, the *Sun* Intelligence, work intensely into the spiritual being of man, then into his soul nature, and finally into his bodily nature. The Michael impulse manifests as *spiritual intelligence, cosmopolitanism,* and *cosmic Christianity.* It is Michael's task to conquer the Ahrimanic Dragon of materialism and to regain control over Cosmic Intelligence, which in earlier ages was instinctive, then became earthly and individualized in man. With the aid of Michael—now the Countenance of the Christ, as formerly he was the Countenance of Jehovah—man will be able to spiritualize his intelligence and the conditions of life that immerse him so deeply in matter. Present impulses, bearing an all-embracing human character that is cosmopolitan and spiritual, arise from the Michael forces as well as from those of the Waterman. Although the flowering of the Aquarian Age is still a long way off, a few forerunners are already sowing the seeds that must be planted now if their fruit— brotherhood—is to ripen in the future.   B.J.

Ego, the Lord from heaven. The developed soul—the Son of Man—meets and merges with the Son of God, the Spirit principles from above, in a divine marriage.

Through baptism with water, John the Baptist, the Waterman, brought to birth in the baptized the needed light of self-knowledge. The one essential urgently needed today is self-knowledge that at the same time is world-knowledge. This true knowledge flows from the fount of the cosmic Christ-ethers by way of the Uranian sign of the Son of Man, Aquarius, for it is in this sign that the individual, soul-matured and Christ-conscious, can say, "I *know* that my Redeemer liveth."

The purpose of Aquarius is fittingly pictured by the symbol of the man pouring water out of an urn upon the earth. This is no ordinary water, but the new Christ-etheric, vivifying, spiritual force. Aquarius has specific rule over the ethers. Increasingly will man's vision be opened to the etheric world. Aquarius might thus be designated "The Etheric Man," although in the Moon Period, the preceding embodiment of the Earth, it was literally correct to call this sign "The Waterman." Prior to this, man-in-the-making had a body consisting only of warmth and air, brought over from still earlier times, the Sun Period and the Saturn Period. In the Moon Period, there was added the fluid element, esoterically known as "water" and, along with this, the astral body, which gave consciousness to man. The influence that brought this about came from the region of the Zodiac which we designate as the Waterman, Aquarius.

It was during the Moon Period that the Hierarchy of the Angels were at their human stage. Now, during our Earth Period, they are a stage higher, being one remove above man, just as the animals are one remove below man. The Angels live in the etheric as we do in the physical. The Christ who appeared in physical form in Palestine nearly two millenia ago in the man, Jesus of Nazareth, may be seen, from our century onward, in an etheric body, visible to those who have raised their consciousness to the etheric. Never again will he appear in an earthly, physical body. Because Aquarius is correlated with the Hierarchy of the Angels, with the Etheric Christ, and with the Angel in man, and furthermore because the fluid-organism in man is esoterically associated with the etheric body, we may rightly designate the Waterman as the Etheric Man.

Intense sensitivity is a pronounced trait of Aquarius, a sensitivity that is mental, psychic, and spiritual. It is likely to hurt or incommode those lacking in true self-knowledge or wisdom. In highly evolved Aquarians, well aware of the wisdom of love and truth of whom Plato still shines forth with rich radiance, along with his last-century expositor, John Ruskin—the light of the solar *Logos* is revealed. Neither man individually, nor mankind as a whole, comes of age in the sense of Christ-soul, until man reaches into the forces of Aquarius and expresses them positively. When this occurs, both man and mankind may be designated as *thinkers* and *knowers of truth*. Aquarius, then, may be set down as the sign representing man become matured in Christ, in virtue of whom he bears a share of the burden of the planet and ever seeks to refresh and restore the parched earthly souls with his spiritual water.

In this fixed air sign, Aquarius, thought power is fixed or concentrated until thinking becomes incandescent or alive in an etheric sense. In connection with this living thinking, we see a reference to the true Aquarian quality of livingness in the words of the Christ, "Because I live, ye shall live also." Aquarius is the sign of the Man, as its symbol indicates, and the word "man" is derived, as some say, from the Sanskrit *manu*, which means "to think." Through making thinking firm and alive in Aquarius, life at last becomes *life* in the sense of the Christ-Spirit, the higher Ego, the true "I." For this reason, John the Baptist says with truth, "He [the Christ-

Ego] must increase, and I [the lower Ego] must decrease."

The hieroglyphic symbol of Aquarius, consisting of two wave-like lines, reveals much more than can mere words to those in whom the mood of meditation is innate. Here the intellect is helpless, but meditation is fruitful. In the cyclic evolution of the Ego through all the signs of the Zodiac in successive earthly lives, Aquarius is the sign where the circle is left behind for the spiralling ascent in mental, psychic, and spiritual progress. In this sign is the needed fixed-air quality and the dual forces of polarity, symbolically expressed by the two wavy lines, indicating the cosmic ethers in constant movement, equalizing and harmonizing the lower earthly Ego and the higher "I." The first symbolizes "the first man Adam made a living soul," whereas the second indicates "the last Adam made a quickening spirit." The first man—the lower Ego and astral man caught up in the senses —"is of the earth, earthy: the second man is the Lord from heaven" (I Corinthians 15: 45, 47). Thus the symbol of Aquarius shows the interplay between the depths and the heights; it conceals the mystery of Man and of the Christ, the mystery of human life and destiny.

In every sign of the Zodiac there are souls that respond to the negative influences, which are the reverse of the awakened response. In Aquarius are many who have not yet been "made a quickening spirit." Among them are swollen egotists, hidebound and pridebound. The higher birth does not take place until the man reverses and raises his rhythm, correcting ill destiny and bringing the lower Ego into a growing power of fine self-control through self-knowledge. All too often, Aquarians display a static quality, an element of inertia, indicating that the soul's awakening has not yet taken place; their promises remain unfulfilled, and they fail to put into practice the truth they readily sense, for instance, the spiritual equality of all men. Because of their laziness, their splendid faculties go to seed. Some of them advocate impractical, utopian ideas, and many are still spiritually asleep. Although the majority of individuals as well as all nations still seek their own interests, the influence of this humanitarian sign is nevertheless making itself felt among the ranks of the people. Acts of altruism, group awareness, and free activity are evident everywhere.

The idealism of God is the inner motive power of advanced Aquarians. They best express their ideals and make them a reality in terms of social life, for a love of human souls is the strongest quality of this sign of humanity. They feel not only the pulse of the people en masse, but the soul of each individual touched or passed; hence arises the living power of genuine friendship and true brotherhood.

Emerson has rightly said, "A friend may well be reckoned the masterpiece of nature." The fifteenth chapter of the Gospel of St. John also makes plain the value of friendship, for there the Christ says, "Greater love hath no man than this, that a man lay down his life for his friends. Ye are my friends, if ye do whatsoever I command you. Henceforth I call you not servants; for the servant knoweth not what his Lord doeth; but I have called you friends" (St. John 15: 13-15). We may add by way of explanation, "The servant [the lower man or personality] knoweth not what his lord [the higher Ego, his Angel] doeth." Man ceases to be in the "servant" class and to be antisocial, once the forces of Christ friendship are found in Aquarius through the spirit of love and truth; and this is the truth that makes man free, for there is no other true freedom. No soul can work its way to this freedom of Christ or be born of the light, until it realizes spiritual intelligence and intelligent love.

He who would seek an understanding of Aquarius to grasp its esoteric significance must meditate much and often upon this fifteenth chapter of St. John's Gospel. It shows what hatred the awakened or Christed Aquarian must take from the world and then transmute, to help the world in its evolution. The Lord says, "If the world hate you, ye know that it hated me before it hated you. If ye were of the world, the world would love its own; but because ye are not of the world, but I have chosen you out of the world, therefore the world hateth you. . . . But this cometh to pass, that the word might be fulfilled that is written in their law, They hated me without a cause" (St. John 15: 18, 19, 25).

No man could murder another if he were aware of and alive to the Spirit of Christ; certainly, no evolved Aquarian could, for his etheric sensitivity relates his individual etheric body with the etheric body of the Earth. This means, the evolved Aquarian is aware of the Etheric Christ who envelops our planet and transforms it and humanity, so that eventually the Earth may re-unite with the Sun. The Christ-born and etheric-conscious Aquarian experiences all humanity in himself. He knows nothing of aliens or foreigners; he actually experiences the truth expressed in the motto of the Great Seal of the United States, "*E pluribus unum*" (out of many, one; or, many in one), which portrays the gift of God into which humanity will come as ever more men open themselves to receive the Christ-Spirit. Since the United States of America—with the Moon in Aquarius and Uranus ascending—is an Aquarian-Uranian country, whose inhabitants are from all races and nations, we find here the early evidences of this spirit.

To Aquarians, no one is a stranger or an alien, not even the person who lacks love entirely, or who loves himself solely, or who isolates himself by race or narrow-minded nationalism. They know that, basically, all human beings are related, despite marked differences in their evolutionary status. Clannish or tribal ideas are anathema to Aquarians; thus they view racial leaders as atavistic, anti-Christ agents, seeking to separate and segregate, to delay if not to thwart, the Christ-freeing, individualizing evolution of millions of Egos. In Aquarius, the sign of the Son of Man, combining the forces of the whole Zodiac, all inequalities of race, color, nationality, creed, or caste disappear, and the glory of God becomes ascendant and manifest in men, cleansed and purified in their soul-body, which confers the gift of white raiment and a consciousness connecting them with the Christ. The advanced Aquarian seeks to have human beings become not only citizens of the world but, what is more, citizens of the cosmos.

In Aquarius, the various influences making up the sum of the Zodiac converge and constitute the power of the Christ-impulse. In this sign is the irradiating core which is the manifesting Son, the Christ-whole. Only if one knows the whole—all the signs of the Zodiac—can one truly know the parts that form the whole. In Aquarius, such knowledge makes man a knower of the truth in proportion to his purity. Thus, evolved Aquarians recognize no race or citizenship, essentially, save that of Christ citizenship. In their eyes, all inequalities of race or religion are effaced by the beautiful unity in diversity, that coat of many colors, which is the glory of God manifesting as men become mature and perfected through the transformation of their soul into the Son of Man, meet to receive the Son of God.

Spiritual intelligence in the sign of the Angel in Man, Aquarius, leads to intelligent love and friendship. It gives the urge to make friendship operative—an urge which everyone's own Guardian Angel impresses every night upon the astral body during dreamless sleep.[2] In our waking hours, it is our vital task to make friendship a fact, spreading creative friendship wherever we go, and recognizing the hidden divinity in every human being.

[2] Rudolf Steiner, *The Work of the Angels in Man's Astral Body* (London: Anthroposophical Publishing Company, 1960).

My Angel comes in sleep each night
To bathe my soul with heav'nly light,
And to imprint upon my heart
The need, on waking, to impart
Real friendship to each soul I meet,
And the divine in each to greet.

B.J.

The pictures imprinted on the astral body by the Angel are to bring man to the realization that in the future no one will find peace in the enjoyment of good fortune while those about him are unhappy or in distress. The Angel gives the impulse to unite the human race in perfect brotherhood —the ideal of this Angel-Man sign that rules universal humanity.

Thus, the most telling trait of Aquarius is a flair for friendship; its essence is altruism, the quality of the Angel in man. Angels outstream love that seeks no return, and they love without ceasing. Through their love for humanity, Aquarians, such as the reformers, knowers, and friends of men, John Ruskin, Charles Dickens, and Abraham Lincoln, become monumental as they revitalize the idea of Christ-truth and the wisdom of love, and practice the friendship of all mankind through spiritual understanding.

Evolved Aquarians, having gained Christ-wisdom, achieve self-knowledge and voluntarily elect to cooperate for the common weal. Under the impulse of the Water-bearer, man does not surrender his unique selfhood to any communistic regime, but offers his gift of God for the use of all, as a service valuable to the entire cosmos. Man must first be properly individualized in Christ before a true collective state or world is possible. All socialistic and communistic experiments at this time will fail, as they deserve to do. Aquarius is the sign of free air. No true Aquarian could conceive or carry the idea of any compulsory labor service, or any subordination or subjugation to the demands of a soulless system, or to the will of some individual. The Christ does not coerce; nor would any soul ripened and evolved in this sign of the Son of Man.

Aquarius is the opposite of the royal and kingly sign Leo, in that it fosters democracy. In Aquarius, we may attain to genuine democracy and, at the same time, to the dignity of man; this will be the more apparent the more men will take in and work with the wisdom of love and the spirit of truth. The creative force of friendship draws together all those of a common mind and purpose. Aquarius makes active the healing bond of genuine brotherhood, that fraternity based not on blood ties but on a kinship of souls alive with intelligent love and spiritual intelligence. Advanced Aquarians are the pacemakers and peacemakers for the spirit of truth, and they are able to provide continual inspiration to their co-workers, associates, and friends who become inert or depressed.

In Aquarius, the ideals of friendship and a successful social system must become concrete fact in operation. More than any other sign of the Zodiac, Aquarius strives to make ideals become real, practical, working facts of life. However, since mankind clings with tenacity to the outmoded, save for machines, clothes, et cetera, Aquarian ideas meet with opposition, as have many inventions also met with intense hostility. When even some mechanical inventions meet with such opposition, it is easy to see why mankind only slowly entertains the truth of repeated earth lives—reincarnation —and the power of man's self-made destiny or karma. But this shows the foil of Luciferic and Ahrimanic powers set against new truth and the Christ-life power in man and Earth. The advanced Aquarian, aware of and responsive to the Christ-etheric world, can never change his conviction of truth or move from his fixed purpose.

The air signs represent man's power to think; the quality

of ideation lies within the air signs. The gift that distinquishes man and raises him above the animal is the power of thought and speech. Not one of the air signs—the Twins, the Scales, and the Man—is symbolized by an animal; the airy element is free of and separate from the earth. Therefore, we see that individuals born under or in air signs, especially those born in Aquarius—the sign of the Son of Man, or the *Man*, he who is the thinker—are least of all influenced by the merely earthy element. In Libra and Aquarius, and to a lesser degree in Gemini, we see a transcendence of earthly logic, the intuition providing a firsthand touch with the realm of truth, the archetypal realm of ideas. Yet, the faith of Aquarius must be rooted and grounded in knowledge; the spirit-lighted reason must be able to solve the riddle of life and death in such a way as to satisfy both the mind and the innate religious sense.

As a sign of fixed air, Aquarius dislikes indecision and disloyalty. The Aquarian has convictions of truth by which he abides with rocklike firmness and according to which he acts, regardless of the world's disapproval. As a Christ-etheric sensitive, he knows that the suggestions he receives are from a realm more rarefied than that of the earth. He obeys such touches with truth, and when his soul is well matured and expresses wisdom, such a Water-bearer can pour from his pitcher into human hearts, or into the parched environment of this time of spiritual inanition, the veritable water of Christ-life.

This creative, cosmic sign is ruled by the awakener, Uranus, which means "heaven." It orbits beyond Saturn, which is the outermost planet arising within our solar system. Uranus, Neptune, and Pluto had a different origin; hence they are referred to as transcendental planets. The retrograding moons of Uranus put it into a different category from the planets inside its orbit. The axis of Uranus is almost at right angles with the axis of the Earth. It is not surprising, there-

fore, that Uranus tends to upset convention and to break up
everything rigid and standardized. It makes non-conform-
ists and reformers. It brings completely new orientation. To
those who can respond, the orientation is cosmic in scope.
The influence of Uranus is lightning-like, always acting with
surprising suddenness and speed, and producing unexpected
events.

Sometimes Saturn is assigned as co-ruler of Aquarius. The
importance of Saturn and Uranus depends on one's stage
in evolution. Weak souls that have not learned the lessons
of the other signs—especially those of Capricorn, which is
ruled by Saturn—may still need the pedagogy of Saturn and
make little response to Uranus. In the course of time, all
human beings will awaken and mature to proper attunement
to Uranus. At present, undisciplined Egos react unfavorably,
unpredictably, and erratically to its influence. The more
mature the individual, the more does he manifest the cosmic,
liberalizing, progressive, and cohering influences of Uranus,
the planet whose name means heaven.

Persons born with the Sun in Aquarius, who have attained
to maturity in their spiritual life, ever seek the life principle,
because Uranus stands for the life-producing causes behind
all things, whereas Saturn, also called Chronos, being the
Guardian of Time, gives the earthly conquest. This planet of
Time, Chronos, seems a strange companion of the Christ-
etheric planet of lightning-like, shockingly sudden, unex-
pected effects, Uranus. The lower qualities that manifest in
the unevolved Aquarians do so because these souls have not
made peace with Saturn, the producer of patience through
lives of helpful hindrance, and because they have not re-
solved in themselves the contradiction caused by these two
contrasting planets, Saturn and Uranus—Time and that
Power beyond Time. Through Uranus, time and the earth-
forces may become invested by the Spirit.

Undeveloped Aquarians choose to live in the personality,

perverting the individuality rather than raising it. These immature, unripened souls sacrifice principle for lustful, egotistical, earthly power and personal aggrandizement. In the negative souls in this sign we see the Uranian influence expressing itself as downright anarchy, and venting itself in a fiery and erratic temper. They show extreme independence and a volcanic, seething unrest and perversity. In some souls the fumes of anger are held in silence, producing a rage far worse than one that is openly released.

It should be noted that periodic states of silence, seemingly strange, are characteristic of Aquarians. In fact, one of the marked traits of this sign is the need and will to be quiet and concentrated, to be utterly alone at times, and to resent any interfering annoyance from others. The maxim given by Rudolf Steiner as an exercise for the month of February, "*Reticence* becomes meditative power," is therapeutic for Aquarians. In silence is their strength.

The truly mature and evolved Aquarians possess all the practical and persevering qualities of the preceding Saturnine sign, Capricorn, yet with the added Uranian power of instant intuition, lofty ideals, and a natural ability and ease in reading character. They are refined, artistic, intelligent, faithful, and humane. Inwardly tranquil, very quiet, but extremely intense, strong, forceful, incandescent souls, they impress one with their innate, etheric, psychic power and marked mentality, combined with a disposition delightfully open and naïve. The joyousness of this angelic sign sometimes gives an air of apparent frivolity, and this tends to mislead others as to the true worth of Aquarians. Being hypersensitive and high-strung, they act with swift speed. Although they are able to resist fatigue, they are apt to injure their health if they apply themselves incessantly to some particular prolonged work. Exposure, likewise, may be a cause for ill health, for Aquarius rules the *sense of warmth*, making Aquarians particularly sensitive to atmospheric changes and fluctuations in temperature. There is a tendency to poor circulation and cold feet. The ankles are the gift of Aquarius to the marvelous physical body of man.

Aquarians have a marked psychic power and an intuitive mind, the effect of the Christ-etheric element, making them as powerful and intense as the natives of Scorpio, yet with a quality and impression far different from that of Scorpio, for in Aquarius there is an airy-etheric-mental something which ever eludes or transcends the understanding of even those souls with fine insight into human character. Evolved Water-bearers who are idealists and inventors possess a force that masters and rises above matter and transcends time, enabling them to think and to be far ahead of the times in which they live. When we survey the innovations and inventions that mankind owes to Aquarians such as Ruskin, Dickens, Lincoln, and Edison, we see the influence of Uranus, the planet of heaven that awakens humanity and unifies the various members of man, to make him whole.

The effect of this sign of the Son of Man is well seen in some of its best representatives. In the last century, the contemporary humanitarians, Charles Dickens and John Ruskin, each in his own unique manner, disclosed a vast understanding of humanity and possessed the literary gift of this sign. Certainly they were reformers and pointed to the need for the raising and regeneration of the race. Ruskin declared the urgent need for scientific human kindness and sought expression for active spiritual intelligence in England during the middle of the last century. How was he able to foretell the woe and sorrow that England was bringing down on her head through intellectualism? Why was his forte—friendship —so active with creative Christ-force? Because he was one of God's messengers and prophets using an Aquarian human garment. He had Aquarius rising, with the Sun and Jupiter therein. The element of universal friendship and brotherhood inheres in this Angel-Man sign, and this becomes as though radioactive in the highly evolved, bestowing on them the art and genius of bringing men together and making them a power for peace. Theirs is the wisdom of love animating the soul to express the divine.

How remarkable the active clairvoyant thought of Charles Dickens and his gift of setting down in extreme caricature the evil conditions in England in the last century! He exposed man's inhumanity, lusts, and lies; he came, as did the other great Uranians, in the role of a reformer, to do away with the outmoded and to bud the new. His work, like that of all the others animated by the same power, declares that special spontaneity which gives electrical, effective action through the vast force of the mighty Uranus.

In America, we see an outstanding Aquarian in Abraham Lincoln. He strove to hold together two hostile factions, the North and the South, at a time of crisis, when the forces of schism were at work. He brought unification to the nation as well as emancipation of a race from slavery, leading to eventual equality before the law. Here we see the fusion-force of friendship, "With malice toward none; with charity for all." He was slain and sacrificed for his great work, as often happens when greatness is not recognized by the ignorant, or is thwarted by the conservative, or eliminated by the envious.

Emanuel Swedenborg, the great scientist, who was born in Stockholm in 1688 and died in London in 1772, had his Aquarian Sun in the degree of "Providence." In 1744, in his fifty-sixth year, he became aware of the spiritual world, gaining etheric clairvoyant vision in virtue of his vast love for knowledge resulting from preparatory work done in preceding lives. Thus, in the last third of his life, he abandoned his scientific pursuits, to use his gracious gift of clairvoyance, with all his energy and industry, in the investigation of the facts and laws of the spiritual world.

Charles Darwin was another Aquarian who was a scientist. He discovered the principle of the evolution of physical forms, but not the spiritual life principle that evolves the forms to ever greater and finer perfection.

He who has ears to hear can detect the love of God and the world of Spirit in the music of Mozart, for his music is simply an up-welling, outflowing force of the divine archetypal heavenly world whose spiritual harmonies he transposed into air-borne earthly sound. Here was an Aquarian angel and a lover of men portraying the sweetness of that love in divine tones. Franz Schubert was another Aquarian who poured forth his soul in his lovely songs and symphonies.

In Aquarius, the sign which synthesizes all the signs of the Zodiac, there comes at last into being the Perfect Man. Through his evolutionary schooling, a mature, evolved Aquarian has at his disposal consummate faculty and facility in body, soul, and spirit. Through such Aquarian force, foremost and always there arises an impulse toward the new, the unexpected, and unique. Aquarius and Uranus are incessantly alive with invention and innovation, and to Aquarian souls is given the building, budding process, bringing renewal to man and planet. This sign symbolizes the Son of Man who pours out living, spiritual water, which gives ongoing, forward-flowing, and upward-spiralling motion. Thus the Waterman serves the evolutionary process in a most positive way.

Aquarius and its ruler, Uranus, stand for and bring "all things new," so that "old things are passed away." Here are the sign and the planet of new outlook and new ideas, beyond the staid and the standardized. They bring the unusual and unique, suddenly, and with unexpected surprise effects. What Aries initiates, Aquarius and Uranus bring to manifestation. To the new that arises in Aries, they give direction, determining the future. Aquarians are innovators and reformers. They seek the etheric essence of all things and, beyond that, the soul-spiritual. The wisdom and beauty they experience they attempt to introduce into a world that is often hostile. We have only to glance at the men who dissolve the past and create the new, whether they be our contemporaries or lived in past ages, to see the forces of this sign of the Son of Man.

One of the greatest and most influential, yet also one of the most misunderstood and most persecuted, Aquarian apostles of freedom and democracy, in both the Old World and the New, was "the man without a country," Thomas Paine. It was he who conceived the idea of the United States of America and who, together with Thomas Jefferson, had much to do in framing the Declaration of Independence. His electrifying writings in the days of the Revolution filled soldiers and civilians with renewed enthusiasm and aroused instantaneous action, so that it was said, "America owes as much to the pen of Paine as to the sword of Washington." His words in *The Crisis* became the battle cry of the new republic:

> These are the times which try men's souls. . . . Tyranny, like hell, is not easily conquered. The harder the conflict the more glorious the victory. That which is won too cheaply is esteemed too lightly. Heaven knows how to put the proper price upon its goods and it would be strange indeed if so celestial an article as freedom be not highly rated. Up! Lay shoulders to the wheel! Show faith by work, that God may bless you. 'Tis the business of little minds to shrink. He whose conscience is firm pursues principles unto death.

How truly Aquarian and Uranian!

Why was Charles Lindbergh the cosmic election to make the first solo flight across the Atlantic to Paris? Or, why was it Douglas Corrigan, of the same Sun sign, who repeated the solo flight, landing in Ireland instead of France? They possessed the impulse for innovation. In these souls there lived the Aquarian element of the new which gave such splendid performance in the air, for this sign rules the ethers and the air.

In the field of inventions, we may note Thomas A. Edison, an Aquarian etheric sensitive. His electrical inventions were numerous, but the achievement that he cherished most was his invention of the phonograph, an instrument connected with sound. Edison's sensitivity to the ethers gave him access to the region of archetypes, the realm of ideas and truth, hence his inventiveness and his urge to produce the new, which has transformed our civilization.

Electricity is light that disintegrated in matter. This sub-material force has revolutionized the world in a very short time, and with this innovation has come the mass of other inventions, all of which are the result of the Sun, by precession of the equinox, coming into an orb of influence with Aquarius.

The innovations of the greatest of musical colorists, the creator of a new mode in music, Richard Wagner, wrought changes that affected the whole musical world. Upon his head descended bitter hate, because he brought new musical ideas, introduced the New Age Christ, and told of this New Day in his music dramas, especially in his last and greatest work, the consecrational "Parsifal." With his Moon joined to the Part of Fortune and the Moon's South Node in Aquarius, and Mars in the same sign, Wagner strove more than all others to unify art, science, and religion—the Aquarian ideal. He died disappointed because people were not yet sufficiently advanced to comprehend this expression of the whole in Aquarian manner.

Aquarius, as the archetypal-force sign, is seen in its universal scope as it acts and expresses itself through men such as those just mentioned. In the Water-bearer, as in no other sign of the Zodiac, we see the union of art, science, and religion and, truly, these three are one, just as God is ever Three in One. The beauty of God's unity in diversity is shown in the universality and comprehensiveness contained in Aquarius, the coat-of-many-colors sign.

The ancient prophets who taught humanity had as their essential make-up this living, spiritual water, the power to light the way and weld mankind through right leadership. The prophet whose initiation was that of the Waterman is the mighty John the Baptist. Under the influence of Aquarius, he tells humanity that something new is entering into man and into the Earth, and that the Lord of all, who makes men free and complete, the Christ, is at hand. John's message called upon people to change their ways. This man was much more than man, as we, who know the living water he poured, can see, for here is the great leader and prophet of the past returned to announce the New Day and Way of the Christ, the very fulfillment of friendship spoken of in the Gospel of St. John 15: 13, 14, "Greater love hath no man than this, that a man lay down his life for his friends. Ye are my friends if ye do whatsover I [the Christ-Ego] command you." This love we see sadly lacking in our own blood-stained century given over to materialism. But this is a passing, temporary phase in evolution, though a necessary one for the development of the earthly Ego, the brain-bound man.

The great men to whom reference has been made portray the progressiveness and the intense humanity that live in the souls of all true Water-bearers. It is a divine compassion that expresses truth through the wisdom of love, which is true philosophy—literally, the love of wisdom. Advanced Aquarians naturally carry this force, which combines the whole range of zodiacal powers, thus making them friends and knowers of men.

In Aquarius, there is instant intuition and the capacity to

read human character with electrical-etheric Uranian effect. If the power of radiance shines through Leo, then the element of etheric incandescence provides the light of Aquarius. With this true insight into souls, the outer veneer of society is swiftly dismissed and the man is seen in his actual worth. Thus the Aquarian beholds the seeming orphan, humanity, for mankind remains orphaned in a very true sense so long as it refuses to take in the Christ-light power and allow love to irradiate the soul. This power to perceive the real man—seeing at the same time the personality yet bypassing it and envisioning the soul of man in its true character—leaves the Aquarian often mentally and psychically isolated. Friendship cannot become a living reality on Earth so long as people remain antisocial, and this is the reason for strife, warfare, and lack of understanding and friendship among nations and races.

Evolution is not only cyclic but spiralling in its periodicity; so it is essential to realize and to bear in mind that the point on the circle of the Zodiac where the spiral starts which lifts man in soul-ascent and mental expansion, is here in this sign, Aquarius, which at the same time provides stability. No man is truly sustained or secure as a law unto himself, certainly not one possessed of the key to heaven admitting him to the light of the Logos, until he vitalizes in himself the Aquarian fixed force of divine stability. Instability results from living solely in the temporal personality; stability is derived from the higher Christ-self, the eternal entity of God. No man is conscious of his higher self until his purity has led him along the way of truth to freedom. In Aquarius there occurs in cyclic fashion that revolution which produces a contingent revelation, the new "take-off" on a new spiral. As in the life of an individual, so in the life of our planet, there comes now a new "take-off" and a new order of things for the world, as by precession of the equinox we are approaching the Aquarian Age. In spite of hatred, fear, and reaction, the world and humanity are moving into a new field of force, the force of the humane sign of friendship and truth, the Water-bearer.

Why is the essence of this sign love itself? Why does it take in all mankind? What makes evolved, matured Aquarians humanitarians, and why do they constantly go out in service to others? What makes them mouthpieces for humanity, and why are they exponents of wise compassion? What is the reason for their belief in, and expression of, the efficacy of intelligent love? Why do they insist on making ideals real now, and not in some distant day far remote? Why are they bearers of "good tidings of great joy to all people"? Why do they preach the gospel of the New Age of Christ, friendship, and brotherhood, and so heal the sick? And why do they teach the truth which man cannot receive until he turns away from the lunar law and accepts the grace and truth of the Christ Sun-Son? The mystery behind, and the answers to, all these questions are implicit in the symbol of this sign, for Aquarius holds the mystery of human destiny, which is inseparable from the Mystery of Golgotha. In this zodiacal sign, man becomes connected with and cognizant of the Christ in himself and in the Earth; man becomes a Christ-man and knows his own Angel; he becomes the "Perfect Man."

Souls who walk in the light of Aquarius cease to be separative and disruptive, and they learn to realize the unifying element which is the Christ-Spirit. He whose evolution ascends to a lofty spiral in Aquarius never seeks for himself but is ever joyously outgoing in true love for others. The forte of Aquarius is friendship, and its keyword is "*I know.*" Friendship implies forces that unify, and in union lies love. Those who live in the love of truth have the wisdom to know. True, living thinking makes the knower. All those highly evolved souls in this sign who are well seasoned by repeated lives well spent in all the signs of the Zodiac know the truth through their conscious connection with Christ. The capacity to know and to manifest friendship, imparted by this sign, gains significance if we remember that this is the sign that rules the ethers, and it is the ether of Christ's body that permeates and envelops the entire Earth.

Aquarius indicates the divine hermaphrodite, combining the male and the female principles inherent in every human Christ-Ego, portrayed in the two wavy lines representing this zodiacal sign. Here we see the forces of the Moon and the Sun, the elements of water and Spirit. Christ Jesus, speaking to Nicodemus, an initiate of the lower degrees, said, "Ye must be born again, ye must be born of water and of the Spirit, if ye would enter into the kingdom of God." This spiritual birth is the sacrament that brings completion to man.

Aquarius stands also for the woman clothed with the Sun, and the Moon under her feet, and upon her head a crown of twelve stars. These twelve stars are the twelve signs of the Zodiac, all of which are so many initiations that come to final expression in this sign, Aquarius. The Moon is the feminine principle, the lower, lunar Ego with imaginative faculty and form-giving power, the brain-bound, earthly man, which we designate as the separative personality. This Ego raises and refines itself to the stage of a Son of Man. The Sun is the higher Ego, the spiritual man or Son of God, who reaches down to the rising Son of Man. Their union is a heavenly marriage taking place in the earthly body, producing the perfected man.

The whole of the Zodiac is expressed in Aquarius, and this is why this sign rules the stellar wisdom and why all advanced souls in Aquarius strive to express life—art, religion, and science—in the sense of a whole and thus as a unity. Aquarius has been called the captain of the host, for it comprehends all the forces of the Zodiac in their sum and substance. In the sign of the Son of Man, man becomes more than man—a "perfect man" who has learned the lessons of all signs of the Zodiac. He who expresses the wisdom of love and truth is consciously or unconsciously clothed with the Christ-etheric forces and thus waters the world of humanity with an intelligent love and is spiritually active.

Always does active Aquarian power give the ability to destroy the old, separative, crystallizing influences in man and planet, releasing forces to produce the new thing, idea, teaching, or process. It parts from the past to fashion the future while the present yet lives. In this meeting place of past, present, and future, there lies concealed the mystery of the eternal now. It is these Aquarian souls, who in some way have touched eternity, who have the power to woo and weld men into a true and lasting unity of peace maintained by the positive, creative, corrective action of the wisdom of love. No true union of mankind in the bonds of peace will be realized till this friendship of Aquarius provides the all-permeating, unifying element.

The fourth chapter of St. John's Gospel describes the meeting of Christ Jesus with the woman of Samaria at the well. He meets her freely, without slight or snobbery, making her wonder why he, a Jew, was conversing with her, a Samaritan woman. Jesus then says to her, "If thou knewest the gift of God, and who it is that saith to thee, Give me to drink, thou wouldst have asked of him, and he would have given thee living water. The woman saith unto him, Sir, thou hast nothing to draw with, and the well is deep: from whence then hast thou that living water? Art thou greater than our father Jacob, who gave us the well?" (The lunar law, symbol of involution and Jehovah). The Christ answered her, saying, "Whosoever drinketh of the water that I shall give him shall never thirst; but the water that I shall give him shall be in him a well of water springing up into everlasting life." Who would not work for this eternal essence of God, this spiritual life of Christ, whose flow wells up, in, and through the solar system, yet whose fountain force is in the water of Aquarius. To attain to height and worth in Aquarius, we must look upon Christ as the living water.

To produce the new on Earth and in man requires the creative budding and building forces of this sign of the Angel-Man, the Son of Man, Aquarius, with the spiritually electrical power ray of Uranus. Whatever the wisdom or work needed to bring true advancement in art, religion, or science, the force that brings the new into manifestation flows into the world from the creative element inherent in the Water-man, the sign of the living water of the Spirit. This sign allows the supra-personality to express itself through the earthly personality; thus the Aquarian can say, "Not I, but Christ liveth in me." But only the spiritually awakened Aquarian is moving upward on the Christ-path. Many Aquarians on the lower rungs of evolution remain static because of the negation, and sometimes, the laziness, which the fixed signs produce.

Although all air signs give mental activity, with little desire for the earthly, Aquarius is the sign that focalizes and fixes ideas and images, so that they become real and concrete. In this sign, the subjective mental image, the thought, develops into objective, concrete reality, and so Aquarians transmute the ideal into the real, making the thought take form in the realm of the physical. Gemini is omnivorous in seeking knowledge and wisdom, and it sets in motion a mental action that irradiates thought as from a point to all parts of the periphery. Libra perceives the whole, then sorts, sifts, and finally seizes upon the real in thought. In Aquarius, however, that which is true becomes the grist for the mental mill. In this sign, thought actually becomes anchored, arrested by the pure force of the will.

No man can become free until he knows the truth, and this freedom may be gained in this sign of the Son of Man, because man may raise himself as a qualified Christ-soul up to the light of the realm where truth abides. In the Gospel of St. John 16: 12-14, Christ says,

> I have many things to say unto you, but ye cannot bear them now. Howbeit when he, the Spirit of truth, is come, he will guide you into all truth: for he shall not speak of himself, but whatsoever he shall hear, that shall he speak, and he will show you things to come. He shall glorify me: for he shall receive of mine, and show it unto you.

Indications of the Aquarian spiritual water are to be found in the Gospels and throughout the rest of the New Testament in statements pointing to the New Age, telling of a humanity reborn and made free through a knowledge of the truth. The forces of the future flow from Aquarius, revealing "things to come," in the true, Uranian, innovating, originating manner, and "turning the world upside down." The Aquarians named in this chapter were men whose lifework shaped events or brought out new concepts of teachings that helped to dissolve the past and to usher in the new. From Aquarius flows that creative life urge which is the Christ-impulse itself.

When man gains liberation from his brain and his senses, he knows the truth and "things to come." At present, man sees objects such as tables, chairs, houses, trees, and clouds as realities of the physical world; but equally real to him will be the realities of the spiritual worlds, which a new vision will open to him when, through self-development, he meets the requisites for this higher sight. The living feeling for the universal all, which man formerly had, he lost centuries ago in order to attain to Egohood and to conscious life on the physical plane, but now the time has come to acquire again the spiritual inwardness of life by means of spiritual-scientific knowledge livingly received, so that something new *lives* in the soul.

There are so few true thinkers because so few are willing to form concentrated, one-pointed, fixed, and intense force in ideation, a requisite of truly living thinking. Only as man trains himself to think livingly will his negation cease, and the blind will no longer be led by the blind. In the evolved Aquarian, the power of living thinking penetrates to reality with truth-telling soul insight, the fruit of intuition, which tells of an *intense inner repose*. This repose may be likened to the relaxed, effortless poise that a cat displays when sitting for hours at the hole of a mouse, with all her muscles relaxed, yet with intense alertness and instant readiness to strike. Without this intensity of inner quiet—a poise that spells patience and power—no messages are received from the higher realms of truth by way of the higher self, and no ideas, inspiration, or invention flow. Indeed, "*Reticence* becomes meditative power."

Our present age bears out the fact that there is a lack of true thinkers, in this time of intellectualism, productive of a materialism which bespeaks no firsthand knowledge of the Christ-truth. Men merely observe data and tabulate findings rather than think. Yet the Christ says, "I am the light of the world," which means that he is the Spirit of our entire solar system, as well as of our planet and of man. A few vanguard scientists of the Spirit have become conversant with the spiritual realms and their beings, and have made the science of the Spirit available in terms which the intellect that is open to truth can comprehend and put to the test of life.

He alone becomes free through knowledge of truth who has learned to think. Such a thinker is so spiritually sensitive and essentially etheric that he grasps a higher reality. Through his Uranian-Aquarian force, he creates a vortex so active, so intensely penetrating that he can raise himself in soul to the archetypal plane, wherein are to be found all those living beings whose singing and weaving word gives expression to everything on our Earth. At such moments of mental intensification, the Aquarian thinker reaches into the great reservoir of archetypal reality and, through the Spirit-quickening Uranus, his mind is vividly vitalized; he receives the creative light of heaven and brings down into the earthly sphere of the mind that which is both new and true.

Only those souls that by their own work and effort through many lives have secured the "oil" for their lamps, are prepared to meet the bridegroom, for they have the light within which is essential to moving consciously in the spiritual worlds. This oil can neither be borrowed nor bought at the last minute; it can only be garnered through wise work well done with glad love through lives. Without this oil, no man becomes a true thinker, conscious of the Christ and aware of the Spirit as an earthly Ego. All those Egos who have not acquired the oil for their lamps will be decidedly disqualified and refused admittance, for without light they remain in darkness and stand without the gate. Many will find themselves thus standing in darkness at this critical turning point of time, when every soul is making its own choice as to its advancement in evolution. Thus does Christ say, "Watch therefore, for ye know neither the day nor the hour wherein the Son of Man cometh" (St. Matthew 25:13).

He who has perfected himself to the point where his personality becomes radiant with his supra-personality, through his lower Ego becoming merged with and amenable to his higher spiritual self, has reached up to the sphere of the Spirit and the consciousness of Christ. Such a soul, though purely human, has made union with the divine and has become a Son of Man conscious of the Spirit in his earthly mind and possessing knowledge of higher realms and spiritual beings.

All men who become consummate and angelic men in Aquarius, do so because their creative work through many lives has earned them the right, and won them the reward of friendly cooperation of the little elemental beings, the wards and children of the Angels, the beings living in the etheric world, which interpenetrates the physical world. There are four ethers, four elements, and four kinds of elemental beings: the gnomes, related to the earth; the undines, to water; the sylphs, to air; and the salamanders to fire. In the etheric world, they have play, a play that at the same time is a service of active duty to Angels, to men, and to the world, for these little elementals form the forces for our earth. They work unseen, for the most part, for only few can see them. Thus these little workers, although they do so much for man, get no credit for their work, as do the bees and beavers.

These elementals fashion all things, from the body of a bee to that of a baby, from the lowliest soil we tread upon to the highest mountain, from the blast of a siren to the most exquisite and sweetest sound our ears can hear. No music, no words, voice, or writing, nought would be formed or finished here on the Earth, whether of earth, water, air, or fire, without the incessant work of these nature spirits, often called the fairies. Everywhere are they to be found, differing in different localities of the world. Man has an etheric body, also called the vital body, life body, or the body of formative forces, which gives him life and makes him what he is today, with all his habits and his memory. The quality of a man can be known by his etheric body. The ethers, so important to know and to study, are ruled by Aquarius.

Aquarians are therefore etherically sensitive and they sense more easily the truth, for truth is anchored in the etheric body. Not only do they know themselves, objectively and detachedly, but knowing themselves they know also all other selves. They instantly perceive the truth in people and in places. They see the designs of others; they divine and discern the true nature and being of anyone standing before them, even if they would shield their soul's gaze from any

false or ugly sight, sound, or scent. They have a deep under-
standing of human nature and are able to help the insane.
They are ever ready to be of service to those who ask for help
or advice, and often they do good in silence. There is latent,
if not active, an interest in man's connection with the cosmos.
Once their attention has been drawn to spiritual science,
they gain a comprehensive grasp of it.

It is through their hypersensitivity and their command of
elemental beings—the fruit of the angelic forces—that the
evolved Aquarians become such consummate artists, teach-
ers, musicians, inventors, reformers, and pacemakers of the
New Age. Such souls have the Christ in some degree evolved
in them through their expression of truth and love, which
brings to their side the invisible hosts of these elemental
beings, working joyously and creatively in fine cooperation
with them. Failure to attain or accomplish is the result of
man's etheric impurity, his deficiency in a love for truth, and
his shortcomings where love is concerned; the man who fails
is not true to himself in the sense of the higher self. Millions
are figuratively chained to the earth because of their mate-
rialism and intellectuality; or, filled with egotism and pride,
they live in an illusory dream world, being unable to main-
tain a balance between the below and the above in the true
Christ-Aquarian sense.

Advanced individuals predominantly under the influence
of Aquarius make touch in some wise with the fount of all
forces, the region of thought and the archetypal realm, so
that new impulses are made a reality in the world. Examina-
tion of these Aquarian innovations usually reveals their
power to bond men more closely in brotherhood and friend-
ship.

An Aquarian, when addressing someone, always gives him
the direct challenge of the eye, ever expecting that his quiet
yet incisive gaze will be returned. The Water-bearer seeks
the truth, knowing that as the truth is sought, the soul is

ennobled and enriched. Only as man begins to discern the sublime and to see himself as a being wrought out of the very substance of the sublime can he recognize his own divinity. It is God's plan for every man to become a master; the apprenticeship, however, to this mastery, is served on Earth as man's Ego evolves through many lives, incarnating in the various signs of the Zodiac and reaching perfection at last in Aquarius, the sign of zodiacal synthesis.

It is fitting, therefore, that Aquarius should be the symbol for the Gospel of St. Matthew, which portrays Christ Jesus primarily as the *Man*. St. John gives us the soaring Scorpio-Eagle thoughts of the Christ. St. Mark presents the Leo-Lion Sun power of the Son of God. St. Luke pictures divine compassion and love, symbolized by the sacrifice of the Taurus-Bull. The three elements of thinking, feeling, and willing are balanced in Man—Aquarius. St. Matthew traces the geneology of Jesus through three times fourteen generations, showing how, through ages of time, a very special body was prepared within the Hebrew race, which thereby performed a mission for the whole of mankind. In the unique Man, Jesus of Nazareth, there incarnated the Christ at the Baptism by John the Baptist. It is significant that St. Matthew is the only gospel writer who relates that Christ Jesus, at the moment of betrayal addressed Judas, his betrayer, as "Friend" (St. Matthew 26:50). Throughout his Gospel St. Matthew describes Christ Jesus as the Son of God in the human form of *Man*. This very highest ideal—man become God-man—became a reality in Christ Jesus. Our remoteness from this divine goal, which is our human destiny, fills us with humility; but the ideal-reality in Christ Jesus gives us hope that we may ultimately attain this highest measure of Man.

GOD'S PLAN—A PERFECT MAN

If I had words, my soul would write
Of wondrous worlds where all is right,
Of realms where revelation lives
To show the Christ who ever gives;
He gives his all to ev'ry soul,
For men are parts of one grand whole,
Which makes our scheme of being true,
He does our life with His indue.
My clumsy hand is too uncouth
To tell the world of realms of truth,
Of finer spheres where love exists
And not a soul the Christ resists.
Yet would I hint this day to you
That purpose real for which you sue:
The plan of God, a Perfect Man,
A spacious soul with heaven's span,
With *heart* so large, embracing all,
With *head* so lighted by His call
That these do merge and balance fine,
And with the *will* make rare align.
Then do these hands at once enhance
To give the soul the healing lance.
If you could read, then I would write
Of heaven's Lords who are the light,
Who ever give their all to man
To aid the Father's mighty plan.
Would you be wise to know the One
Who is the Christ, alone his Son?
Would you upon your own feet stand?
Then trust yourself and give a hand
And heart, and love the least of these,
For love and truth provide the keys
Which open doors to sweeter sphere

Where all is love without a fear.
If you would live to lift the curse,
Then you must give, must reimburse
At last these Lords, who give you all.
Now through the Christ there comes the call
To live with him, who is the Way;
For now He speaks to us to say:
Mankind shall not be separate,
Only one fold can consummate
This lovely Age of Waterman,
Which Christs the man—the Father's Plan.

THE HIGHEST ART

The highest art is Christ to know:
To send out love and let it flow
To all mankind throughout the Earth;
His truth will end the Spirit-dearth—
His love and truth renew the Earth.

Pisces - The Fishes

I. PISCES AND MANKIND — THE PISCEAN AGE

PISCES, The Fishes, the twelfth sign, completes the circle of the Zodiac. The symbol consists of two crescent-shaped fishes swimming in opposite directions yet tied to each other by a connecting cord, indicating the restricting nature of this sign. The dualism is obvious, and one may assume a third element, the water in which the two fishes swim, the universal solvent. One interpretation is that the soul is bound to the body within the ocean of the Spirit.

One cannot easily fathom the Zodiac and its signs, least of all this sign of mystery, Pisces, the loftiest note in the sublime symphony. Here is pure Spirit, virgin divinity, undifferentiated, yet to be made into manifest forms, spoken into being by the creative Word. Something of the mystery of Pisces is sensed in the picture of the Earth, when it "was without form and void, and darkness was upon the face of the deep. And the Spirit of God moved upon the face of the waters." The manifestation of the Great Unmanifest is the result of union between the Piscean feminine formless with the masculine form of the Saturnine Capricorn. The ultimate ideas expressed in forms come to manifestation through the Son—Aquarius. Capricorn, Aquarius, and Pisces are designated as Father, Son, and Mother, the Divine Trinity, yet One. The trident of Neptune, one of the rulers of Pisces, is a symbol of the Trinity in manifestation.

Pisces represents "The Great Deep," the water that is the universal solvent. It stands for Chaos, as against Christ-Aquarian Cosmos. Thus, in Pisces may be seen the power of the unresolved, that which is to be born and built and brought to life and form through the instrumentality of the Christ, that all may be fructified with *self*-consciousness, yet clothed with Spirit-life.

At present, Pisces is especially important for all mankind, for we are passing through the Piscean Age; that is, by precession of the equinox, the vernal Sun now rises in the Fishes, the twelfth sign of the Zodiac, the sign of destiny as duty. Through the formless Spirit's imprisonment in flesh, there has now developed a phase of life so dense that the divinity in man has been largely forgotten. This has produced a mode of consciousness stepped down to such an extent by the brain as to make man unresponsive to, and unaware of, the spiritual realms and beings, and of his true nature of soul and spirit. In the development of the intellect, man lost touch with the truth and his own soul. The result is chaos, which Pisces gives in its negative phase. This phase we see today in this cleansing era, with its separativeness, confusion, ubiquitous fear, lies and errors, every one seeking only his own interests, the all-pervasive poison gas of incessant war talk, even when war is not actively fought, and ultimately the negation of God. This time of transition, terribly testing for all mankind, shows profound misunderstanding and the consummation of human sorrow and self-undoing, the purchase of pain self-wrought by man and being brought to a head now in this Piscean Age.

Pisces being the loftiest note in the Zodiac, the power of pure Spirit, the unexpressed essence of God, it is small wonder in an age so intensely intellectual and godless, that many people fail to express the spiritual and gravitate more easily toward intellectualism and materialism. When the negative expression of this sign of divinity inverts the power of God, then must matter be raised from the dead by the Spirit, through the topmost facet of the zodiacal diamond, the pure Spirit of Pisces.

Having experienced the initiation of Pisces, and having received into himself those spiritual impulses that are the instruments of the Fishes-initiation, Jesus of Nazareth was prepared for the reception of the Christ and was enabled to baptize not only with water, as did John the Baptist, but to baptize in the higher sense designated by John as the "baptism of the Holy Spirit." It was no chance event that some of the disciples of Christ Jesus were fishermen. There is deep significance in his calling them to be fishers of men, indicating their work in preparing for the Piscean Age, and also in the fact that the early Christian symbol for Christ Jesus was a fish.

So few as yet have been baptized by the Holy Spirit; many are obsessed by inferior spirits. The negative, unindividualized members of Pisces are souls whose forces are scattered. Some are actually usurped by spiritual thieves, spirit-controls, hypnotists, and earthbound dead human souls who victimize, steal from, and use vicariously the physical forces of such derelicts. Moreover, the power of Pisces is to perfect the man through his life of feelings and emotions; the inner, silent, secret, subtle soul life is made subject to intense sympathies, feelings, and emotions in the earthly and astral environment. Large numbers of Pisceans are thus unknowingly, or knowingly, subject to control by souls seen and unseen, to their great detriment in true evolutionary growth; they become mere psychic servants and astral carriers for the so-called "dead." Frequently do they become burdened with the earthbound dead, so that life for them becomes a terrible, wretched experience. When people are so negative in Pisces, there is a lag in proper development, a retention of a vestige of atavistic clairvoyance. A large number of mediums are to be found in this sign, some of whom have made doubters, sceptics, and materialists change their entire life of thought and action, converting such scientists as Sir Oliver Lodge and Sir William Crooks. Through this avenue, however, one cannot reach the true goal, for mediumism is not the proper path to the Spirit. "I AM the door of the sheep" (St. John 10:7) and "He that entereth not by the door [the solar 'I AM' power] into the sheepfold, but climbeth up some other way [lunar mediumism and spirit-control], the same is a thief and a robber" (St. John 10:1).

Some Pisceans become a dismay and disappointment to themselves, for often their souls in truth do not belong to them. They are moved by all and sundry, by people here or in the unseen worlds, because of their scattered, uncollected, decentralized, psychic forces, their undifferentiated, diffused nature. This is why they are so often mediums and why so many of the unevolved souls become degraded and dissolute. The secret of their defeat, the source of sorrow and of the often sinister destiny in Pisces and through Neptune, lies in the lack of cohering Christ-will, which makes the man master of his life, and makes him whole. Piscean souls need to learn how to retain a grip on their own Ego and thus bring into focus their thinking and their self-consciousness. When this is achieved, they can direct their own lives and give moral help and direction to others.

The purpose of Pisces is in large degree the purpose of pain. In this restricting, inhibiting sign of sorrow, man is spiritualized, perfected, and purified through intense, subtle, silent, secret emotional suffering, the most exquisitely agonizing and poignant. None but those allied to Pisces can know the power of this pain, and only those who have dedicated themselves to Christ and have given their soul in full surrender, can know the magnitude of this mood of suffering, or the awful burden of a long drawn-out life incessantly frustrated by lack of achievement. Thus the term "sorrow and self-undoing" for this truly acute, inevitably destiny-dealing sign is quite apt, yet this purification by sorrow reaches a maximum of pure pain in Pisces only when Saturn and Neptune dominate the nativity. These forces compel renunciation of whatever is designated by them. The very essence of this silent note, Pisces, is, "If any man will come after me, let him deny himself, and take up his cross, and follow me. For whosoever will save his life shall lose it: and whosoever will lose his life for my sake shall find it" (St. Matthew 16: 24, 25).

Because the pedagogy of pain fructifies soul forces for the spirit, man may truly rejoice in his pain, knowing that every pang of it builds his inner man, the psychic-spiritual being, whereas this cannot be true for the animals. They derive no building power from pain. Unconsciously do most Pisceans love and protect the dumb creatures. Yet all persons may rediscover this fine feeling, this all-embracing compassion for animals. One can resuscitate such a universal feeling in this meditation upon Pisces, as the soul correlates with primeval wisdom, which mankind once possessed as original knowledge of all things and thus also of the animals. Man has lost remembrance of his connection with the animals; he has forgotten his relation to them and pays now his debt to them in terrible coin—he destroys their bodies and eats them!

By understanding the sign Pisces and its pedagogy of pain through Neptune via Saturn, we learn the nature of human death, and how through repeated earthly deaths the Father's force works through Saturn in and on the soul of man, so that eternal life and Christ-youth are at last achieved. Thus does St. Paul declare with truth, "the last enemy that shall be destroyed is death" (I Corinthians 15:26). Most people fear death in this era of Pisces when the Spirit-light in man is relatively inactive. Crucifixion of the Christ-Spirit in man continues when man, because of his intense intellectual darkness, believes that with the loss of his physical body by death all is lost and all is finished.

This is the paradox of this dual sign of the Fishes in the present Age of Pisces, for this is the sign of faith, and its keyword is 'I believe"; but many today do not retain faith in God. Quite recently, I had a letter from a Piscean woman, seventy-six years of age, asking me to pray for her that she might regain her faith. Although we might call this an age of faithlessness, at the same time, in this sign as in no other, the most definite firsthand evidence of spiritual worlds and beings is possible, ranging from the least, negatively psychic mediumism to the very highest degree of positive clairvoyance.

Not only Pisceans but all persons are moved and moulded by the forces of the invisible worlds and their beings, from the lowliest elementals to the highest Spiritual Hierarchies. This influence is the result of Neptune, one of the rulers of

Pisces. Our good or bad relations with the invisible beings and worlds—the reward or ruin—is shown by the position and power by sign, house, and aspect, of the planet of divinity and destiny, Neptune, and also by the twelfth house, by the place of Pisces, and by its other ruler, Jupiter. No man or woman would drink, take drugs or dope, nor in any other way degrade and negate the free Christ-Spirit within, were it not for the inversion of God that takes place here, creating darkness and lust, the narcotizing of the soul, which deprives the person of his earthly privilege and true work of driving out the dross of the lower nature and achieving spiritual freedom.

Every human Ego has created its own destiny. There is no such thing as a helpless lot dealt out by life in some fatalistic scheme. There is a design, in virtue of which the human Ego conditions by its own free will and accord the way it will walk. Every thought, every feeling, and every action creates after its own pattern and calls for an appropriate compensating destiny, just as a gun that has been aimed and fired must needs send its projectile to the target. The working of destiny or karma takes place in this sign of destiny. It is part of man's destiny, in Christ, to attain to full Ego- or "I AM"-consciousness and to freedom. This has entailed a descent into matter, with all the consequences of not just one "Fall," but many falls. In the course of incarnations, there comes to realization the means to regenerate the man, to resolve the karma, and to emerge from the prison house of the physical body as a liberated soul, willing to make any sacrifice for the progress of humanity. In this meditation on Pisces, we should ponder on the fact that, from our time onward, Christ is to be the Lord of karma, that is, he will bring order into karma and align individual destiny with the entire Earth-karma. Our destiny will thus be balanced in such a way as best to promote general human progress.

Many souls feel the whiplash of Piscean destiny, a destiny that so often degrades in unspeakable ways, often because of total blindness to the purpose of life, but sometimes because of a refusal to work rightly with those forces that produce the marriage of the soul with the heavenly bridegroom in a human earthly body. In the intense materialism today it is not the clever thing to do to live in the Spirit and to work consciously with the Christ-impulse. This is the outcome of the present dormancy of divinity in man. His conscious life is concerned solely with the senses and the physical world; the entire range of higher planes of consciousness and higher planes of being, free of the flesh, are lost to him, except for remnants of distorted dreams, which are of very little use to him as definite information. Yet, when we know how sublime, how divine, Pisces and Neptune are, and when we see the great unformed, uninformed, unfinished, laggard development of mankind, we do not marvel that there are so few evolved Egos, but are surprised that so many have already appeared. In every age, this testimony of God and divinity has been vouchsafed. Now, however, that time has come when there is to be made a leap in evolution, for many have matured and are ready to meet the Master; they have sufficient oil in their lamps to get the light.

The Light of the World, from the Father through the Christ, cannot be mirrored into the earthly brain of man in true and exact reflection, unless the desire or astral body of man is first cleansed. With the purification of this soul body, a commensurate cleansing quality is passed on to the etheric body, which in turn conditions man's sensitivity to spiritual truth. The coordination of the various members of man indicates the union of the Holy Spirit, Pisces, with the purified astral body, which St. John, finding it impossible to compass and confine by an earthly name, calls "the Mother of Jesus" or the Virgin Sophia, Virgo. In this wise, are the complementary signs, Pisces and Virgo, closely related as their influences work in man. They are referred to also in the feeding of the five thousand with the five barley loaves and two fishes—Virgo and Pisces—indicating the inexhaustible nourishment to be derived from these spiritual realms. The Fishes, the twelfth sign, is the occult symbol denoting the division between the night signs and the day signs.

Luciferic selfishness and Ahrimanic error must first be purged from the soul, to enable the will of man to manifest true feeling and exact thought, and so to attain purity. We see, then, why so many—not only in the sign Pisces, but in all signs during this Piscean Age—spurn the Spirit, become derelicts, render themselves destitute of will, and allow themselves to be commanded either by leaders of laggards wherever there are dictators, or by bureaucratic and socialized systems of government in supposedly democratic countries. Signal problems confront humanity now in the Piscean Age, its severe tests affecting all humanity, everyone on our planet, not just the people in Pisces.

Pisces remains a paradox and puzzle to those who have not understood the dualism inherent in this destiny sign, which indicates the formless, undifferentiated Spirit that is to become the formed and informed, differentiated man. This perfecting process is peculiarly the power of Saturn working in man through the last three signs of the Zodiac. The formless Piscean element is prepared through Saturnine Capricorn experiences, the sign that cradles the Christ through physical lessons in intense egotism. After this experience in egotism, man must be refined and matured in the experience of altruism in the sign Aquarius, where he is raised to the power of a perfected Saturn quality. Then can he pass on to Pisces as a self-directing, free Ego, as the more mature type of a Piscean.

When the last three zodiacal sign forces become a unified trinity, the "Dumb Note," Pisces, becomes articulate, the formless having become the formed. Thus those with subtle sight will see how Saturn brings the ballast that balances and how it provides a place of rest upon which the Spirit-motion moulds with its intense forces to make the man whole and perfect for Christ. We see how the virgin element for this Christing process is provided out of Pisces. The shaping, finishing forces work through all signs, but they are brought to fruition in the union of the last three signs in the sign of the Son of Man, Aquarius.

From what is here revealed about the sign of human destiny, Pisces, it is easier to realize why so few attain true alignment here, save with the Christ-cohering ballast brought by Aquarius. In Pisces, the all-conscious, unconditioned virgin element of God must become moulded by the Ego into the self-conscious, fully individualized Christ-man. It is the mission of the evolutionary process in this Piscean Age to develop the consciousness soul, or spiritual soul, through willed activity in a physical body in the physical world, thus mastering matter and enabling man to become a law unto himself, a self-directing Ego living in accord with spiritual laws, hence mindful of the interests of other Egos.

The mood most manifest in the mutable signs is the dual activity of thought aroused by experience in feeling and emotions. Common signs prominent in the nativity make one reason and meditate much upon emotional experiences and upon the feeling life. In consequence of such thinking, man advances in evolution when thought is illumined by truth. This present Piscean Age is, however, an age of intellectualism, expressing itself as the age of materialism. It is intellectualism, unlighted by Spirit, that causes chaos all over the globe and incites hatred through systems of thought that are either false or too limited, too narrowly conceived. When one's thinking does not accord with truth, the dissonance produces disease. The time is at hand when it will be known to be "*immoral to hold a false theory.*" Then the refusal to recognize the truth of the law of rebirth will be a moral issue. The time is now here when increasingly the intellect is being lighted by a higher faculty, which imparts knowledge of the higher worlds. With such illumination, man no longer lives loveless and in error.

In the years since the beginning of World War I, man has been to some degree in a state of soul meditation, realizing more and more acutely, through thought derived from experience of feeling, the maladjustment, or lack of connection, between the inner, real self, and the lower, earthly man and mind. Intellect has been highly evolved in the Piscean Age, but *spiritual* intelligence in the large mass of humanity has yet to be realized. When there is a marriage between the intellect and the Spirit, the large work of Pisces will have been consummated, with growing numbers of souls becoming Christ-conscious and thus free from fear, hatred, selfishness, and error. The pain wrought in this Piscean Age is the travail of purification that is bringing to the Earth in our time the gift of God indicated by Christ Jesus when he spoke of a woman's sorrow of travail in childbirth (Age of Pisces), but after that travail (this present transition), the *joy* that a man (Christ-Aquarius) is born into the world (St. John 16:21).

The mute note of Pisces produced brain-bound corpse-consciousness, the consciousness common now. But man has come of age in this era, and the new Christ-note is now to make man truly articulate. In Pisces occurs the great renunciation and great resolution that raises all earthly souls in this testing time. This twelfth sign of human destiny is also the loftiest sign of divinity and mystery.

The power of Pisces is shown in St. John 14, "Let not your heart be troubled; *ye believe* in God [the Father], *believe* also in me [the Son] . . . Peace I leave with you, my peace I give unto you: not as the world [brain-bound thinking] giveth, give I unto you. Let not your heart be troubled, neither let it be afraid." Today men's hearts are filled with fear and are troubled through lack of faith and devotion, the Piscean elements, and because of the absence of Aquarian truth-knowledge. Yet the cleansing alchemy of pain in this Piscean Age is changing the consciousness of man. This metamorphosis of man's soul enables him to gain Christ-peace, whatever the outer circumstances of life may be. Such peace is real—not "peace when there is no peace," nor peace at any price, nor compromise with principle. Such peace is the power and gift of the Christ active in man. This gift of peace is the mainspring of the evolved Piscean's life. It enables him to radiate a power far transcending all worldly power.

II. PISCES AND MAN

There is no sign more elusive to try to describe than Pisces, the Fishes, for this section of the Zodiac is as mobile as the astral world. On the physical plane, the oceans are its counterpart, the seas that toss and surge in sounding, raging fury; yet, the same waters may sometimes reveal the placid power of sweetest peace in idyllic, silvery calm, and the lovely lull and lakelike beauty that make cognizable the tune, tempo, and harmony of the spiritual worlds, calling up a vision of the divine, a touch with the transcendental, a union with the one life of love through the Word of the world, sounding as tranquil tone. This sign of spirituality is fittingly called "The Great Deep or Depth."

The signs of the Zodiac most intimately connected with the psychic nature of man, the side least seen, yet incessantly active for good or ill, are the water signs, which with their houses and the planets therein, may be called the dispensers of destiny. In persons lacking in spiritual discernment, these forces may seem to suppress the personality, whereas in truth they enhance and enlarge the soul.

In Cancer, Scorpio, and Pisces, those who are awakened

recognize not only the building of the soul, but the builder also, for in these signs of soul-sensitivity are encompassed all inherent qualities of soul, the psychic-spiritual fruit and heritage of past lives, eventuating in the man himself. As these water signs show the soul quality and tendencies, so do their houses—the fourth, eighth, and twelfth—indicate the personal earthly conditions, which are invariably restrictive, limiting, and sorrow-producing. Their effective scope and power consist in personal activity that appears ineffectual: through denial, when the influence is in the twelfth house; or after long delay, at the end of life, in the fourth house; and even after death, in the eighth house.

Pisces is a dual sign, as the two fishes indicate. The fishes are bound to each other, denoting the destiny restriction, which gives less freedom of choice than is granted in the outstanding dual sign, Gemini. The twins have a free relationship; not so the fishes. Dual experiences arise in Pisces, bringing extremes in kind and nature, the native often being torn to shreds between two conflicting emotions. The Piscean rarely gains a true grasp of himself, for emotions play through his soul as the winds through an aeolian harp; his soul is easily influenced, or played upon by sympathy, for it is easy for him to put himself in the soul of another who suffers. This is the sign that causes one to be keenly receptive and impressionable to the moods and soul-conditions of others. Psychic supersensitivity and immense emotionalism are forces that need control and direction, for Pisces puts the soul *en rapport* with the soul world. As a result, one feels the forces of other souls here or elsewhere, be they embodied, moving on the physical plane, or in the world of the so-called dead.

In Pisces, as in all the signs of the Zodiac, one finds souls at all stages of evolution. Some Pisceans impart love, irradiating as spiritual light and supernal feelings. Others in this sign are imperfectly prepared for personal attachments.

They may evince an intense thirsting desire for devotion and confidence with one part of their nature, while with their other part they show too weak a faith, too little trust, and have a tendency to withdraw. A lack of balance is in evidence, which points again to the dual quality of this sign. Too often, for want of proper perspective and right balance, the very reverse of what was envisioned as the ideal is achieved.

In this dual sign there sound the forces of *destiny* and *divinity*. It is here that the lowest and the loftiest reside—the darkness in which the light shines, and the light which ultimately transmutes the darkness of human brain-bound egotism. Man is chained to an earthly destiny so long as the darkness prevails and earthy desires are not exhausted. When the Ego begins to transmute its earthy desires and evolves toward the purity needed for a spiritual birth, then the light is perceived shining in the darkness, the light that "lighteth every man that cometh into the world." This is the direction toward divinity.

In this sign of destiny one realizes the need for earthly birth. The limiting conditions of personal earthly expression are picked up here as the "moral bundle" of past lives, the moral bundle that was checked in the soul world after the last death, before one entered the spiritual world. It is taken up again as one returns once more through the soul world to earthly incarnation. That which constitutes the "moral man" and his make-up in the aggregate from his past lives, passes over into his experience as destiny, through the twelfth sign, Pisces. Jupiter and Neptune, rulers of Pisces, indicate the moral-spiritual quality and power of the Ego—the good and the ill—nay, more, they show what our relations are with the heavenly host. By their position and condition, we know whether we have earned their favor or disfavor.

The esoteric Christian teaching of the laws of rebirth and of destiny, the dual laws that lead man to the goal of godhood, take effect in Pisces. The law of rebirth, of repeated earthly lives, each one of increasing fineness, has nothing fatalistic attached to it. On the contrary, it shows the definite and deliberate way toward the light that leads to liberation. The working of destiny speaks of the God within, forever guiding and leading man toward the goal. In esoteric Christian teaching, the negative idea of "sorrow and self-undoing" becomes changed into the spirit that charges the soul with spiritual power, enabling one to lose one's egotism and to find the spiritual love of the Lord of life, surrendering the lower, physical man to the spiritual Lord from heaven.

Magnificent Christ-alchemy shows itself in the spirit of sacrifice inherent in Pisces, the real royalty that originates in this sign of renunciation, for *renunciation* and *sacrifice* must be made either freely or perforce. The house on which Pisces stands, and also the position of Neptune, indicate the quality and type of sorrow, self-surrender, or sacrifice demanded. No matter what the talent or genius of a Piscean personality, there is always a background of obstacles and adversities. In Pisces, consecration through crucifixion leads to the consummate man. People in the Fishes are seldom understood, or truly appreciated, yet these are the most self-effacing souls, giving with a joy in giving. None ask less for themselves than they do, and none can be trusted more implicitly when living in the higher side of the sign.

In Pisces, one can realize the Great Ocean or Deeps of the Spirit and be aware of the spiritual man and the life hidden away and buried within the physical man—the Christ who lives in the Earth and in the souls of humanity. The sense of universality makes Pisces the least personally possessive sign. It calls forth marked hospitality and *generosity*. The generosity of Pisceans extends not only to goods, but also to judgments; they are ever ready to forgive and to manifest their good will in loving deeds. Some Pisceans have an attitude of other-worldliness; yet, in emergencies and crises, no better help can be given than by the people of this sign of deep inner understanding and compassionate self-surrender and sacrifice.

The divinity of Pisces is such that those strong in this sign have a constant aching yearning, an intense urge, to merge the soul entirely and completely with the souls of others, to form one universal spiritual union. Pisceans, or those truly under the Neptunian light, experience spiritually; thus they have the faculty and forte to commune and to unite with others on the mental and psychic planes. The purer the Piscean, the more profound the communion and union with the feelings and thoughts of people and places and, yes, with the planet itself!

In this mergence with others on Earth and on the invisible planes, there lies danger and often damage, for if the Piscean soul is not positively endowed with the strong factor of a developed mind, if it is still tainted with atavistic clairvoyance—and these today are still legion—the risk of obsession by spirit controls and so-called guides, is great, and these forces are evil. One must not remain negatively psychic. So many, too many, born in or under this sign, or with the Moon in Pisces, are the victims of invisible spirits and of mediumism. Then the sense of *hearing*, which is ruled by it, is perverted to undesirable hearing of what astral entities convey.

As Aquarius and Uranus emphasize the one in all, the individual as a part of the whole, so Pisces and Neptune declare the all in which the individuality is merged in the collectivity of the Christ. "That they all may be one; as thou, Father, art in me, and I in thee, that they also may be one in us; that the world may believe that thou hast sent me. And the glory which thou gavest me I have given them; that they may be one, even as we are one" (St. John 17: 21, 22). To grasp the secret of Pisces incisively, one must unite with the Spirit-life and love and light. If one would search into the meaning and mystery of this spiritual sign, let him search the scriptures, particularly St. John's Gospel and, specifically, chapter seventeen, the priestly prayer of Christ Jesus.

As Aquarius individualizes and identifies the man in and through the Christ, so Pisces universalizes and unites the man in and with the whole Christ-life. Thus the soul that has become Christ-identified or individualized, can never become lost in the ocean of Christ-life. At present, there are not enough Christ-individualized men and women on the Earth. The world is witness to this deplorable fact in this time of Communism and of socialized schemes of life for mankind. Man must first establish his Christ-egohood, his true self-identification in the Spirit, before he can universalize his love as a world and cosmic citizen, in the new and true citizenship that awaits him. Enforced fusion is danger-ous. The Christ-"I" and the Christ-"YOU" are both para-mount in the soul that is keeping pace with man's proper evolutionary development.

Pisces is called the "Universal Solvent" or the "Great Deeps or Depths." It shows the inhibited, the silent, the secret, and all that is mute and powerless of expression. Pis-ces is unlike Cancer, where feelings are awakened, and un-like Scorpio, where desires and feelings are brought to a center and concentrated, for Pisces turns everything into muted emotion, deep and silent as the ocean. This great ocean of emotion is permeated with sympathy and love, as universal solvents. This is the sign of Parsifal, the "pure fool," the guileless one, mute, timorous, and helpless, until through search and suffering, "by pity enlightened," he attained to knowledge, self-knowledge, spiritual enlighten-ment, and the power to discriminate between good and evil. Then he became the "help-bringing knowing one," the savior bringing salvation.

Very few Pisceans are egotists; in fact, they are in many instances deficient in self-esteem. The quality of humility that abides here can in positive souls create a mystic mood and beautiful reverence. Divinity and devotion reside here; but what if these forces are reversed? That reversal too often occurs and it tears the soul into shreds, rendering it lost and without true color, definition, or self-identification. Few souls can manage the mighty mood of this divine spiritual essence. It is easy for many to become materialists, or worse, utter derelicts on the sea of life. The psychic forces are too often negative and the sympathies unwise. Without firm inner direction in the Piscean soul, dereliction in some form may easily ensue; thus the highest may become the very lowest.

Zodiacal signs are difficult to explain in mere earthly language, for the language of the stars cannot be compassed or compressed into intellect, or into mere earthly words. The signs are better understood by observing people who are in the various signs or under their influence. Pisces has been called by some "the dust bin of humanity," with some relevancy. It has also been called "the dumb note" of the Zodiac, and this, too, rightly. This so-called "dumb note" has, however, become expressive in marvelous music, a music that voices what "The Heavens Are Telling," such as the mighty music of Handel, whose Sun was in Pisces. Truly did Handel refer to himself as a musical amanuensis for the divine beings and for mankind, when he said, "the heavens opened to me." The Neptunian note and the Piscean power—the utterance of divinity—are heard in Handel's interpretation of the Spirit through the concordance of sound. Chopin, too, makes audible the music of heaven as it flows from the Neptunian fount of his Piscean Sun, expressed in intricate, yet exquisitely beautiful, ethereal tones.

The ear that is attuned to the divine knows instantly when Neptune and Pisces provide the power and inspiration, be it in literature, poetry, art, or music. There is a limpid purity of style, placid and picturesque, and a flow of utterance that speaks of the highest reach of heaven, and an element so holy and ethereal as to declare the divine. However, when that which is holy and heavenly becomes inverted, evil is set in motion, and so Neptune and Pisces, in this Age of Pisces, invert the godly to produce monstrosities in art and in music—that devil's delight, jazz—which have a disorganizing and destructive, rather than an upbuilding effect upon the vital formative forces and the soul of man. The paradox of Pisces is the light and the darkness.

Dual forces inhere in all the common signs, but they do to a marked degree in the Fishes. In this sign we see the strong expression of the logical mind with great intellectual development, and also the priestly, spiritual element. On the one hand, we see an Einstein, an exponent of the mathematical mind, the intellect calculating space while not truly knowing space. On the other hand, we see a combination of the logical and the spiritual in the great master man, priestly soul, seer, teacher, architect, artist, scientist of the visible and invisible, the spiritual virtuoso, Dr. Rudolf Steiner. His thinking was scientific and precise in a very real sense; his whole life and teaching were highly spiritual, and his knowledge tells at firsthand of the spiritual Christ-content of space and its significance for all future evolutionary cycles of time.

We meet a very highly evolved Piscean in this Christ-initiate, Rudolf Steiner, who had three planets in Pisces: the Sun in the degree of "Testing," in the sense of examining and proving; and Mercury and Neptune conjunct at twenty-eight degrees, giving him a "direct, open line" to higher worlds. His disciplined intellect was illuminated by divinity, so that through his writings and nearly six thousand lectures there flowed the wisdom of the Spirit, the power of a positive, exact seership, with a capacity for skilled, firsthand spiritual investigation. So far as it is possible to make luminous the Mystery of Christ in language, Rudolf Steiner remains without a peer. He elucidated the mystery of mankind, which is inseparable from the Mystery of Golgotha, the unique Christ-event for the Earth. Steiner leads mankind to the Christ and to the reality of Spirit, the worlds of soul and Spirit, and their beings, in virtue of his self-earned expression of divinity in his earthly man.

True Pisceans are true teachers, for they carry within them a real priestly wisdom and love. Understanding and wisdom are not the fruit of the intellect alone. It is a strange paradox that, inherent in this sign of divinity, ruling this time, our present Piscean Age, there lie concealed the forces and facts of the cosmos, yet confusion and world misunderstanding occur. Cosmos and chaos lie hidden here, in this sign of mighty mystery. The light is not recognized by the physical, brain-bound personality, fear-filled and tormented and tossed by seething secret hates and emotions.

There are intellectual, worldly Pisceans, and there are chaotic, other-worldly members of this dual sign of the Fishes. For perfect expression one must gain perspective both in the lower Ego and the Earth, and in the world of Spirit. True balance between this world and the worlds of soul and Spirit must be found if one would be whole, and this wholeness, this true health, is our need. The Christ came for those who need a physician, to make them whole. It is essential for Pisceans to become far stronger as physically conscious earthly Egos, and to use the mental forces far more effectively, so that they may stand stabilized as self-protected personalities. If not self-protected through this proper I-consciousness, they are apt to become the sport and prey of evil entities in the flesh or in astral bodies, seen or unseen. They then lack stability and logic, and are devoid of a sound social sense. They often become lost to themselves in the surrender of their souls to others, for the great difficulty in their sacrifice and self-giving is to retain, at the same time, their own personality. They need to learn to give themselves spontaneously in self-surrender, and yet to be their own selves and not to neglect themselves.

In the sign of the Fishes, there is an immense, intense desire to help others and to give to all in need, especially to those who suffer and are ill-treated, to the extent of even denying themselves the comforts of life, sharing their "widow's mite," depleting themselves and making great sacrifices. There is a desire actually to make an oblation, an offering to the Lord as it were, in sacrifice for others. In one who is negative, this leads to the loss of himself in his own personality. This must be avoided or corrected, for the personality needs to be made positive and Christ-constructive in Pisces more than in any other sign. The greater the purity of the soul, the finer and fuller will be the flower of the Spirit in full Ego-consciousness, and the greater the capacity to comfort, to harmonize, and to consummate peace in the environment. This sign is correlated with the beatitude, "Blessed are the peacemakers, for they shall be called the children of God." Here is expressed and applied the spirit of forgiveness and love toward all, and the overcoming of evil through transmutation by the good, the only solvent.

Pisces is a psychic-sensitive sign that evokes spirituality and tends sometimes to other-worldliness. Pisceans are impressionable, and they ever seek to understand their impressions and intuitions, intimations that arise quite free of the brain and are realized, more often than not, as a psychic sensing. Many Pisceans get lost in the maze of the multitudinous ideas and impressions they continually receive from all worlds. They tend to become bewildered when there is confusion and pressure. Their best qualities are evident when there is an undisturbed atmosphere; then their mood of peace is powerful and profound, and their inspiration most active. The sign of the Fishes rules the feet, which bear some resemblance to attached fish. The feet denote an inner understand-ing of life, also "treading the Path," and making progress. In this respect, they are symbols of the spiritual life, and they also indicate what we mean when we say that the feet should be firmly planted on the earth. They give us our stance.

No sign more than Pisces needs to make itself positive on the physical plane, to allow the spiritual light to produce a true practicality on the personal, physical plane. The practical thinking of scientific logic is needed to insure a proper, wholesome, balanced personality. Without this correction, the soft, indulgent Piscean will too readily comply with the wishes and even the self-indulgence of others around him. Pisces is always ready to forgive and overlook all errors, mistakes, and sometimes even the effort which man must make to approach and pursue the Spirit of truth. "To know all is to forgive all" is right if one is Christ-constructive in such an absolution; but, if such forgiveness degrades, and draws out further negation in the character, leading to worse chaos by neglecting to impart right truthful ideas and conduct, the resulting Piscean compassion will not be a *wise* compassion. It will be an unwise sympathy, degrading and destroying the soul, rather than exalting and elevating it.

Jupiter and Neptune rule the Fishes. The benevolent Jupiter is a planet of bonding good will, reverence, and creative cosmic thought. Neptune denotes idealistic devotion. In general, one may say of Pisceans, that they are sympathetic, emotional, benevolent, good-natured, easy-going, patient, generous, hospitable, and that they love beauty and refinement in all things. Evolved Egos have a wonderful capacity for quiet, tactful persistence when dealing with others. In spite of being shy and timid, they can show considerable dignity if anyone presumes to take advantage of their good nature and inoffensiveness; they detest anything vulgar or violent. Many have healing power, sometimes through their hands, but largely through their presence, which emanates peace and piety. The less evolved Pisceans, however, are themselves in need of healing of soul, for they are confused, disorderly, worried, mediumistic; they suffer from illusions, they have a weak will, and they are too easily influenced by others. There is usually a deep religious feeling. Destiny is paid out in this sign which gives the destiny of sacrificial service. Renunciation is either offered willingly or imposed by destiny.

The true delight of this sign of detachment, discipleship, devotion, and divinity, is a devotion to the divine. Yet it is only by way of one's self-designated and self-invoked destiny that one can approach this divinity. In this mute sign, one carries out a prolonged self-meditation, passing judgment upon one's own self as a Christ-Ego, until at last the lower Ego merges with the higher, cosmic Ego, "the twain become one" and enter into the light. Then does one have the power more quickly to dissolve one's own ill destiny and to provide the light that dispels the darkness in the world.

There are centered in Pisces those forces that confer the archetypal value of the man, the formgiving cause, which brings him into earthly incarnation. Birth in a physical body is not ill fate if we take in the Christ; it is a real opportunity to grow in God through his Christ. The choice is ours! Destiny, or karma, will not be deplored if we realize that it is a progressive, developing force, bringing the experiences that are corrective and drawing us nearer to the goal. What is essential is that we have a right attitude. *Poise in the presence of destiny* is most needful to discharge the destiny rightly and to enhance the growth of soul.

The dual effect of the Fishes becomes evident in the fact that, on the one hand, this sign holds the destiny that leads the Ego to an earthly birth and, on the other, it provides the means to overcome the evil destiny conditions, liberating one from the individual need for rebirth. However, so long as the planet is not redeemed, the Christed soul will want to reincarnate for the sake of humanity and to aid the Christ in the work of redemption. Pisces, the sign of ready *renunciation* and *sacrifice*, produces such saviors, as well as *The Savior*, Jesus of Nazareth, who, at the Baptism in the Jordan, sacrificed his body, so that the Christ could incarnate in it and consummate the Mystery of Golgotha, the greatest event of all Earth-evolution—the Sacrifice Supreme that brings salvation to our Earth and to mankind. In Pisces, the destiny of repeated earthly births, according to true Christian teaching, becomes not ill fate, but the joyous avenue of Christ-alchemy leading to mankind's *illumination* and *liberation*.

O freighted I with love so great
That I with ease dissolve my "fate"!
So laden I with love alive,
My destiny doth come deprived
Of hate and hurt, of painful sting,
Of ev'ry bitter, tragic thing.

For all these pains I give full meed
Of praise to Thee, though I did bleed.
For ev'ry pang I thank Thee, Lord,
Not else could I sit at Thy board,
To take Thy Bread and drink Thy Blood
Which doth my soul with Thine full-flood.

Deep gratitude to Thee alone,
That I did reap as I had sown.
'Twas Thou, my life who made the Way
To this royal magnitude today.
For now Thy light doth flood through me
And all I see is nought but Thee.

*   *   *

O stagger not but stand and take
Thy destiny which thou didst make!
Still thy complaint, and understand
'Tis Christ who guides with loving hand.
O wander not with wounded air,
Nor longer grieve through mind's despair.
Accounts do come for settlement
Today, that give Christ-betterment.

It matters not how rough my road,
How uphill be its climb each day;
It matters not how large the load
With Christ within to point the Way.
It matters much that I should hear
At ev'ry moment of my life
Thy voice, so clear, without a fear,
For Thou, my Lord, Thou art my life.

So is my life a wondrous one!
Now through my pains Thy place is won.
Thus doth my soul evaluate
Aright all things, so estimate
The lot and load my life must bear,
So that I take from Thee a share
Of Earth's full burden here below
That sooner comes Thy fiery flow,
For this gross Globe must Gold become
When Thou art come in all the Sum.

The Zodiac

The encircling Zodiac doth tell
Of Hierarchies who there dwell;
God gives the gift that circles here,
The stellar girdle of each year.

The Zodiac shows, too, a ring
Of animals which slay and sting,
Until the soul arouse, and wake
The God within, the spell to break.

Who tames the ring of beasts shall birth
A Higher Man of heaven's worth;
The Zodiac embracing thee
Shall birth at last, The MAN, Christ-free.

Who bears the burden and the strife
Through years and lives forever rife,
Shall birth at last "The Perfect Man,"
The circle shall the center span.

Only the soul who knows the Word
Unites his life with what is heard;
He finds the light and in its glow
Can say with Job, "I know, I know."

The pictures of the Zodiac
Depict the man upon the rack
Of space and time, the torture borne
Upon the cross till dawns the Morn.

"Ye must be born again," He said,
Who suffered in the Earth and bled;
The center of the circle shows
The Risen Lord, who life bestows.

The Shepherd of the flock is He
Who entered Earth mankind to free.
He teaches all and tames the beast
So all may tend the wedding feast.

The Christ controls, He guards the flock,
He tends them all and takes the shock;
He is the Lord, the central Life,
Whose Love and Light dissolve the strife.

Within the center of the ring
Is seen the Christ, our God and King;
He doth perfect, make tame the wild,
Until the savage find the Child.

John Jocelyn